Intellectual Property Law in Canada

Third Edition

Mistrale Goudreau

This book was originally published as a monograph in the International Encyclopaedia of Laws/Intellectual Property Law.

Founding Editor: Roger Blanpain
General Editor: Frank Hendrickx
Volume Editor: Hendrik Vanhees

Wolters Kluwer

Published by:
Kluwer Law International B.V.
PO Box 316
2400 AH Alphen aan den Rijn
The Netherlands
Website: lrus.wolterskluwer.com

Sold and distributed in North, Central and South America by:
Wolters Kluwer Legal & Regulatory U.S.
7201 McKinney Circle
Frederick, MD 21704
United States of America
Email: customer.service@wolterskluwer.com

Sold and distributed in all other countries by:
Air Business Subscriptions
Rockwood House
Haywards Heath
West Sussex
RH16 3DH
United Kingdom
Email: international-customerservice@wolterskluwer.com

ISBN 978-90-411-9474-9

e-Book: ISBN 978-90-411-9495-4
web-PDF: ISBN 978-90-411-9516-6

The Author

Prof. Mistrale Goudreau holds an LLL from the University of Montréal, Quebec, Canada (Faculté de Droit, 1979) for which she received the Governor General's Academic Medal. She also holds an LLM in Commercial Law from the London School of Economics and Political Science (Department of Law, London, England, 1981). She is a member of the Quebec Bar since 1981 and is full professor at the Civil Law Section of the University of Ottawa, Ontario, Canada where she has been teaching since 1982. She has been also lecturer and visiting professor at the Faculty of law of the University of Montréal, at the Faculty of Law of the University of Nantes, France, and at the Canadian Foreign Service Institute (CFSI) in Ottawa, as well as research fellow at the Max-Planck-Institut für ausländisches und internationales Patent-, Urheber- und Wettbewerbsrecht, Munich, Germany and consultant for the Government of Canada. In the past, Mistrale Goudreau has acted as executive director of the Council of Canadian Law Deans, assistant dean for clinical and applied teaching and vice-dean of the Civil Law Section of the University of Ottawa. She published numerous articles on copyright, unfair competition, legislative drafting and legal theory.

The Author

Table of Contents

Table of Contents

List of Abbreviations

A.C.	Law Reports, Appeal Cases (U.K.)
All E.R.	All England Reports (U.K.)
Alta.	Alberta
Alta. Reg.	Alberta Regulations, available at www.qp.alberta.ca
B.C.	British Columbia
BCCA	Neutral citation[a] for the decisions of the Court of Appeal for British Columbia – recent decisions available at www.bclaws.ca
B.C.L.R.	British Columbia Law Reports
B.C. Reg.	British Columbia Regulations, available at www.bclaws.ca
Berkeley Tech L.J.	Berkeley Technology Law Review (U.S.A.)
C.A.	Court of Appeal; Cour d'appel
CBSA	Canada Border Services Agency
CanLII	Canadian Legal Information Institute, online www.canlii.org
CETA	Comprehensive Economic and Trade Agreement
Ch.	Law Reports, Chancery (U.K.)
C.I.P.R.	Canadian Intellectual Property Reports
C.I.P. Rev.	Canadian Intellectual Property Review
C.C.S.M.	Continuing Consolidation of the Statutes of Manitoba, available at http://web2.gov.mb.ca/laws/statutes/index_ccsm.php
C.N.L.R.	Consolidated Newfoundland and Labrador Regulations, available at http://assembly.nl.ca/legislation/sr/titleindex.htm
C.P.R.	Canadian Patent Reporter (Canada)
C.Q.	Cour du Québec; Court of Quebec, recent decisions available at www.jugements.qc.ca
CQLR	Compilation of Québec Laws and Regulations, available at http://legisquebec.gouv.qc.ca/en/Search?t=a
C.S.	Cour supérieure; Superior Court, recent decisions available at www.jugements.qc.ca
CRC	Consolidated Regulations of Canada, available at http://laws-lois.justice.gc.ca/eng//

D.	Recueil Dalloz (France)
D.L.R.	Dominion Law Reports (Canada)
Ex. C.R.	Canada Law Reports: Exchequer Court (Canada)
F.C.	Canada Federal Court Reports (Canada), available at http://reports.fja.gc.ca/eng/index.html
FCA	Neutral citation for the Federal Court of Appeal – Recent decisions available at http://decisions.fca-caf.gc.ca/en/index.html
F.C.A.	Federal Court of Appeal
F.C.R.	Federal Court Reports (Canada), available at http://reports.fja.gc.ca/eng/index.html
F.C.T.D.	Federal Court Trial Division
Fox Pat. C.	Fox's Patent, TradeMark, Design and Copyright Cases (Canada)
FTC	Neutral citation[a] for the Federal Court (Trial Division) – recent decisions available at http://decisions.fct-cf.gc.ca/fc-cf/en/nav.do
F.T.R.	Federal Trial Reports (Canada)
Geo. V	Statutes enacted during the reign of George V
H.L.	Appeals (House of Lords) (U.K.)
IDEA	The Journal of Law and Technology (United States)
I.P.J.	Intellectual Property Journal (Canada)
J.E.	Jurisprudence Express (Canada, Quebec)
J.Q.	Judgments du Québec (Database from the commercial legal research service provider LexisNexis Canada Inc.)
Man.	Manitoba
Man. Reg.	Manitoba Regulations, available at http://web2.gov.mb.ca/laws/regs/index.php
NAFTA	North American Free Trade Agreement
N.B.	New Brunswick
N.B. Reg.	New Brunswick Regulations, available at http://laws.gnb.ca/en/BrowseTitle
N.R.	National Reporter (Canada)
N.S.	Nova Scotia
NWT Reg	Northwest Territories Regulations, available at www.justice.gov.nt.ca
O. Reg.	Ontario Regulations, available at http://www.e-laws.gov.on.ca/
Ont.	Ontario
Pat. App. Bd.	Patent Appeal Board
PBRO	Plant Breeders' Rights Office
P.C.	Privy Council (U.K.)

List of Abbreviations

PLR	Public Lending Right
O.R.	Ontario Reports
QCCA	Neutral citation[a] for the Court of Appeal for Québec, recent decisions available at www.jugements.qc.ca
Qué.	Québec
r.	Règlement; regulation
Reg.	Regulation
R.J.Q.	Recueil de jurisprudence du Québec
R.P.C.	Reports of Patent Cases (U.K.)
R.Q.	Règlements du Québec; Quebec Regulations, available at www.publicationsduquebec.gouv.qc.ca
R.R.S.	Revised Regulations of Saskatchewan, available at www.publications.gov.sk.ca
R.S.A.	Revised Statutes of Alberta, available at www.qp.alberta.ca
R.S.B.C.	Revised Statutes of British Columbia
RSC	Revised Statutes of Canada, available at http://laws-lois.justice.gc.ca/eng/
R.S.N.B.	Revised Statutes of New Brunswick, available at http://laws.gnb.ca/en/BrowseTitle
R.S.N.L.	Revised Statutes of Newfoundland and Labrador, available at www.assembly.nl.ca/legislation/sr/consolidation/
R.S.N.S.	Revised Statutes of Nova Scotia, available at http://nslegislature.ca/legc/index.htm
R.S.N.W.T.	Revised Statutes of Northwest Territories, available at www.justice.gov.nt.ca/legislation/SearchLeg&Reg.shtml
R.S.O.	Revised Statutes of Ontario available at www.e-laws.gov.on.ca/index.html
R.S.P.E.I.	Revised Statutes of Prince Edward Island, www.gov.pe.ca/law/statutes/
R.S.S.	Revised Statutes of Saskatchewan, available at www.publications.gov.sk.ca
R.S.Y.	Revised Statutes of Yukon, available at www.gov.yk.ca/legislation/
S.B.C.	Statutes of British Columbia
SC	Statutes of Canada, available on http://laws-lois.justice.gc.ca/eng/
S.C.R.	Supreme Court Reports (Canada), recent decisions available at http://scc.lexum.org/en/index.html
SI	Statutory Instrument (Canada)
S.N.B.	Statutes of New Brunswick, available at http://laws.gnb.ca/en/BrowseTitle

S.N.L.	Statutes of Newfoundland and Labrador, available at www.assembly.nl.ca/legislation/sr/consolidation/
S.N.S.	Statutes of Nova Scotia, available at http://nslegislature.ca/legc/index.htm
S.N.W.T.	Statutes of Northwest Territories, available at www.justice.gov.nt.ca/legislation/SearchLeg&Reg.shtml
SOR	Statutory Orders and Regulations (Canada)
S.Q.	Statutes of Québec
S.R.Q.	Lois refondues du Québec; Revised Statutes of Quebec available at www.publicationsduquebec.gouv.qc.ca
S.S.	Statutes of Saskatchewan, available at www.publications.gov.sk.ca
Times L.R.	Times Law Reports (U.K.)
T.M. Opp. Bd.	Trademarks Opposition Board
U.K.	United Kingdom
UPOV	Union for the Protection of New Varieties of Plants
Vict.	Statutes enacted during the reign of Victoria
WPPT	WIPO Performances and Phonograms Treaty
WT/DS	WTO Document – Dispute Settlement
W.W.R.	Western Weekly Reports (Canada)
YOIC	Yukon Orders in Council

[a] On the concept of neutral citation, *see* the explanations of the Canadian Citation Committee at https://lexum.com/ccc-ccr/neutr/index_en.html.

Preface

This study seeks to provide a concise text, aimed at those interested in a succinct overview of the present state of intellectual property in Canada. Although international agreements have been influential in the shaping of the Canadian regime, our study does not examine the details of the international intellectual property conventions but focuses instead on the basic traits of the domestic rules. The text refers not only to the relevant legal provisions but also to major Canadian courts decisions or some cases most illustrative of the legal issues. It is worth noting that office consolidations of federal and provincial legislations, as well as recent Canadian courts decisions, are for the most part accessible for free on the Internet. The reader will find in the list of abbreviations references to the relevant governmental websites.

The law is stated as of 1 January 2017.

General Introduction

§1. General Background

I. Geography

1. Canada, with its 9,984,670 km^2, is the second largest country in the world. It occupies most of the North American Continent and is north of the United States of America. It is divided into ten provinces and three territories, each having their own capital city. Due to its wide east–west extent, Canada comprises of six time zones. Its only international land boundary is with the United States of America. Also, the majority of Canada's population lives in the country's south, near the US border.

2. Canada is rich in natural resources and is an important manufacturing country. Its main natural resources are natural gas, oil, gold, coal, copper, iron ore, nickel, potash, uranium, zinc, food and water. Its principal industries include automobile manufacturing, pulp and paper, iron and steel work, machinery and equipment manufacturing, mining, extraction of fossil fuels, forestry and agriculture.[1] Canada is a member of the G8, the group of eight leading industrialized nations and is the United States of America's largest trading partner.

3. Canada is a net importer of intellectual property.[2] The manufacturing of high-technology products is one of Canada's leading export sectors. Canada also has a high percentage of internet users: in 2009, nearly 80% of the population aged 16 and over had used internet communications for personal reasons.[3]

1. One can find this data as well as other useful information about Canada's economy on the Statistics Canada website www.statcan.ca, or on those of the Global Affairs Canada www.dfait-maeci.gc.ca and of Innovation, Science and Economic Development Canada www.ic.gc.ca.
2. CIPO, *A Guide to Patents*, (2009), p 6 http://publications.gc.ca/collections/collection_2009/ic/Iu71-4-3-2008E.pdf.
3. Statistics Canada, *Information and communications technology*, 30 September 2011, http://www.statcan.gc.ca/pub/11-402-x/2011000/chap/information/information-eng.htm.

II. Cultural Compositions

4. Migrations and resettlements of populations are central to Canadian History.[4] Canada belongs to the group of the most ethnically and racially diverse countries in the world.[5]

5. The earliest European settlers came from Britain and France and today both English and French are Canada's official languages. Immigrants in the past were primarily from European countries and the United States of America, but today most immigrants come from Asia.[6] According to the 2011 Census Canada's foreign-born population represents 20.6% of the total population.[7] Among Canadians, 20.6% have a mother tongue other than English or French.[8]

6. English is the main official language spoken in Canada. The 2006 Census showed that Anglophones represent 57.8% of the population while Francophones share is 22.1%.[9]

7. The report on the 2011 Census also estimated at 4.3% of the population, those reporting to have Aboriginal origins.[10] The indigenous population of Canada includes North American Indians, Métis (descended from persons of mixed blood) and Inuit.

8. In 2011, people predominantly reported that they were affiliated with a Christian religion, the Roman Catholics being the largest religious group in Canada.[11]

III. Political System

9. Canada is a constitutional monarchy within the British Commonwealth and a federation that is a union of ten provinces and three territories. The core of the constitution is contained in the *British North America Act, 1867*,[12] (renamed in 1982

4. Harold Troper, rev Maude-Emmanuelle Lambert, *Immigration in Canada*, The Canadian Encyclopedia, 14 July 2015, http://www.thecanadianencyclopedia.ca/en/article/immigration/#top.
5. *Ibid.*
6. Statistics Canada, Immigration and Ethnocultural Diversity in Canada - National Household Survey, 2011 www12.statcan.gc.ca/census-recensement/2006/as-sa/97-557/p1-eng.cfm .
7. *Ibid.*
8. Statistics Canada, Linguistic Characteristics of Canadians Language, 2011 Census of Population http://www12.statcan.gc.ca/census-recensement/2011/as-sa/98-314-x/98-314-x2011001-eng.cfm.
9. Statistics Canada, 2006 Census: Immigration, citizenship, language, mobility and migration, The Daily, Tuesday, 4 Dec. 2007, www.statcan.gc.ca/daily-quotidien/071204/dq071204a-eng.htm.
10. Statistics Canada, 2011 National Household Survey: Aboriginal Peoples in Canada: First Nations People, Métis and Inuit http://www.statcan.gc.ca/daily-quotidien/130508/dq130508a-eng.htm.
11. Statistics Canada, Immigration and Ethnocultural Diversity in Canada - National Household Survey, 2011, *supra* note 6.
12. (1867) 30-31 Vict., c. 3 (U.K.).

the *Constitution Act, 1867*[13]), which set the framework for the division of powers between the provinces and the federal institutions.

10. The Federal Government, headed by the Prime Minister, is responsible, among other things, for foreign policy, national defence, trade, the monetary system and intellectual property.

11. The provinces are largely self-governing; they enact their own laws. Legislative powers extend to education, cultural affairs, commercial activities and private law. The province of Québec has a legal system still based on civil law principles for private matters, while the other provinces have adopted the common law system. The territories exercise the powers which have been delegated to them by the Government of Canada.

IV. Population Statistics

12. On 10 May 2011, Canada's population was estimated at 33,476,688 people.[14] From 2006 to 2011, the growth rate was 5.9%, mainly due to migratory increase.[15]

13. The majority of the population lives in urban areas[16] and more than a third of Canadians live in one of Canada's three largest metropolitan areas: Toronto, Montréal and Vancouver.[17]

§2. Historical Background

14. After the discovery of Canada by John Cabot (1497) and the exploration of the St. Laurence River by Jacques Cartier (1534–1542), Samuel de Champlain founded Québec (1608) and colonization by the French population began. European conflicts (known as the Seven Years' War) spread to the new territory and after the French defeat in Québec (1759) and Montréal (1760), the *Treaty of Paris* (1763) ceded the French colony of Canada to Great Britain. The British tried to impose their own legal system into the colony and the *Proclamation of 1763* abolished the Canadian laws. These efforts to impose the English regime were met with great resistance from the French colonists. In 1774, at the request of the local population, the *Quebec Act, 1774* re-established the French legal rules to deal with property and private matters, while public law and criminal law remained governed by the English legal system.

15. Mainland Acadia (modern Nova Scotia) passed to the British Crown in 1713 by the treaties of *Utrecht*. The fate of New Brunswick as part of the English colony was confirmed after the defeat of the French forces at Fort Beauséjour (1755) and the signature of the *Treaty of Paris* (1763). It was administered as a part of Nova Scotia until 1784 when it became a separate colony.

---

13. *See* No. 1 of the Schedule to the *Constitution Act, 1982*, being Schedule B of the *Canada Act 1982*, (U.K.) 1982, c.11.
14. Statistics Canada, The Canadian Population in 2011: Population Counts and Growth, http://www12.statcan.gc.ca/census-recensement/2011/as-sa/98-310-x/98-310-x2011001-eng.cfm.
15. *Ibid.*
16. *Ibid.*
17. *Ibid.*

16. After the American Revolution (1775–1783), the loyalists immigrated to Canada, colonized Nova Scotia and New Brunswick. In the old Québec, to accommodate the wishes of the new English settlers, the territory was divided in 1791 into two parts: the Upper Canada (modern Ontario), which adopted the common law system and the Lower Canada (modern Québec), still governed in private matters by the principles of French civil law. Each had its own legislature. The two provinces were later reunited by the *Act of Union* (1840). Finally in 1867, *British North America Act, 1867*,[18] (renamed in 1982 the *Constitutional Act, 1867*)[19] united the provinces of Canada, New Brunswick and Nova Scotia. The other provinces were added subsequently: Manitoba (1870), British Columbia (1871), Prince Edward Island (1873), Alberta and Saskatchewan (1905) and Newfoundland (1949). In 1898, the Yukon Territory was separated from the Northwest Territories, and in 1999 Canada created the new territory of Nunavut. All three territories have a legislative assembly and a territorial government exercising the powers that have been transferred to them by the Federal Government.

18. (1867) 30-31 Vict., c.3 (U.K.).
19. *See* No. 1 of the Schedule to the *Constitution Act, 1982*, being Sch. B of the *Canada Act 1982*, (U.K.) 1982, c.11.

Chapter 1. Copyright and Neighbouring Rights

§1. Sources: Legislation

17. In 1867, the *British North America Act, 1867*,[20] (renamed in 1982 the *Constitution Act, 1867*)[21] granted legislative power over copyright to the Federal Parliament.[22] In accordance with the statute, the Parliament adopted in 1921, a new *Copyright Act*,[23] which is still now the governing legislation in Canada. Although the texts are not identical, the Canadian *Act* of 1924 borrowed extensively from the English *Copyright Act, 1911*.[24]

18. Canada is a party to several multinational conventions. Since 26 June 1998, it is bound by the *Berne Convention for the Protection of Literary and Artistic Works* (hereafter named the *Berne Convention*), as revised in Paris in 1971.[25] Canada also adhered to the *Universal Copyright Convention* as formulated in 1952, but not to its Paris revision of 1971.[26] Canada has entered into the *Agreement Establishing the World Trade Organization* (WTO), which includes the *Agreement on Trade-Related Aspects of Intellectual Property Rights* (hereafter named the *TRIPs Agreement*).[27] Canada is also a party to the *North American Free Trade Agreement*, (hereafter named the *NAFTA*), which regroups in a specific chapter on intellectual property, provisions similar to those adopted in *TRIPs Agreement*[28] and to the *International Convention for the Protection of Performers, Producers of Phonograms and Broadcasting Organizations* (hereafter named the *Rome Convention*).[29] Canada has signed in 1997 the *WIPO Copyright Treaty* (hereafter named the *WCT*) and the *WIPO Performances and Phonograms Treaty* (hereafter named the *WPPT*)[30] but Canada has only deposited its

20. (1867) 30-31 Vict., c. 3 (U.K.).
21. *See* No. 1 of the Schedule to the *Constitution Act, 1982*, being Sch. B of the *Canada Act 1982*, (U.K.) 1982, c.11.
22. Section 91 (23).
23. *An Act to Amend and Consolidate the Law Relating to Copyright*, (1921) 11-12 Geo. V, c. 24; RSC 1985, c. C-42.
24. (1911)1-2 Geo. V, c. 46; *see also* H.G. FOX, *'The Law of Industrial and Intellectual Property: 1923-1947'* Can. Bar Rev. 26 227, at 243(1948).
25. Canada's accession was on 26 Mar. 1998, but the entry into force of the convention for Canada was on 26 Jun. 1998. *See* Index, *Canada Treaty Series 1998*, 1, Ottawa (1998).
26. Canada ratified the agreement on 10 May 1962: *see* (1962) 22 *Fox Pat C.* 245.
27. The agreement was signed by Canada on 15 Apr. 1994 and ratified on 30 Dec. 1994. It was enacted into domestic law by the *World Trade Organization Agreement Implementation Act*, SC 1994, c. 47.
28. 32 I.LM. 296. It was enacted into Canadian domestic law by the *North American Free Trade Agreement Implementation Act*, SC 1993, c. 44.
29. It was enacted by the *Act to amend the Copyright Act*, SC 1997, c. 24.
30. Both treaties were signed on 22 Dec. 1997 (*see* the information on the WIPO web site www.wipo.int/portal/index.html.en.

instruments of ratification on 13 May 2014.[31] Finally, in 2016, Canada adhered to the *Marrakesh VIP Treaty*.[32] The implementation legislation received royal assent and came into force on 22 June 2016.[33]

§2. Subject Matter of Protection

19. According to section 5 of the Canadian *Act*, copyright subsists in Canada in every literary, dramatic, musical and artistic work. Section 2 also provides a definition of 'copyright', which adds three types of subject matter, those being the performer's performance, the sound recording and the communication signal. In order to attract copyright, a work must fall into one or more categories of the works listed in those sections.[34] In Canada, copyright law is purely statutory law.[35] The 1924 *Act* introduced the rule that the common law copyright (which protected unpublished works[36]) no longer exists.[37] Therefore new rights or new subject matters of protection have to be secured from the legislature.

20. Section 2 of the Canadian *Act* also provides a definition of 'every original literary, dramatic, musical and artistic work', which appears to have been taken from the Rome revision of the *Berne Convention*.[38] The expression is said to include, among other things, every original production in the literary, scientific or artistic domain, and sketches and plastic works relative to geography, topography or science.

I. Different Categories of Protected Works

21. Section 5 enumerates four classes of protected works: literary, dramatic, artistic and musical works. Each class of work is defined by statutory provision or has been the subject of judiciary comments.

31. WIPO, WCT Notification No. 81, http://www.wipo.int/treaties/en/notifications/wct/treaty_wct_81.html and WIPO, WPPT Notification No. 86, http://www.wipo.int/treaties/en/notifications/wppt/treaty_wppt_86.html The Treaties entered into force, with respect to Canada, on 13 August 2014.
32. WIPO, Marrakesh Notification No. 20, http://www.wipo.int/treaties/en/notifications/marrakesh/treaty_marrakesh_20.html. The treaty entered into force on 30 September 2016.
33. *An Act to amend the Copyright Act (access to copyrighted works or other subject-matter for persons with perceptual disabilities),* SC 2016, c 4.
34. *Cuisenaire v. South West Imports Ltd.*, [1968] 1 Ex. C.R. 493, at 511, aff'd [1969] S.C.R. 208.
35. *Compo Co. v. Blue Crest Music Inc.*, [1980] 1 S.C.R. 357, at 373; *Télé-Métropole Inc. v. Bishop*, [1990] 2 S.C.R. 467, at 477.
36. *See* for example *Massie & Renwick v. Underwriters' Survey Bureau Ltd.*, [1940] S.C.R. 218, at 227.
37. The rule is now set out in s. 89 of the *Copyright Act*.
38. *Cuisenaire v. South West Imports Ltd.*, [1968] 1 Ex. C.R. 493, at 509, aff'd [1969] S.C.R. 208.

A. Literary Works

22. According to section 2, the literary works include tables, computer programs and compilations of literary works. Book, lecture, delivery (in relation to a lecture) are all terms also defined in section 2.

23. In order to be a literary work, a work does not need to be possessed of literary merit or to belong to the realm of literature.[39] Many works which cannot claim to rank as literature have been protected. A work will not be denied protection simply because the copy is not in a human readable form.[40]

B. Artistic Works

24. This category include paintings, drawings, maps, charts, plans,[41] photographs, engravings, sculptures, works of artistic craftsmanship, architectural works and compilation of artistic works.[42] Furthermore, statutory definitions are provided for the terms: 'architectural work', 'engraving', 'photograph', 'plate' and 'sculpture'.[43]

25. In order to fall into this category, a work does not require an artistic element: the term 'artistic work' is used merely as a generic description of the type of works which find expression in a visual medium as opposed to works of literary, musical or dramatic expression.[44]

26. Some types of works, such as architectural works and photographic works, call for some comments. Before 1988, the definition of architectural work restricted the copyright protection to building or structure having an artistic character or design, which brought some judges to look for distinctive features or some uniqueness in the building before granting protection. The 1988 legislative amendment seems to have eliminated this requirement of distinctiveness or uniqueness.

27. The definitions of photograph have also been changed. Previously the term 'photograph', included in the category of artistic work,[45] was said to include 'photo-lithograph and any work produced by any process analogous to photography'.[46] The legislative definition was amended in 1993:[47] the legislator now refers to any work

---

39. *Underwriters Survey Bureau Ltd.* et al. *v. American Home Fire Assurance Co. and Central Fire Office Inc.*, [1939] Ex. C.R. 296, at 303.
40. *Apple Computer, Inc. v. Mackintosh Computers Ltd.*, [1988] 1 F.C. 673 (F.C.A.), at 686; aff'd [1990] 2 S.C.R. 209.
41. Before the 1988 adoption of the *Act to amend the Copyright Act and to amend other Acts in consequence thereof*, SC 1988, c. 15; RSC 1985, c. 10 [4th Supp.], s. 1, maps, charts and plans were included in the definition of literary work.
42. Section 2.
43. Section 2.
44. *DRG Inc. v. Datafile Ltd.*, [1988] 2 F.C. 243, at 253, aff'd on other grounds (1991) 35 C.P.R. 243 (C.F.A.).
45. Section 2.
46. *Copyright Act*, RSC 1985, c. C-42, s. 2. The live telecasting of sporting events were said not to be analogous to a photographic process: 'a photograph is something concrete, something in a material form that cannot only be seen but handled, and involves the creation of a negative': *Canadian Admiral Corp. v. Rediffusion, Inc.*, [1954] Ex. C.R. 382, at 398.
47. *North American Free Trade Agreement Implementation Act*, SC 1993, c. 44 subs. 53(2).

'expressed by any process analogous to photography' and commentators argued that this legislative amendment has substantially broadened this category of work.[48]

C. *Dramatic Works*

28. According to section 2, this category encompasses two types of works: first, pieces for recitation (or plays), choreographic works and pantomimes, and second, cinematographic works. The section also provides a definition for 'choreographic work' and 'cinematographic work'. A choreographic work does not require a story line.[49]

29. A cinematographic work includes any work expressed by a process analogous to cinematography[50] and may or may not be accompanied by a soundtrack.[51]

D. *Musical Works*

30. Musical works are works of music or musical compositions, with or without words.[52] Before 1993, the definition was more restrictive: it included only 'any combination of melody and harmony, or either of them, printed, reduced to writing, or otherwise graphically produced or reproduced'.[53]

II. Works Excluded of Protection

31. The Canadian *Copyright Act* does not protect information or ideas, but solely the form in which they are expressed.[54] However, the case law has extended traditional copyright principles to protect works against non-literal reproduction. The Supreme Court of Canada has expressly stated that the *Act* protects authors against both literal and non-literal copying and decided that the copyright in a proposal for an educational children's television show had been infringed because the overall architecture of the submission and the specific personality traits of the characters had been copied without authorization.[55]

32. As a corollary of the idea/expression distinction, judges have developed the merger notion: for example, copying of parts of computer programs may not be

48. *See* John S. McKeown, *Fox Canadian Law of Copyright and Industrial Designs* 217 (3d ed., Carswell 2000).
49. Section 2.
50. *Tom Hopkins International, Inc. c. Wall & Redekop Realty Ltd.*, (1984), 1 C.P.R. (3d) 348 (B.C. S.C.), aff'd, (1985), 64 B.C.L.R. 245 (B.C. C.A.).
51. Section 2. Before 1993, cinematograph films were treated as 'dramatic work' only if the arrangement or acting form or the combination of incidents represented has given the work an original character: *Copyright Act*, RSC 1985, c. C-42, s. 2. Without this original element, they were protected as a series of photographs – an artistic work: *Canadian Admiral Corp. v. Rediffusion, Inc.*, [1954] Ex. C.R. 382, at 401.
52. Section 2.
53. *Copyright Act*, RSC 1985, c. C-42, s. 2.
54. *Cuisenaire v. South West Imports Ltd.*, [1968] 1 Ex. C.R. 493, aff'd [1969] S.C.R. 208.
55. *Cinar Corporation v. Robinson*, 2013 SCC 73, [2013] 3 S.C.R. 1168.

copyright infringement, 'if there is only one or a very limited number of ways to achieve a particular result in a computer program, (since) to hold that that way or ways are protectable by copyright could give the copyright holder a monopoly on the idea or function itself'.[56]

III. Special Categories of Works

A. Computer Software

33. As mentioned earlier, computer programs are included in the category of literary work, and the expression is defined in section 2 as meaning 'a set of instructions or statements, expressed, fixed, embodied or stored in any manner, that is to be used directly or indirectly in a computer in order to bring about a specific result'. The statutory definition of computer programs thus provided more or less confirms the Canadian case law.[57]

B. Databases

34. According to the copyright provisions of *NAFTA* and *TRIPs Agreement*, Canada must grant protection to 'compilations of data or other material, whether in machine readable or other form, which by reason of the selection or arrangement of their contents constitute intellectual creations'.[58]

35. The *Copyright Act* was amended on two occasions to provide protection to compilations: the first amendment, in 1988, included the compilations into the category of literary works.[59] In 1993 the *NAFTA Implementation Act*[60] introduced a more coherent approach. A definition was added to section 2 of the *Copyright Act*: a compilation means either a work resulting from the selection or arrangement of literary, dramatic, musical or artistic works of parts thereof, or a work resulting from the selection or arrangement of data. All of the definitions of literary, musical, dramatic or artistic works were changed as to include compilations of works of those categories.[61] If a compilation contains works of two or more of the categories, it shall be deemed to be a compilation of the category making up the most substantial part of the compilation.[62] The *Copyright Act* also clarifies the status of works incorporated in a compilation:

---

56. *Delrina Corp. v. Triolet Systems Inc.* et al. (2002), 17 C.P.R. (4th) 289 (Ont. C.A.), at 307, affirming 47 C.P.R. (3d) 1 (Ont. S.C.).
57. *Mackintosh Computers Ltd. v. Apple Computer Inc.* (1987), 18 C.P.R. (3d) 129 (F.C.A.), aff'd [1990] 2 S.C.R. 209.
58. *NAFTA*, Art. 1705(1)(b), *TRIPs Agreement*, Art. 10.
59. *An Act to Amend the Copyright Act and to amend other Acts in consequence thereof*, SC 1988, c. 15, subs. 1(2).
60. S.C. 1993, c. 44.
61. Section 2.
62. Subsection 2.1(1).

their incorporation does not increase, decrease or otherwise affect the copyright protection or moral rights conferred by the *Act* in respect of those works.[63]

C. *Title of the Work*

36. By section 2 of the *Copyright Act*, the title is to be treated as part of the work when such a title is original and distinctive.[64] Normally, a title alone will not enjoy a copyright protection. Applying the general principles of copyright protection, the case law has established that the copying of the title constitutes infringement only when what is copied is a substantial part of the work.[65]

§3. Conditions of Protection

I. **Formal Requirements**

37. Since 1924, the grant of protection is independent of any formalities. The statute does not call for copyright notices. Registration is permissive only; the subsistence of copyright in no way depends upon registration. There are some legal obligations to deposit copies of works published in Canada,[66] but those requirements are not a precondition to copyright protection.

38. Even though registration is not compulsory, the author or the copyright owner, an assignee or the grantee of an interest may apply for the registration of a copyright at the Copyright Office.[67] Rectification of an entry wrongly made or wrongly omitted can be ordered by the Federal Court at the request of the Registrar or any interested person.[68] The registration gives rise to presumptions concerning ownership, and subsistence of copyright[69] as well as knowledge of the copyright by an infringer.[70] The statute also gives priority to the assignee or the grantee who registered first its interest.[71]

---

63. Subsection 2.1(2).
64. *See* s. 2, definition of 'work'.
65. *King Features Syndicate, Inc. et al. v. Lechter*, [1950] Ex. C.R. 297.
66. *See* for instance the *Library and Archives of Canada Act* (SC 2004, c. 11), s. 10 and the *Legal Deposit of Publications Regulations*, SOR/2006-337; *An Act Respecting Bibliothèque et Archives nationales du Québec*, S.R.Q. c. B-1.2, ss 20.0.1–20.10.
67. Sections 55–57.
68. Subsection 57(4).
69. Subsection 53(2). s. 34.1 creates a statutory presumption that the author was the owner of the copyright. A certificate of registration under subs. 53(2) could be sufficient to rebut the statutory presumption: *Circle Movie Enterprises Inc. v. C.B.C.*, [1959] S.C.R. 602, at 604–607.
70. Section 39.
71. Subsection 57(3).

II. Substantive Requirements

39. The subsistence of copyright depends upon whether the work is original, whether it meets the fixation requirements and whether it presents the connecting factors with Canada.

A. Originality

40. Section 5 requires that a work be original to be protected. To define originality, the Canadian courts have often said to be in agreement[72] with the analysis of the High Court (Chancery Division) in the UK decision *University of London Press Ltd. v. University Tutorial Press Ltd*,[73] who stated:

> The word 'original' does not in this connection mean that work must be the expression of original or inventive thought. Copyright Acts are not concerned with the originality of ideas, but with the expression of thought in print or writing. The originality which is required relates to the expression of the thought. [...] the Act does not require that the expression must be in an original or novel form, but that the work must not be copied from another work – that it should originate from the author.[74]

41. In the case *CCH Canadian Ltd. v. Law Society of Upper Canada*,[75] the Supreme Court of Canada clarified the notion of originality, stating:

> I conclude that an 'original' work under the Copyright Act is one that originates from an author and is not copied from another work. That alone, however, is not sufficient to find that something is original. In addition, an original work must be the product of an author's exercise of skill and judgment. The exercise of skill and judgment required to produce the work must not be so trivial that it could be characterized as a purely mechanical exercise. While creative works will by definition be 'original' and covered by copyright, creativity is not required to make a work 'original'.[76]

The Court, applying the standard of skill, judgment and/or labour, found that headnotes of reported judicial decisions, the case summary and the topical index of law reports were original works and protected by copyright.[77] Also the reported judicial decisions, that is the arrangement of the case summary, the catchlines, the case title, the case information (the headnotes) and the judicial reasons, set in a specific manner, were also original work attracting copyright protection.

72. *See* for instance *Canadian Admiral Corp. v. Rediffusion, Inc.*, [1954] Ex. C.R. 382.
73. [1916] 2 Ch. 601.
74. *Ibid.*, at 608.
75. *CCH Canadian Ltd. v. Law Society of Upper Canada*, [2004] 1 S.C.R. 339.
76. *Ibid.*, at para. 25.
77. *Ibid.*, at para. 36.

However, the editing of the judicial reasons without the headnotes were not original works, because the correction of minor grammatical errors and spelling mistakes and the addition of only basic factual information were mere mechanical exercises: those changes were too trivial to attract copyright protection.[78]

B. Fixation

42. There are no general standards of fixation in the *Copyright Act*. However, the issue of fixation is addressed in some statutory provisions. For instance, the legislative definition of computer programs and dramatics works requires fixation.[79] Until 1993, the statute also specified that musical work had to be 'printed, reduced to writing or otherwise graphically produced or reproduced'.[80] According to section 3(1.1), a work that is communicated to the public by telecommunication is fixed even if it is fixed simultaneously with its communication.

43. Although some learned authors argue strongly that the copyright does not require a general precondition fixation in material form,[81] the courts have asked that the work be embodied in a permanent form on a number of occasions. In *Canadian Admiral*,[82] the Court decided that the live broadcast of sports events were not covered by the *Copyright Act*, since the process by which broadcasting produces pictures or images on a screen is not analogous to cinematography or photography. The Exchequer Court (Ex. C.R.) stated:

> … for copyright to subsist in a 'work' it must be expressed to some extent at least in some material form, capable of identification and having a more or less permanent endurance.[83]

In *Gould Estate v. Stoddard Publishing Co.*,[84] the Ontario Court of Appeal agreed with the judge of the first instance that the artist who gave an interview had no copyright in his oral utterances. In *Théberge v. Galerie d'Art du Petit Champlain inc.*,[85] the Supreme Court of Canada declared that:

> 'Fixation' […] distinguishes works capable of being copyrighted from general ideas that are the common intellectual 'property' of everyone[86] and that: 'Fixation of the work in a medium is a condition sine qua non of the production of a work.'[87]

---

78. *Ibid.*, at para. 35.
79. Section 2.
80. S.R.C. 1985, c. C-42, s. 2.
81. Y. Gendreau, *'The Criterion of Fixation in Copyright Law' R.I.D.A.* 110, 159 (1994).
82. *Canadian Admiral Corp. v. Rediffusion, Inc.*, [1954] Ex. C.R. 382.
83. *Ibid.*, at 394.
84. (1998) 161 D.L.R. (4th) 321 (Ont. C.A.); (1998) 39 O.R. (3d) 555 (Ont. C.A.).
85. *Théberge v. Galerie d'Art du Petit Champlain Inc.*, [2002] 2 S.C.R. 336.
86. *Ibid.*, at para. 25.
87. *Ibid.*, at para. 145.

All those dictum seem to support the view that there is a general requirement of fixation in Canadian law.

C. Connecting Factors

44. Canada is a party to the Berne Convention, to the Universal Copyright Convention and to the Agreement on Trade-Related Aspects of Intellectual Property Rights (TRIPs Agreement).[88] All three international conventions are based on the principle of national treatment. Each country party to those conventions must grant the same protection to nationals of the other member countries as it grants to its own nationals.

45. As a consequence of Canada's membership to those conventions, the Canadian *Copyright Act* grants protection not only to works produced by Canadians or published in Canada but also to works connected to countries party to those conventions. Section 5 specifies that copyright shall subsist in a work, published or not, if the author, at the time of the making of the work, was a 'qualified person', that is a citizen, a subject, a habitual resident of a treaty country, (a country party to *Berne Convention*, to the *Universal Copyright Convention* or to the *TRIPs Agreement*).

46. The place of first publication can also serve as a connecting factor. The Canadian *Act* will protect published works if the first publication (made in such a quantity as to satisfy the reasonable demand of the public, having regard to the nature of the work), has occurred in a treaty country.[89] If publication occurs in two countries within thirty days, and only one is a treaty country, the publication can still be used as a connecting factor.[90] Special rules apply for cinematographic works and architectural works.[91] The *Copyright Act* provides for a legislative definition of publication. Publication means making copies available to the public.[92] Will not be sufficient, the performance in public of the work, or the communication to the public by telecommunication.[93] The construction of an architectural work constitutes a publication of that work. In the case of an artistic work, the incorporation of such work into an architectural work is also treated as a publication, but not the exhibition in public of such artistic work.[94] The copyright protection can also be extended to works of other countries on condition of reciprocity, to be certified by the Minister of Industry.[95]

§4. OWNERSHIP

47. The *Copyright Act* deals with the initial ownership, the joint authorship and works for hire.

88. *See* para. 19 of this chapter.
89. Subsection 5(1).
90. Subsection 5(1.1).
91. *See* s. 5.
92. Section 2.2.
93. Subsection 2.2(1).
94. *Ibid.*
95. Subsection 5(2).

I. The Author (Initial Authorship)

48. In principle, the author of the work is the first owner of the copyright.[96] The author is the one that creates the work by writing it, drawing it or composing it.

49. The *Copyright Act* has created special rules of ownership for certain categories of work, such as photographs, engravings, portraits, cinematographic works and works commissioned by the Crown. In the case of a photograph, the *Act* previously granted the first ownership to the first owner of the negative or photograph, or to the person who had commissioned and paid for a photograph.[97] The Act was amended to eliminate this special regime,[98] but there is now an exception for the private use of a photograph or portrait.[99] In the case of a cinematographic work, the *Act* defines the maker as the person by whom the arrangements necessary for the making of the work are undertaken.[100] However, the copyright ownership should be assessed using the general principles.[101]

50. Section 12 provides that, without prejudice to any rights or privileges of the Crown, the copyright in any work prepared or published by or under the direction or control of Her Majesty or any government department, subject to any agreement with the author, belongs to the government.

II. Joint Works/Works Created by Several Persons

51. The *Copyright Act* deals separately with works of joint authorship, collective works and compilations.

A. Collective Work and Compilation

52. Collective works are according to section 2, either:

> (a) an encyclopaedia, dictionary, year book or similar work, or (b) a newspaper, review, magazine or similar periodical, or (c) any work written in distinct parts by different authors, or in which works or parts of works of different authors are incorporated.

Compilation is also the object of a legal definition in section 2. It means:

> (a) a work resulting from the selection or arrangement of literary, dramatic, musical or artistic works or of parts thereof, or (b) a work resulting from the selection or arrangement of data.

---

96. Section 13.
97. David Vaver, *Intellectual Property Law* 122 (2d ed., Irwin Law 2011).
98. *An Act to amend the Copyright Act*, SC 2012, c. 20, s. 6.
99. Section 32.2 (1) f).
100. Section 2.
101. John S. McKeown, *Fox Canadian Law of Copyright and Industrial Designs* 332 (3d ed., Carswell 2000).

Often a collective work, such as a newspaper, will also be characterized as a compilation.[102] To be protected by copyright, both need originality, which can exist in either the selection or the arrangement of the different components.[103] The copyright covers the selection and arrangement of the components and following the Supreme Court's decision in the *Robertson* case, the copyright holder in the collective work can reproduce the work without infringing the copyright of the individual contributors.[104] However, the right holder in the collective work cannot claim copyright in the individual parts of the collective work,[105] so he or she is not entitled to reproduce those works separately.

B. Work of Joint Authorship

53. A work of joint authorship is a work produced by the collaboration of two or more authors in which the contribution of one author is not distinct from the contribution of the other author or authors.[106] Some courts also require some 'mutual intent' or an 'intent to co-author' the work, but the case law is not all in agreement.[107]

III. Works Made for Hire

54. The *Act* lays down a special rule when an author is in the employment of some other person under a contract of service or apprenticeship: unless there are contractual provisions to the contrary, the *Copyright Act* grants the employer copyright in all works produced by the employee in the course of employment.[108] A contract of service is to be distinguished from a contract for services where the author, as independent contractor, keeps the copyright on the work commissioned. The work must also be made in the course of employment.[109]

55. Section 13(3) also provides a limited right for employees who contribute to newspapers, magazines or similar periodicals of their employer to restrain publication of their works otherwise than as part of the periodical. The section applies only to employees. In the case of freelance authors, the Supreme Court of Canada ruled that they have an exclusive right on the reproduction of their works in online databases, but not on the CD-ROM version of the periodical.[110]

---

102. *Robertson v. Thomson Corp.*, [2006] 2 S.C.R. 363, at para. 31.
103. *Ibid.*, at para. 37.
104. *Robertson v. Thomson Corp.*, [2006] 2 S.C.R. 363. This right does not cover the reproduction of the work in a database.
105. *See* subs. 2.1(2) and *CCH Canadian Ltd. v. Law Society of Upper Canada*, [2004] 1 S.C.R. 339, at para. 33; *Robertson v. Thomson Corp.*, [2006] 2 S.C.R. 363, at paras. 36–37.
106. Section 2.
107. *See Neugebauer v. Labieniec*, 2009 FC 666, at paras 40–52, aff'd 2010 FCA 229.
108. Subsection 13(3).
109. John S. McKeown, *Fox Canadian Law of Copyright and Industrial Designs* 342 (3d ed., Carswell 2000), referring again to *Stevenson Jordan and Harrison, Ltd. v. Macdonald*, [1952] 1 The Times L.R. 101.
110. *Robertson v. Thomson Corp.*, [2006] 2 S.C.R. 363.

§5. Transfer

56. The *Copyright Act* deals separately with the economic rights and the moral rights of the author. It is therefore necessary to present the different rules of transfer applicable to each type of rights.

I. Assignment of Copyright

57. As far as economic rights are concerned, section 13(4) of the *Copyright Act* states:

> The owner of the copyright in any work may assign the right, either wholly or partially, and either generally or subject to limitations relating to territory, medium or sector of the market or other limitations relating to the scope of the assignment, and either for the whole term of the copyright or for any other part thereof.

The section also requires that any assignment of copyright be in writing and signed by the owner of the right. This requirement has been treated as a substantive rule of law, not as a simple rule of evidence.[111] However, oral contracts will be enforced under the general rules of law.[112]

58. The *Act* imposes a limitation on the term of the assignment where the author was the first owner of the copyright: twenty-five years after the death of the author, the copyright will revert to the legal representatives of the deceased.[113]

59. Assignment can be registered[114] and a certain priority is given to assignees who registered their rights first.[115]

60. The *Copyright Act* also specifies that the holder of any right, title or interest in a copyright may start proceedings to protect and enforce rights conferred by the *Act.*[116] The *Act* adds:

> *For greater certainty, it is deemed always to have been the law that a right of action for infringement of copyright may be assigned in association with the assignment of the copyright or the grant of an interest in the copyright by license.*[117]

111. D. Vaver, *Copyright Law* 242 (Irwin Law 2000); John S. McKeown, *Fox Canadian Law of Copyright and Industrial Designs* 368 (3d ed., Carswell 2000).
112. D. Vaver, *Intellectual Property Law* 584 (2d ed., Irwin Law 2011).
113. Subsection 14(1). The section does not apply to a collective work. *See* s. 14(2).
114. Subsection 57(1).
115. Subsection 57(3).
116. Subsection 41.23(1). In some cases, the copyright owner must be made party to the proceedings: *see* subs. 41.23(2).
117. Subsection 13(6).

61. With regard to moral rights, the rules of transfer are different. Moral rights are personal rights and consequently inalienable.[118] They may be transferred only on death.[119] Nevertheless, the *Act* declares that moral rights may be waived in whole or in part.[120] An assignment of copyright in a work does not necessarily mean that the assignor has waived his or her moral rights.[121] Finally, in the absence of any contrary stipulation, a waiver of a moral right made in favour of an owner or a licensee of copyright may be invoked by any person authorized by the owner or licensee to use the work, unless there is an indication to the contrary in the waiver.[122]

II. Licences

62. Since moral rights cannot be licensed,[123] the *Act* deals only with the licensing agreements of economic rights. The copyright owner can grant two types of licences: a licence coupled with the 'grant of an interest' (this terminology is the one used in subsections 13(4), 13(6) and subsection 13(7) of the *Act*) and a mere licence which is an authorization to do something that would otherwise amount to infringement. The *Act* specifies that the grant of an exclusive licence[124] in a copyright confers to the licensee an interest in the copyright.[125] If coupled with an interest, the licence must be put in writing.[126] However, it seems that the exclusive licensees have only a limited proprietary interest, enabling them to sue third parties but not the owner-licensor for copyright infringement, and granting them no right to stop parallel imports of copies of the protected work.[127] The other licences, the non-proprietary authorizations or permissions, do not need to be put in writing[128] and even implied licences have been enforced by the courts.[129]

63. Like assignments, licences coupled with an interest will end at the end of a period of twenty-five years after the death of the author, if the author was the first

118. Subsection 14.1(2)
119. Subsection 14.2(2)(3).
120. Subsection 14.1(2).
121. Subsection 14.1(3).
122. Subsection 14.1(4).
123. Since, according to subs. 14.1(2), moral rights cannot be assigned, logically they cannot be licensed either.
124. Section 2.7 indicates that for the purposes of the Act, 'an exclusive license is an authorization to do any act that is subject to copyright to the exclusion of all others including the copyright owner, whether the authorization is granted by the owner or an exclusive licensee claiming under the owner'.
125. Subsection 13(7).
126. Subsection 13(4).
127. So reasoned three judges of Supreme Court in the decision *Kraft Canada Inc. v. Euro-Excellence Inc.*, [2007] 3 S.C.R. 20.
128. *Robertson v. Thomson Corp.*, [2006] 2 S.C.R. 363, at para. 56.
129. *Netupsky v. Dominion Bridge Co.* [1972] S.C.R. 368; *Robertson v. Thomson Corp.*, [2006] 2 S.C.R. 363, at para. 56.

copyright holder.[130] Those proprietary licences can also be registered[131] and a certain priority is given to the licensees who registered their rights first.[132]

§6. Scope of Exclusive Rights

64. The Canadian *Act* grants moral rights and economic rights to the author. As the Supreme Court of Canada correctly remarked, the 'separate structures in the Act to cover economic rights on the one hand and moral rights on the other show that a clear distinction and separation was intended'.[133]

I. Moral Rights

65. The *Copyright Act* recognizes two forms of moral rights: the paternity right (i.e., generally the right of the author to be identified as such) and the integrity right (i.e., the right to object to a derogatory treatment of the work prejudicial to the honour or reputation of the author).

A. Paternity Right

66. Section 14.1(1) states that the author of a work has, in connection with an act mentioned in section 3, the right, where reasonable in the circumstances, to be associated with the work as its author by name or under a pseudonym. The author also has the right to remain anonymous. Those rights can only be exercised in connection with an act mentioned in section 3, for instance an act of reproduction or communication or publication of the whole or a substantial part of the work.

B. Integrity Right

67. Section 28.2(2) states that the author's right to the integrity of a work is infringed if the work is, to the prejudice of the honour or reputation of the author, (a) distorted, mutilated or otherwise modified; or (b) used in association with a product, service, cause or institution. In the case of a painting, sculpture or engraving, the prejudice shall be deemed to have occurred as a result of any distortion, mutilation or

130. Subsection 14(1), the section does not apply to a collective work. *See* s. 14(2).
131. Subsection 57(1).
132. Subsection 57(3).
133. *Théberge v. Galerie d'Art du Petit Champlain Inc.*, [2002] 2 S.C.R. 336, at para. 59. The Court decided that economic rights should not be so expanded that they cover the same ground as the moral rights. So a creator who has authorized the reproduction of his works on cards, photolithographs and posters and who objects to the transferring of these reproductions onto canvas is claiming a moral right, not an economic right. Moreover, since there is only a transfer of his artistic works from a paper support to a canvas substrate for purposes of resale, no reproduction of the work is made and no infringement is committed.

other modification of the work.[134] However, it will not be considered a modification of the work covered by a moral right, if the only change is in the location of a work, in the physical means by which a work is exposed or in the physical structure containing a work. Steps taken in good faith to restore or preserve the work are also by themselves not considered a modification of the work infringing moral rights.[135]

68. The integrity of the work is infringed only if the work is distorted, mutilated or modified to the prejudice of the honour or reputation of the author.

II. Exploitation Rights

69. Sections 3 and 27 establish the exploitation rights of the author. With respect to a literary, musical, dramatic and artistic work, section 3(1) prescribes that the copyright includes the right: to produce or reproduce the work in any material form, to perform the work in public, to publish, adapt, translate the work, to communicate the work by telecommunication, to sell or otherwise transfer ownership of a tangible copy of the work, and a whole series of other rights specific to certain categories of works. Section 3 also recognizes the right to authorize an exploitative right. Section 27(2) is concerned with practices known as secondary infringements where a person deals commercially with copies of a work that he or she knows or should have known infringe copyright.

70. For an infringement to occur, the defender must make use of the whole work or of a *substantial par*t of it.[136] The test of substantiality is qualitative rather than quantitative. As the Supreme Court explained in the *Cinar* decision:

> [26] A substantial part of a work is a flexible notion. It is a matter of fact and degree. 'Whether a part is substantial must be decided by its quality rather than its quantity': Ladbroke (Football), Ltd. v. William Hill (Football), Ltd., [1964] 1 All E.R. 465 (H.L.), at p. 481, per Lord Pearce. What constitutes a substantial part is determined in relation to the originality of the work that warrants the protection of the Copyright Act. As a general proposition, a substantial part of a work is a part of the work that represents a substantial portion of the author's skill and judgment expressed therein.[137]

To assess substantiality, the courts will use a number of factors, such as:

> the quality and quantity of the material taken; (b) the extent to which the defendant's use adversely affects the plaintiff's activities and diminishes the value of the plaintiff's copyright; (c) whether the material taken is the proper subject-matter of a copyright; (d) whether the defendant intentionally appropriated the plaintiff's

134. Subsection 28.2(2).
135. Subsection 28.2(3).
136. *See* the wording of s. 3.
137. *Cinar Corporation v. Robinson*, 2013 SCC 73, [2013] 3 S.C.R. 1168, at para. 26.

work to save time and effort; and (e) whether the material taken is used in the same or a similar fashion as the plaintiffs.[138]

71. Will Canadian courts sanction the appropriation of the non-literal portions of a work, such as a computer program? The courts may in some circumstances refer to the American 'abstraction-filtration-comparison' method of deciding infringement of copyright in computer programs.[139] In the *Cinar* decision,[140] the Supreme Court of Canada, while refusing to apply the method in the case at hand, acknowledged its potential value in other instances:

> [35] The approach proposed by the Cinar appellants is similar to the 'abstraction-filtration-comparison' approach used to assess substantiality in the context of computer software infringement in the United States: see Computer Associates International, Inc. v. Altai, Inc., 982 F.2d 693 (2d Cir. 1992); B. Clermont, 'Les compilations et la Loi sur le droit d'auteur: leur protection et leur création' (2006), 18 C.P.I. 219, at p. 237; B. Tarantino, ""I've Got This Great Idea for a Show. . ." — Copyright Protection for Television Show and Motion Picture Concepts and Proposals' (2004), 17 I.P.J. 189, at pp. 199-200. It has been discussed, though not formally adopted, in Canadian jurisprudence: [Delrina Corp. v. Triolet Systems Inc. et al. (2002), 17 C.P.R. (4th) 289 (Ont. C.A.)], at paras. 43-47. I do not exclude the possibility that such an approach might be useful in deciding whether a substantial part of some works, for example computer programs, has been copied. But many types of works do not lend themselves to a reductive analysis. Canadian courts have generally adopted a qualitative and holistic approach to assessing substantiality. 'The character of the works will be looked at, and the court will in all cases look, not at isolated passages, but at the two works as a whole to see whether the use by the defendant has unduly interfered with the plaintiff's right': J. S. McKeown, Fox on Canadian Law of Copyright and Industrial Designs (loose-leaf), at p. 21-16.4.

The Court in the Cinar case also indicated that a 'substantial part of a work is not limited to the words on the page or the brushstrokes on the canvas. The Act protects authors against both literal and non-literal copying, …'.[141] So the copyright in a proposal for an educational children's television show is infringed if the overall architecture of the submission and the specific personality traits of the characters have been copied without authorization. Also, when there is only a limited number of ways to express an idea, the court may refer to the merger notion to determine if the portions taken amount to a substantial part of the work. In Delrina Corp. v. Triolet Systems Inc., the Ontario Court of Appeal stated:

---

138. *U & R Tax Services Ltd. v. H & R Block Canada Inc.* (1995), 62 C.P.R. (3d) 257 (F.C.T.D.), at 268.

139. *Conexsys Systems Inc. v. Aime Star Marketing Inc.*, [2003] R.J.Q. 2875 (Qué. C.S.); *Delrina Corp. v. Triolet Systems Inc.* (2002), 17 C.P.R. (4th) 289 (Ont. C.A.); *Matrox Electronic Systems Ltd. c Gaudreau*, [1993] R.J.Q. 2449, (C.S. Qué.).

140. *Cinar Corporation v. Robinson*, 2013 SCC 73, [2013] 3 S.C.R. 1168.

141. *Cinar Corporation v. Robinson*, 2013 SCC 73, [2013] 3 S.C.R. 1168, at para. 27.

> The merger notion is a natural corollary of the idea/expression distinction which [...] is fundamental in copyright law in Canada, England and the United States. Clearly, if there is only one or a very limited number of ways to achieve a particular result in a computer program, to hold that that way or ways are protectable by copyright could give the copyright holder a monopoly on the idea or function itself.[142]

A. Reproduction Right

72. This right is perhaps the most important prerogative granted by section 3 of the *Copyright Act*. It means that no one other than the copyright owner may make any production or reproduction of the work in any material form. Even a copy or reproduction of the work in a non-human readable form will be covered by the reproduction right.[143] Thus computer programs embedded in a silicon chip are a reproduction of the programs in assembly language protected as literary work.[144] Section 3(1)(*d*) is even more specific in stating that in the case of a literary, dramatic or musical work, the reproduction right encompasses the right to make any sound recording, cinematograph film or other contrivance by means of which the work may be mechanically reproduced or performed. In 2015, the Supreme Court of Canada decided that broadcast-incidental copying activities do engage the reproduction right, and that the Copyright Board must consider the principle of technological neutrality when fixing the licence fees for those broadcast-incidental copies.[145]

B. Performing Right

73. The *Copyright Act* distinguishes two types of performance rights: the public performance right, which allows the copyright holder to control the performance of the work in front of a public audience, and a transmission right, which involves the right to communicate the work to the public by telecommunication. In Canadian law, those two rights are distinct, being set in two separate subparagraphs of section 3.[146]

142. (2002), 17 C.P.R. (4th) 289 (Ont. C.A.), at para. 52, affirming 47 C.P.R. (3d) 1 (Ont. S.C.).
143. *Apple Computer Inc. v. MacKintosh Computers Ltd.*, [1987] 1 F.C. 173 (F.C.T.D.), at para. 79, varied by [1988] 1 F.C. 673, (F.C.A.), aff'd [1990] 2 S.C.R. 209.
144. *Ibid.*
145. Canadian Broadcasting Corp. *v.* SODRAC 2003 Inc., 2015 SCC 57, [2015] 3 S.C.R. 615.
146. In two decisions, the F.C.A. had decided that a broadcast transmission could also be considered a public performance: *see Canadian Cable Television Assn. v. Canada (Copyright Board)*, [1993] 2 F.C. 138 (F.C.A.); *CTV Television Network Ltd. v. Canada (Copyright Board)*, [1993] 2 F.C. 115 (F.C.A.). The legislator overruled those decisions by enacting s. 2.3 which states that a person who communicates a work to the public by telecommunication does not by that act alone perform it in public.

1. Public Performance Right

74. Section 3 grants to the author the exclusive right to perform the work or any substantial part of it in public. A 'performance' encompasses any acoustic or visual representation of the work, including a representation made by means of any mechanical instrument (such as a disc player), radio receiving set or television receiving set. Section 2.3 specifies that a person who communicates a work to the public by telecommunication does not by that act alone perform it in public.

75. The work must be performed in public. To determine if a performance is to be considered public, the court will look at the nature of the intended and potential audience for a performance. Thus a performance in a private home, does not amount to a performance in public since the audience is purely a domestic one.[147]

2. Transmission Right

76. Subparagraph 3(1)(f) grants to the author the right to communicate the work to the public by telecommunication. A telecommunication means any 'transmission of signs, signals, writing, images or sounds or intelligence of any nature by wire, radio, visual, optical or other electromagnetic system'.[148] The *Copyright Act* specifies that 'communication of a work or other subject matter to the public by telecommunication includes making it available to the public by telecommunication in a way that allows a member of the public to have access to it from a place and at a time individually chosen by that member of the public'.[149] So broadcasts, cable transmissions and internet transmissions[150] are all telecommunications of works. However a videogame distributor who sells copies to consumers and transfers to the purchasers the file for download using the internet is not communicating the works.[151] As the Supreme Court of Canada explained:

> *... the term 'communicate' in s. 3(1) (f), which has historically been linked to the right to perform, should not be transformed by the use of the word 'telecommunication' in a way that would capture activities akin to reproduction. Such transformation would result in abandoning the traditional distinction in the Act between performance-based rights and rights of reproduction.*[152]

77. The transmission must be made to the public. The *Act* specifies that occupants of apartments, hotel rooms or dwelling units situated in the same building are part of the public, and a communication intended to be received exclusively by such persons

147. *Canadian Admiral Corp. v. Rediffusion Inc.*, [1954] Ex. C.R. 382.
148. Section 2 definition of 'telecommunication'.
149. Subsection 2.4 (1.1).
150. *Society of Composers, Authors and Music Publishers of Canada v. Canadian Assn. of Internet Providers*, [2004] 2 S.C.R. 427.
151. *Entertainment Software Association v. Society of Composers, Authors and Music Publishers of Canada*, 2012 SCC 34, [2012] 2 S.C.R. 231.
152. *Entertainment Software Association v. Society of Composers, Authors and Music Publishers of Canada*, 2012 SCC 34, [2012] 2 S.C.R. 231, at para. 39.

is a communication to the public.[153] To be 'to the public' a communication must be targeted at the public in general or at a segment of the public, such as the customers of a wireless carrier.[154] It also means that the streaming of files from the Internet by individual users constitutes a communication to the public made by the online music services that make the files available for streaming.[155] However, sending a single copy to a single individual is not a communication to the public[156]

78. Finally, the *Act* deals with communications of works by enterprises part of a network: all the transmissions are presumed to be a single communication to the public for which those persons are jointly and severally liable.[157] On the other hand, because the *Act* exempts cable retransmitters (and similar enterprises) from the normal application of the transmission right, section 2.4(3) confirms that a work is not communicated to the public when a signal is retransmitted to a person who is a retransmitter.

C. Adaptation Right

79. The copyright holder has the exclusive right to convert a dramatic work into a novel or other non-dramatic work, or to convert a novel or other non-dramatic work into a dramatic work, or to make a cinematographic work from another type of work.[158]

80. As the Supreme Court of Canada stressed, there is no explicit and independent concept of 'derivative work' in the Canadian *Act.*[159] The general principles apply: a work borrowing from a pre-existing work should be protected by copyright if the originality requirement has been met, that is, if sufficient skill and judgment have been used to produce the derivative work.[160]

D. Translation Right

81. The translation right is expressly granted in section 3(1)(a).

---

153. Subsection 2.4(1).

154. *Canadian Wireless Telecommunications Association v. Society of Composers, Authors and Music Publishers of Canada*, 2008 FCA 6; quoted with approval by the Supreme Court of Canada in *Rogers Communications Inc. v. Society of Composers, Authors and Music Publishers of Canada*, 2012 SCC 35, [2012] 2 S.C.R. 283, at para. 31.

155. *Rogers Communications Inc. v. Society of Composers, Authors and Music Publishers of Canada*, 2012 SCC 35, [2012] 2 S.C.R. 283.

156. *CCH Canadian Ltd. v. Law Society of Upper Canada*, [2004] 1 S.C.R. 339, at para. 78; *Rogers Communications Inc. v. Society of Composers, Authors and Music Publishers of Canada*, 2012 SCC 35, [2012] 2 S.C.R. 283, at paras 25–26.

157. Subsection 2.4(1)(c).

158. *See* subss 3(1) (b), (c) and (e).

159. *Théberge c. Galerie d'Art du Petit Champlain inc.*, [2002] 2 S.C.R. 336, at para. 73.

160. *See* s. IIA of this chapter.

E. Other Rights

1. Droit de Suite

82. There is no droit de suite in the Canadian copyright regime.

2. Public Lending Right

83. The *Copyright Act* does not recognize as such a public lending right (PLR). However the federal *Status of the Artist Act*[161] stresses the importance of compensating artists for the use of their works, including the public lending of them.[162] In 1986, a PLR regime was established by a Cabinet decision: under the regime, the payments are provided by the Federal Government and a PLR Commission is responsible for setting the general policies of the programme.[163]

3. Others

84. The Act grants the authors a right to authorize an exploitation act, a right of action to stop secondary infringement of their copyright, and a first public distribution right. In addition, it provides, in favour of certain copyright holders, for an exhibition right and a right to rent out copies. Some provisions also recognize additional rights of action.

a. Right to Authorize an Exploitation Right

85. In the last line of section 3(1) of the *Copyright Act*, copyright is said to include the exclusive right to authorize any of the rights enumerated in section 3. The word ‘authorize’ has been judicially construed to include anyone who ‘sanctions, approves, or countenances’.[164] So a company who orders, without consent from the copyright holder, the manufacturing of records of protected works, is infringing the right to authorize the mechanical reproduction of the works.[165] However, the Supreme Court of Canada specified that an ‘officer of a corporation cannot be held personally liable for copyright infringement merely on the basis of his hierarchical status as officer’.[166] Similarly, providing equipment that could be used to infringe copyright is not authorizing infringement: one can presume that the equipment will be used in accordance with the law.[167] However once a notice of infringing activities is given, liability may arise if the activities are not stopped. In *Society of Composers, Authors*

161. S.C. 1992, c. 33.
162. Subsection 2(e).
163. For further information, *see* the reports of the PLR Commission on the website www.plr-dpp.ca.
164. *CCH Canadian Ltd. v. Law Society of Upper Canada*, [2004] 1 S.C.R. 339, at para. 38.
165. *Compo Co. Ltd. v. Blue Crest Music Inc.* et al., [1980] 1 S.C.R. 357, at 373.
166. *Cinar Corporation v. Robinson*, 2013 SCC 73, [2013] 3 S.C.R. 1168, at para. 64.
167. *CCH Canadian Ltd. v. Law Society of Upper Canada*, [2004] 1 S.C.R. 339, at para. 38.

and Music Publishers of Canada v. Canadian Assn. of Internet Providers, the Supreme Court of Canada explained:

> The knowledge that someone might be using neutral technology to violate copyright (as with the photocopier in the CCH case [CCH Canadian Ltd. v. Law Society of Upper Canada, [2004] 1 S.C.R. 339]) is not necessarily sufficient to constitute authorization, which requires a demonstration that the defendant did '(g)ive approval to; sanction, permit; favour, encourage' (CCH, at para. 38) the infringing conduct. I agree that notice of infringing content, and a failure to respond by 'taking it down' may in some circumstances lead to a finding of 'authorization'.[168]

Specific regimes cover or will cover the liability of network services providers, such as internet access providers, web hosting service providers and providers of information location tools.[169]

b. Secondary Infringement

86. Subsection 27(2) enumerates the acts constituting secondary infringements of copyright:

> *It is an infringement of copyright for any person to:*

(1) *sell or rent out;*
(2) *distribute to such an extent as to affect prejudicially the owner of the copyright;*
(3) *by way of trade distribute, expose or offer for sale or rental, or exhibit in public;*
(4) *possess for the purpose of doing anything referred to in paragraphs (a) to (c); or*
(5) *import into Canada for the purpose of doing anything referred to in paragraphs (a) to (c)*

> *a copy of a work, [...] that the person knows or should have known infringes copyright or would infringe copyright if it had been made in Canada by the person who made it.*

Moreover, the Act prohibits the importation or exportation of counterfeit goods.[170]

87. There is no secondary infringement if the copy was made outside Canada in circumstances which if made in Canada would have been covered by an exception.[171] Specific provisions apply to imports of books.[172]

168. In *Society of Composers, Authors and Music Publishers of Canada v. Canadian Assn. of Internet Providers*, [2004] 2 S.C.R. 427, at para. 127.
169. *See* para. 90 of this chapter.
170. Sections 44 and ff.
171. Subsection 27 (2.1).
172. Section 27.1.

88. Is also liable for infringement of copyright anyone who provides through the Internet, or another digital network, a service that is designed primarily to enable acts of copyright infringement if actual infringement occurs as a result of the use of that service.[173]

c. Exhibition Right

89. Because artistic works, unlike other types of work, could not really be 'performed', the *Copyright Act* was amended in 1998 to provide them with an exhibition right. According to section 3(1)(g), the display without authorization of an artistic work at a public exhibition for a purpose other than sale or hire is an infringement of copyright. This exhibition right applies for any artistic work other than a map, chart or plan. Because of the potential impact of this new provision on museums' activities, the legislator attached this new right only to works created after 7 June 1988.[174]

d. Right to Rent Out Copies

90. In order to comply with section 1705 of *NAFTA*,[175] the right to rent out computer programs was added to the list of the exclusive rights of the authors.[176] A similar right to rent out sound recordings, also set out in *NAFTA*,[177] was granted to the holders of copyright in musical works.[178] The rental must be made with the motive of gain.[179] The *Act* specifies that a person who rents out a computer program or sound recording with the intention of recovering no more than the costs, including overhead, associated with the rental operations does not by that act alone have a motive of gain.[180]

e. First Public Distribution Right

91. The copyright holder has, in the case of a work that is in the form of a tangible object, the right to sell or otherwise transfer ownership of the tangible object, as long as that ownership has never previously been transferred in or outside Canada with the authorization of the copyright owner.[181]

f. Additional Rights of Action

92. The *Act* prohibits the act of circumventing a protective measure that controls access to a work or restricts the doing of some reproduction or communication of the

173. Subsections 27 (2.3) (2.4).
174. Subsection 3(1)(g).
175. *See* para. 18 of this chapter.
176. *North American Free Trade Agreement Implementation Act*, S.C. 1993, c. 44 subs. 55(2), introducing subs. 3(1)(h) *of the Copyright Act*.
177. Article 1706.
178. *See* subs. 3(1)(i) of the *Copyright Act*.
179. *See* the definition of rental in subs. 2.5(1).
180. Subsection 2.5(2).
181. Subsection 3 (1) (1)(j)of the *Copyright Act*.

work.[182] It is also forbidden to remove or modify rights management information (identifying the rights holder, terms and conditions of use, etc.) embedded in a protected work.[183] The copyright owner has a right of action against anyone who contravenes those prohibitions and is entitled to all remedies available for copyright infringement.[184] These prohibitions are subject to limitations,[185] some of which will be determined by regulations.[186]

§7. Limitations or Exemptions to the Scope of Copyright Protection

93. The exploitation rights are not without limits: they are for instance limited by the fair dealing provision and several other specific limitations set forth in the *Copyright Act*. The main exceptions to the exclusive rights of authors are enumerated in sections 29 et seq. Those exceptions can be regrouped under the following headings: fair use, educational use, use by libraries, archives, or museums, private copying and other specific exceptions. Finally, the Canadian *Competition Act*[187] may impose some limits to the rights of a copyright owner.

94. It is important to note that the specific exceptions are very detailed provisions setting very precise limits to the users' rights and imposing strict conditions to satisfy. For instance, some exempted activities for educational use must be done on the premises of the educational institution; distance education is excluded. It is also necessary to satisfy strictly each one of the conditions specified in the provision: if for instance, a suitable support is accessible on the market, exceptions are usually not applicable. The fair dealing exception is a little more flexible.[188]

I. Fair Use

95. The most important exception relates to fair dealing. It is not an infringement of copyright to make a fair dealing of a work for the specific purposes enumerated in

182. Sections 41–41.22.
183. Section 41.22.
184. Subsections 41.1 (2) and 41.22 (2).
185. To protect personal information (s. 41.14); in matters of law enforcement and national security (s. 41.11); for interoperability of computer programs (s. 41.12); for encryption research (s. 41.13); for security of computer system or network (s. 41.15); for persons with perceptual disabilities (s. 41.16); for broadcasting undertakings (s. 41.17); for radio apparatus to gain access to a telecommunication service (s. 41.18).
186. Section 41.21.
187. RSC 1985, c. C 34.
188. *See CCH Canadian Ltd. v. Law Society of Upper Canada*, [2004] 1 S.C.R. 339, where the Court applied the fair dealing provision to exempt the defendants' photocopying practices, whereas s. 30.3 withdraws the exception if a certified tariff or agreement exists or if a proposed tariff has been filed with the Copyright Board.

the *Act*.[189] In some cases, the exception requires that the source and author be properly identified.[190]

96. In order to show that a dealing is fair under section 29 of the *Copyright Act*, a defendant must prove: (1) that dealing comes within one of the enumerated purposes; and (2) that it is fair. To determine if an utilization is fair, courts will look at: (1) the purpose of the dealing; (2) the character of the dealing; (3) the amount of the dealing; (4) alternatives to the dealing; (5) the nature of the work; and (6) the effect of the dealing on the work.[191] The specific purposes for a fair dealing are identified in the statute: research, or private study, education, parody and satire (section 29), criticism or review (section 29.1), or news reporting (section 29.2).). The provision was interpreted as allowing elementary and secondary schools to make, at the teachers' initiative, copies of works as reading material for the students[192] or as permitting online music service providers to allow customers to listen to free previews of musical works in order to identify which music to purchase.[193]

II. Educational Use

97. The law creates exemptions in favour of educational institutions and people acting under their authority, such as teachers or pupils. The term 'educational institution' is defined in the *Act* and would not cover an establishment not licensed or recognized by or under a federal or provincial statute to provide pre-school, elementary, secondary or post-secondary education.[194]

98. The law allows these establishments of teaching to reproduce or present protected works within very precise limits and under strict conditions. In general, the exempted activities must be done in the premises of the educational institution for educational or training purposes and not for profit.[195] The audience must consist primarily of members of the educational institution. In some cases, copies are to be kept for short periods of time, unless royalties are paid.[196] Moreover, if a suitable support is accessible on the market, exceptions are usually inapplicable. It will also be specified that the exceptions do not apply if done by unlawful means or from illegal sources.[197]

99. The list of authorized acts for the educational institutions is: reproduction for instruction,[198] reproduction for examination,[199] live performance or direct transmission

189. Sections 29–29.2.
190. Section 29.1.
191. *CCH Canadian Ltd. v. Law Society of Upper Canada*, [2004] 1 S.C.R. 339, at paras 53–60.
192. *Alberta (Education) v. Canadian Copyright Licensing Agency (Access Copyright)*, 2012 SCC 37, [2012] 2 S.C.R 345.
193. *Society of Composers, Authors and Music Publishers of Canada v. Bell Canada*, 2012 SCC 36, [2012] 2 S.C.R. 326
194. Section 2.
195. Section 29.3.
196. *See* for instance subss 29.7(2) and 30.01(5) (6).
197. Sections.29.8 and 30.04 (5).
198. Subsection 29.4(1).
199. Subsection 29.4(2).

of works,[200] public performance of sound recordings,[201] reproduction and performance of news programs or news commentary programs (excluding documentaries),[202] reproduction in a casebook,[203] reproduction by photocopying machines in open areas.[204] Some exceptions also apply to distant teaching activities[205] and to works available through internet.[206] Educational institutions that have a licence for the reprographic reproduction of works are also allowed to make and communicate digital reproductions but they have to take measures to prevent communication of those reproductions to the public.[207]

III. Use by Libraries, Archives or Museums

100. The law creates a set of exceptions in favour of libraries, archives, museums and people acting under their authority.[208] These derogations are reserved to establishments that are not constituted to make profit.[209] The statute allows those institutions to make some reproductions for the management and maintenance of their collection.[210] They are also entitled to benefit from the fair dealing exemption applicable to their users' practices,[211] and from the exception relating to the reproduction of works by photocopying machines in open areas.[212]

IV. Private Copying

101. Since 1997, the private copying of musical works embodied in a sound recording is legal. The exception is limited: only the act of reproducing the music onto an audio recording medium for the private use by the person who makes the copy does not constitute an infringement of the copyright in the musical work, the performer's performance or the sound recording.[213] A commercial dealing of the copy will fall outside the exemption.[214] It does not cover the copying in a permanently embedded or

200. Section 29.5.
201. Section 29.5.
202. Section 29.6.
203. Section 30.
204. Section 30.3.
205. Section 30.01.
206. Section 30.04.
207. Sections 30.02 and 30.03.
208. Sections 30.1–30.3. A special exception applies to the Librarian and Achivist of Canada; *see* s. 30.5.
209. Sections 29.3.
210. Section 30.1.
211. Sections 30.2, 30.21.
212. Section 30.3.
213. Subsection 80(1).
214. Subsection 80(2).

non-removable memory, incorporated into a digital audio recorder, since such a device is not an 'audio recording medium'.[215]

102. To compensate the right holders, the *Act* has created a right to receive remuneration from manufacturers and importers of blank audio recording media.[216] The royalties are determined by a tariff certified by the Copyright Board. To be eligible, the authors, artists and makers of sound recordings, must satisfy the connecting requirements set up by section 85. The remuneration scheme operates on the basis of reciprocity rather than national treatment, so a right holder coming from a country which does not have a private copying scheme is not entitled to the remuneration.

V. Others Specific Exceptions in the Copyright Act

103. Some specific exceptions, subject to strict conditions, apply to reproduction of computer programs,[217] incidental inclusion of works,[218] ephemeral recordings by broadcasting undertaking,[219] retransmission of local television and radio signals,[220] reproduction and performance for people with perceptual disability,[221] disclosure and reproduction imposed by statutory provisions,[222] some use and reproduction of artistic works,[223] reporting of lectures or political speeches,[224] public recital of extracts of published works,[225] performance in an agricultural or agricultural-industrial exhibition or fair,[226] performance by religious or charitable organization,[227] and radio performances in places other than theatres.[228]

104. Amendments were introduced in 2012 to adapt the *Copyright Act* to technological changes: those exceptions cover temporary reproductions for technological processes facilitating a legal use,[229] or reproduction for encryption research,[230] for security purposes,[231] for time shifting,[232] format shifting and private copying of music

215. *Canadian Private Copying Collective v. Canadian Storage Media Alliance* (2004), [2005] 2 F.C.R. 654 (F.C.A.); *Re Private Copying 2008–2009*, 2008 FCA 9.
216. Section 81.
217. Section 30.6, 30.61.
218. Section 30.7.
219. Sections 30.8–30.9.
220. Section 31. The retransmission of distant signals is subject to the payment of royalties determined in a tariff certified by the Copyright Board: *see* ss 31 and 71.
221. Section 32.
222. Section 32.1.
223. Subsections 32.2(1)(a)(b)(f).
224. Subsections 32.2(1)(c)(e).
225. Subsections 32.2(1)(d).
226. Subsection 32.2(2).
227. Subsection 32.2(3).
228. Subsection 69(2). The royalties compensating for this use are set in a tariff certified by the Copyright Board and are paid by the radio broadcasting stations.
229. Section 30.71.
230. Section 30.62.
231. Section 30.63.
232. Section 29.23.

on the various devices that a person owns,[233] use of an existing published work for insertion in a non-commercial user-generated content (the so-called YouTube exception);[234] however, these exceptions will generally not allow people to circumvent a technical measure.[235] The liability of network services providers, such as internet service providers and host server providers, and information location tools operators is also limited[236] but the *Copyright Act* will require those enterprises to participate in the 'notice and notice' regime if they want to keep their immunity.[237]

VI. Limitations Imposed by the Competition Act

105. The *Competition Act*[238] seeks to maintain and encourage competition in Canada.[239] As intellectual property rights can be used in anti-competitive conducts that inappropriately create, enhance or maintain market power or are likely to substantially lessen or prevent competition among firms, the exercise of intellectual property rights is subject to the *Competition Act* provisions. The *Act* itself prescribes that if a right is used to restrain trade, the Federal Court can make an order to void an agreement, stop its execution, grant a licence or may order any measure necessary to prevent the anti-competitive use.[240] Also an agreement involving an intellectual property rights can constitute a criminal offence of the *Competition Act*[241] or a reviewable (civil) matter.[242] The Competition Bureau of Canada has published the *Intellectual Property Enforcement Guidelines*[243] in which it indicates when it will consider that a conduct involving intellectual property raises an issue under the *Competition Act.*

§8. Duration of Protection

106. The standard duration of a copyright is the life of the author plus fifty years.[244] In the case of a joint authorship, the copyright runs for fifty years after the

233. Section 29.22.
234. Section 29.21.
235. *See* for instance sections 29.22, 29.23 and 29.24.
236. Section 31.1 and 41.27.
237. Sections 41.25–41.26.
238. RSC 1985, c. C-34.
239. Section 1.1, *Competition Act.*
240. Section 32, *Competition Act.*
241. They include conspiracy (s. 45), bid-rigging (s. 47), false or misleading representations and other deceptive marketing practices in telemarketing, multi-level marketing plan, pyramid selling and contests (s.52–55.1).
242. Reviewable matters include deceptive marketing practices (s. 74.01), refusal to deal (s. 75), price maintenance (s. 76), exclusive dealing, tied selling and market restriction (s. 77), abuse of dominant position (s. 79), mergers (s. 92), and anti-competitive agreements (s. 90.1).
243. They were issued in 2000, revised in 2016, and are available on the Competition Bureau website www.competitionbureau.gc.ca.
244. Section 6.

last author dies.[245] The copyright in anonymous and pseudonymous works lasts for the shorter of fifty years from first publication or seventy-five years from the making of the work.[246]

107. Copyright terms differ in duration in a number of specific cases. For works that have not been published or performed, the rule was that the copyright could be perpetual.[247] A new provision removes that duration of protection and allows the standard term to apply.[248] Some transitional provisions were adopted to allow for some exploitation of the works which were losing protection.[249] The Crown copyright runs for fifty years after the first publication of the work.[250] Cinematographic works enjoy different terms of protection; except for cinematographic works in which the arrangement or acting form or the combination of incidents represented give the work a dramatic character,[251] the term of protection is fifty years after the publication of the work, or fifty years after the creation of the work, should the publication not have occurred during those fifty years.[252]

§9. Neighbouring Rights

108. The *Copyright Act* deals with the right of three beneficiaries: performers, sound recordings makers and broadcasters.

I. Performer's Rights

109. Canada is a member of the *Rome Convention*,[253] which generally imposes a national treatment obligation,[254] but allows for a number of reservations and exceptions, where the nations can, for instance, make the right to remuneration subject to reciprocity.[255] The *TRIPs Agreement* includes some, but not all the obligations of the *Rome Convention.* Canada has now ratified the *WIPO Performances and Phonograms Treaty (WPPT)*[256] country and has modified the *Copyright Act* to satisfy the minimum requirements of the WPPT.[257] Thus Canada has three regimes of protection for performances, one for the performances having a relevant connection with countries that are members of the

245. Subsection 9(1).
246. Section 6.2
247. The copyright subsisted for fifty years after publication or performance in public or transmission to the public. *See* subs. 7(1).
248. Subsection 7(2).
249. Subsections 7(3)(4).
250. Section 12.
251. In which case, the general rule applies.
252. Section 11.1.
253. For details concerning the Canada's accession, *see* para. 18 of this chapter.
254. Article 2 of the *Rome Convention.*
255. Article 16(1)(a) of the *Rome Convention.*
256. For details concerning the *WPPT*, *see* para. 18 of this chapter.
257. *Copyright Modernization Act*, SC 2012, c. 20.

Rome Convention,[258] one for the performances which took place in a *WTO* country[259] and one for the performances having the relevant connection with a *WPPT* country.[260]

110. For the performances which took place in a *WTO* country, performers have exclusive rights over the fixation in a sound recording and the communication to the public of their live and unfixed performance, the reproduction of the sound recording of their performance if made without their authorization, and the authorization of those acts.[261] Notwithstanding an assignment of a performer's right, the performer, as well as the assignee, may (a) prevent the reproduction of any unauthorized fixation of the performer's performance, or any substantial part of it, and may (b) prevent the importation of any such fixation or reproduction that the importer knows or ought to have known was made without the performer's consent or the assignee's consent.[262] Those rights are subject to the same limitations as the copyright in literary, artistic, musical and dramatic works.[263]

111. For performances protected under the *Rome Convention* regime, performers have the exclusive rights on the:

- broadcasting of their live and unfixed performances;
- public performance of their live and unfixed performances (when the public performance comes from a telecommunication otherwise than by communication signal);
- fixation of their unfixed performances;
- reproduction of their fixed performances if the reproduction was outside the purposes for legal exceptions, was unauthorized or made for purposes different from those for which they gave their consent;[264]
- rental of a sound recording;
- authorization of those acts.[265]

They are also entitled, where a sound recording of their performance has been published,[266] to be paid equitable remuneration for the performance in public or the communication to the public by telecommunication.[267] All these rights are subject to the same limitations as the copyright in literary, artistic, musical and dramatic works.[268]

112. For performances related to a *WPPT* country, performers have two additional rights: to make a sound recording available to the public over the Internet and to sell

258. Subsection 15(2) of the *Copyright Act*. If a country grants to Canadians substantially similar neighbouring rights, it can be covered by the *Rome Convention* regime; *see* s. 22 of the *Copyright Act*.
259. Section 26 of the *Copyright Act*.
260. *See* ss 5 and 8–17 of the *Copyright Modernization Act*, SC 2012, c. 20.
261. Section 26 of the *Copyright Act*.
262. Subsection 26(7).
263. *See* s. 7 (Limitations or exemptions to the scope of copyright protection) of this chapter.
264. Note the exception for the performance embodied in a cinematographic work at s. 17.
265. Section 15.
266. A sound recording 'made available to the public' through interactive networks, such as Internet, is deemed to be published: *see* ss 19.1–19.2.
267. Section 19; note that they have no right to remuneration for a retransmission.
268. *See* s. 7 (Limitations or exemptions to the scope of copyright protection) of this chapter.

or transfer the ownership in a physical recording for the first time.[269] They are also entitled, where a sound recording of their performance has been published, to be paid equitable remuneration for the performance in public or the communication to the public by telecommunication of the record.[270]

113. For performances related to Canada or to a WPPT country, a performer of a live aural performance or a performance fixed in a sound recording will also enjoy moral rights.[271]

114. The concept of performance is defined by the statute. It covers any of the following acts when done by a performer:

> *(a) a performance of an artistic work, dramatic work or musical work, whether or not the work was previously fixed in any material form, and whether or not the work's term of copyright protection under this Act has expired;*
>
> *(b) a recitation or reading of a literary work, whether or not the work's term of copyright protection under this Act has expired; or*
>
> *(c) an improvisation of a dramatic work, musical work or literary work, whether or not the improvised work is based on a pre-existing work.*[272]

115. The performer is the first owner of the copyright in a performance,[273] which can be assigned or licensed.[274] The copyright and right to remuneration last for fifty years after the first performance. If the performance is fixed in a sound recording before the copyright expires, the copyright continues for fifty years after the first fixation.[275] If the sound recording is published before the copyright expires, the copyright continues until the earlier of the end of seventy years after the first publication and the end of hundred years after the performance occurred.[276] The copyright on a performance which is subject to the *WTO* regime runs for fifty years after the performance took place.[277]

II. Sound Recording Maker's Rights

116. The maker of a sound recording has a copyright in the sound recording, consisting of the exclusive rights to: (a) publish it for the first time; (b) reproduce it

269. Subsection 15 (1.1) (d)–(e).
270. Subsection 19 (1.2).
271. Sections 17.1 and 28.1.
272. Section 2.
273. Section 24.
274. Sections 25, 26(6).
275. . Section 23.
276. *Ibid.*
277. Subsection 26(5).

in any material form; and (c) rent it out; and (d) to authorize any of those acts.[278] The maker, that is the person by whom the arrangements necessary for the first fixation of the sounds were made,[279] is entitled to the copyright protection if the sound recording has a relevant connection with a country that is member of the *Berne Convention*, or the *Rome Convention,* or the *WTO*, the *WPPT*.[280] Two additional rights are recognized to the makers protected under the Canadian or WPPT regimes: (1) to communicate it to the public by telecommunication in a way that allows a member of the public to access it from a place and at a time individually chosen by that member of the public; and (2) to sell or otherwise transfer ownership of it, in the case of a sound recording made by the sound recording maker that can be put into circulation as a tangible object and whose ownership has never previously been transferred with the authorization of the sound recording maker in or outside Canada.[281] The maker is also entitled, where the sound recording has been published, to be paid an equitable remuneration for the performance in public or the communication to the public by telecommunication of the recording.[282]

117. All these rights are subject to the same limitations as the copyright in literary, artistic, musical and dramatic works.[283] The duration of the protection is set at fifty years after the first fixation of the sound recording.[284] However, if the sound recording is published before the copyright expires, the copyright continues until the earlier of seventy years after the first publication and a hundred years after the first fixation.[285]

III. Broadcaster's Rights

118. The first owner of this neighbouring right is the broadcaster, defined in the *Act* as:

> a body that, in the course of operating a broadcasting undertaking, broadcasts a communication signal in accordance with the law of the country in which the broadcasting undertaking is carried on, but excludes a body whose primary activity in relation to communication signals is their retransmission.[286]

To be able to benefit the copyright protection, the broadcaster must, at the time of the broadcast, have its headquarters in Canada, in a country that is a *WTO* Member or in

278. Section 18.
279. Section 2 definition of 'maker'.
280. Subsections 18(2) and (2.1). If a country grants to Canadians substantially similar neighbouring rights, the protection will be available for the makers of sound recordings that are citizens, subjects or permanent residents of that country, or if corporations, have their headquarters in that country; *see* s. 22.
281. Subsection 18 (1.1).
282. Section 19.
283. *See* s. 7 (Limitations or exemptions to the scope of copyright protection) of this chapter.
284. . Subsection 23 (1.1).
285. *Ibid.*
286. Section 2, definition of 'broadcaster'

a *Rome Convention* country; and must broadcast the communication signal from that country.[287]

119. Broadcasting organizations enjoy the exclusive rights to fix their broadcasts, to reproduce any fixation that was made without their authorization, to communicate to the public their broadcasts if such communication is made in places accessible to the public against payment of an entrance fee and to authorize any of those acts.[288] The exclusive rights run for fifty years after the signal was broadcast[289] and are subject to the same limitations as the copyright in literary, musical, artistic, and dramatic works.[290]

§10. Infringement and Remedies

120. The *Copyright Act* grants to right holders civil and criminal remedies. The *Act* also establishes the framework for the collective management of copyright.

I. Civil Remedies

121. In case of copyright or moral right infringement, the right holder (including the holder of an interest by assignment or grant in writing[291] or the partial assignee[292]) can initiate proceedings at the federal or provincial courts,[293] and is entitled to all remedies such as injunction, damages, accounts, delivery up, etc.[294] The *Act* also provides for the seizure of imported copies of works.[295] The Act provides for a limitation or prescription period of three years for civil remedies.[296]

A. Presumptions

122. The *Act* creates a number of presumptions in favour of the author and copyright owner. It specifies that in an action for infringement, copyright is presumed, unless the contrary is proved, to subsist in the work, and the author, is unless the contrary is proved, to be presumed to be the owner of the copyright.[297] Also, as explained earlier, a certificate of registration of copyright is evidence that the copyright subsists

287. Subsection 21(2). If a country grants to Canadian substantially similar neighbouring rights, the protection will be available for the broadcasters that are citizens, subjects or permanent residents of that country, or if corporations, have their headquarters in that country; *see* s. 22.
288. Section 21.
289. Section 23.
290. *See* s. 7 (Limitations or exemptions to the scope of copyright protection) of this chapter.
291. Subsection 41.23(1). In such cases, the copyright owner must be joined with the proceedings, unless an exception applies. *See* subs. 41.23(2).
292. Subsection 13(5).
293. Section 41.24.
294. Section 34.
295. Sections 44–45.
296. Section 43.1.
297. Subsection 34.1(1).

and that the person registered is the owner of the copyright.[298] A similar presumption exists for a certificate of an assignment of copyright and a certificate of a licence granting an interest in a copyright.[299] Those statutory presumptions are only prima facie evidence, liable to be rebutted by the introduction of evidence for the contrary.[300]

B. *Injunctions*

123. Once the infringement has been established, the right holder can ask for a permanent injunction.[301] Interlocutory injunctions are also possible as long as the plaintiff can satisfy the test established by the courts.[302] Courts have also on occasion granted Anton Piller orders[303] and Mareva injunctions.[304] According to section 39 of the *Copyright Act*, in an action for infringement of an unregistered copyright, no remedy other than an injunction will be available if the defendant proves that at the date of the infringement he or she was not aware, and had no reasonable ground for suspecting that copyright subsisted in the work. If the copyright was duly registered, the defendant shall be deemed to have had reasonable ground for suspecting that copyright subsisted in the work.[305] The courts will not often accept this defence of good faith since 'no person is entitled to assume, without inquiry, that a work published anonymously is not the subject of copyright'.[306] Note that the owner of the copyright is not entitled to obtain an injunction to stop the construction of a building or structure

298. Subsection 53(2).
299. Subsection 53(2) and (2.1).
300. *Circle Film Enterprises Inc. v. Canadian Broadcasting Corp.*, [1959] S.C.R. 602. The prima facie evidence provided by the certificate of registration was held to prevail over the presumption created by subs. 34.1(1) that the author was the owner of the copyright.
301. Section 34.
302. The test is composed of three questions: (1) Is there a serious issue to be tried? (2) Can the plaintiff demonstrate that irreparable harm will ensue if the injunction is not granted? and (3) Does the balance of convenience favour the plaintiff or the defendant?: *RJR-MacDonald Inc. v. Canada (Attorney General)*, [1994] 1 S.C.R. 311.
303. The courts have confirmed the conditions established by Lord Ormrod L.J. in the case of *Anton Piller KG v. Manufacturing Processes Ltd.*, [1976] 1 Ch. 55 (C.A.) at 62: 'First, there must be an extremely strong prima facie case. Second, the damage, potential or actual, must be very serious for the applicant. Third, there must be clear evidence that the defendants have in their possession incriminating documents or things, and fourthly it must be shown that there is a real possibility that they may destroy such material before any application inter partes can be made'. *See Celanese Canada Inc. v. Murray Demolition Corp.*, [2006] 2 S.C.R. 189, at para. 35; *British Columbia (Attorney General) v. Malik*, 2011 SCC 18, [2011] 1 S.C.R. 657 at para. 29.
304. In *Aetna Financial Services Ltd. v. Feigelman*, [1985] 1 S.C.R. 2, the Supreme Court of Canada established that Canadian courts have jurisdiction to grant the order. The applicant must establish a strong prima facie case and that there is a real or impending threat by the defendant to remove assets from the jurisdiction, or to dissipate assets.
305. *See* . s. 39.
306. *Slumber-Magic Adjustable Bed Co. v. Sleep-King Adjustable Bed Co.* (1984) 3 C.P.R. (3d) 81 at 118, referring to *Gribble v. Man. Free Press Co.*, 40 Man. R. 42, [1931] 3 W.W.R. 570 at 575, [1932] 1 D.L.R. 169 (Man. C.A.), at paras 28–30.

or to order its demolition once the construction has started, even if the construction infringes a copyright or would infringe a copyright where completed.[307]

C. Damages

124. Damages can be measured on the basis of the loss of revenues resulting from the defendant's illegal use of the protected work or the fee normally charged for the production of work. Where it is customary to license the use of a work, damages can equal the usual royalty or licence fee. Nominal and exemplary damages are also available.

125. As permitted by section 38.1 of the *Copyright Act*, the right holder may elect an award of statutory damages in a sum of not less than CAD 500 or more than CAD 20,000 as the court considers just. Individuals caught doing an infringement for non-commercial purposes, such as downloading copyrighted files, could be fined only between CAD 100 and CAD 5000.[308]

D. Account of Profits

126. The right holder can also claim, in addition to damages for infringement, such part of the profits that the defendant has made from the infringement and that were not taken into account in calculating the damages as the court considers just.[309] The *Act* specifies that in proving profits, the plaintiff must only prove the receipts or revenues derived from the infringement and the defendant must prove every element of the cost.[310]

E. Seizure of Imported Copies of Works

127. The *Combating Counterfeit Products Act*[311], which came into force 1 January 2015, has strengthened the enforcement regime for counterfeit goods. The *Act* provides now for a procedure of 'requests for assistance', which allows right holders to file requests asking for the Canada Border Services Agency (CBSA) to temporarily detain suspected counterfeit goods while they seek remedy in civil court. The *Act* also indicates that copyright holders knowing that infringing copies are to be imported, may deliver notice to the CBSA that they wish the copies to be intercepted. Such goods will be deemed subject to tariff item No. 9897.00.00 under the Schedule to the Customs Tariff, and their importation will be prohibited under that provision.[312]

---

307. Section 40.
308. Subsection 38.1(5) sets the relevant factors to consider in the statutory damages calculation.
309. Section 35. When profits were made on infringing and non-infringing components of a work, the plaintiff can claim only the profits which have a causal link with the infringement. However, it is the infringer who bears the onus of proving that some of the profit are attributable to the non-infringing components: *see Cinar Corporation v. Robinson*, 2013 SCC 73, [2013] 3 SCR 1168, at para. 76–80.
310. Subsection 35(2).
311. SC 2014, c. 32
312. Section 44.11

If the court concludes in the applicant's favour, the court may order that the copies of the work be destroyed or that they be delivered up to the plaintiff as the plaintiff's property absolutely.[313]The *Act* lays out some exceptions in favour of people importing for specific use such as some private use or educational use.[314]

F. Recovery of Possession and Delivery Up

128. The copyright owner can also ask for the recovery or the destruction of the infringing copies and the plates used or intended to be used for the production of these infringing copies.[315] If the copies also contain non-infringing material, the court, before making the order, will consider the importance and severability of the non-infringing part.[316] Damages for conversion are no longer available.[317]

II. Criminal Remedies

129. According to the section 42 of the *Copyright Act*, commits an offence, whoever knowingly makes some specific commercial dealings of an infringing copy of a work or other subject matter in which a copyright subsists, although some exceptions are provided for.[318] Criminal provisions also cover the possession of a plate for illegal purposes,[319] an illegal public performance,[320] some improper modifications of a dramatic or operatic or musical work[321] and the circumvention of a technological protection measure (TPM) for commercial purposes,[322]

130. In 1988, the penalties for some offences were increased: a person convicted under section 42 is liable, on summary conviction, to a fine not exceeding CAD 25,000 or to imprisonment for a term not exceeding six months or to both, or on conviction on indictment, to a fine not exceeding CAD 1,000,000 or to imprisonment for a term not exceeding five years or to both. The court has also the power to order the destruction or the delivery up, to the copyright owner, of the copy of the infringing copies and the plates used or intended to be used for the production of these infringing copies.[323]

131. The general provisions of the *Criminal Code*[324] also apply to the conscious violation of copyright and can lead to a conviction if all the elements of the offence

313. . Subsection 44.12(9).
314. Section 45.
315. Sections 34 and 38.
316. Subsection 38(4).
317. Subsection 38(5).
318. Subsections 42(1) and (5).
319. Subsection 42 (2)(a). Section 2 provides a definition of the term 'plate'.
320. Subsections 42(2)(b) and 43(1).
321. Subsection 43(2). It covers alteration of the title or name of the author or any changes in the work or composition itself for the purpose of public performance for private profit.
322. Subsection 42 (3.1).
323. Subsection 42(3).
324. R.C.S. 1985, c. C-46, s. 380.

are established.[325] Also an amendment was made in 2007 to the *Criminal Code* to create a separate offence for the unauthorized recording of a movie.[326] The unauthorized use of a computer, made fraudulently and without colour of right, is also a punishable offence under the *Criminal Code*.[327]

III. Collective Management of Copyright

132. Authors will also form collective societies to help them collect their royalties from users. The first copyright collective society who dealt with public performance of music was introduced to Canada in 1925. Because of the fear that the society could act against the public interest, it was decided in 1936 to set up the Copyright Appeal Board, which was replaced in 1989 by the Copyright Board of Canada.[328] At first, the Board's mandate was to establish the royalties to be paid for the public performance of music. Later the communication of music to the public by telecommunication, as well as the remuneration rights for the performance or communication of sound recordings (i.e., the neighbouring rights), were added to the jurisdiction of the Board. Under this regime, known as the *Socan regime*,[329] the collective societies are required to get their tariffs approved on a regular basis by the Board.[330] Once the tariff is approved, the collective society may collect and sue for the royalties specified in the tariff. However no other proceeding may be brought for the infringement of the right concerned in the tariff.[331]

133. The *Act* also created other regimes, where the royalties are fixed either mandatorily, or at the request of an interested party. These other compulsory regimes apply to the retransmission of distant television and radio signals,[332] some educational use of works[333] and the private copying.[334] These regimes are mandatory in the sense that the copyright owners' rights are reduced to receiving remuneration for the use of their work.[335] Under some of these regimes, even copyright holders who are not members of a collective society are entitled to receive from the collective the royalties specified in the tariff.[336]

325. *See* for example *R. v. Kirkwood*, (1983) 73 C.P.R. (2d) 114 (Ont. C.A.); *R. v. Fitzpatrick* (1984), 11 C.C.C. (3d) 46 (B.C.C.A).
326. *See* an *Act to amend the Criminal Code (unauthorized recording of a movie)*, SC 2007, c. 28, introducing s. 432 of the *Criminal Code*.
327. *See* s. 342.1.
328. *See* the *Act to amend the Copyright Act and to amend other Acts in consequence thereof*, SC 1988, c. 15, consolidated RSC 1985, c. 10 [4th Supp.], s.12.
329. SOCAN, the *Society of Composers, Authors and Music Publishers of Canada*, is the collective society which now manages these royalties in Canada.
330. Section 67.
331. Subsection 68.2(1). *See* also subs. 67.1(4) which prohibits any action for infringement without the written consent of the Minister of Industry, if a proposed tariff is not filed.
332. Section 71.
333. Section 71.
334. Section 83.
335. *See* subss 31(2)(d), 29.7(3), 80 and 81.
336. Section 76.

134. Under the optional regimes, the collective societies that are not subject to a specific scheme have two choices: they may reach agreements with individual users or ask the Board to certify a tariff.[337] Once a tariff is approved, there can be no action for infringement against a person who paid or offered to pay the royalties specified in the tariff.[338] Furthermore, when a society and a user are unable to agree on the terms of a licence, either of them can apply to the Board to have the royalties set.[339] These regimes are purely optional since the parties may reach an agreement which then takes precedence over the tariff.[340]

135. The Board also assumes other jurisdictions such as the licensing of uses of published works whose owners cannot be located.[341] Also it helps the collective societies to clear the status of their agreements under the competition legislation: a collective may file an agreement with the Board within fifteen days of its conclusion and, in so doing, avoids any prosecutions pursuant to section 45 of the *Competition Act*.[342] Under the *Copyright Act*, the Commissioner of Competition has access to those agreements and may request the Board to examine the agreement and set the royalties.[343]

§11. Overlapping and Relation to Other Intellectual Property Laws

136. In principle, there is no reason why several intellectual property rights may not attach to the same article. As long as the respective conditions of protection are met, the intellectual property rights must be enforced by the courts. However, the courts will try to identify what is the proper subject matter of each right and restrict the protection accordingly. Thus patent laws are said to be concerned with processes belonging to a useful art as distinct from a fine art.[344]

137. In some cases, the *Copyright Act* eliminates any duplication. It indicates that copyright protection will not extend to utilitarian features of a work[345] and it expressly excludes the copyright protection for topographies.[346] Also in 1988, the legislator created a new regime to avoid the double protection of the *Copyright Act* and the *Industrial Design Act*[347] for the same act of copying a design.[348] If, with the authorization of the copyright holder, a design or an artistic work is used for the manufacture of more than fifty copies of a useful article, then it is not a copyright infringement to manufacture the article, to make a drawing or a reproduction in any

337. Sections 70.12–70.191 of the *Act.*
338. Section 70.17
339. Section 70.2.
340. Section 70.191.
341. Section 77.
342. *Competition Act*, RSC, 1985, c. C-34. *See* s. 70.5.
343. Section 70.6.
344. *Tennessee Eastman Co. et al. v. Commissioner of Patents* (1970), 62 C.P.R. 117 (Ex. Ct.), 154–155, aff'd [1974] S.C.R. 111.
345. Section 64.1, *Copyright Act*, S.R.C. 1985, c. C-42.
346. Section 64.2, *Copyright Act*, S.R.C. 1985, c. C-42.
347. S.R.C. 1985, c. I-9.
348. For further explanations, *see* s. 10 of c. 6 of this monograph.

material form of the article. Equally, anyone may do anything with the article that the copyright holder has the sole right to do, without committing a copyright violation.[349] Exceptions are provided; notably, when the *Copyright Act* restores the full copyright protection of a design used for the manufacture of multiple copies of a useful article, when the work is a trademark or label.[350]

138. Provided that the conditions are met, a logo can be protected as a trademark and as an artistic work. However, judges have expressed their doubts when parties have tried to transform their copyright protection 'into an instrument of trade control not contemplated by the *Copyright Act*'.[351] Thus, for several judges of the Supreme Court of Canada, the merely incidental presence of the copyrighted works on the wrappers of the chocolate bars may not be used to stop the parallel import of these chocolate bars.[352] As they explained:

> *[...] the* Copyright Act *ought not only to be interpreted with an eye to the internal coherence of its own scheme; it must also not be interpreted in a fashion which is inconsistent with the* Trade-marks Act, *[...]. Trade-mark law protects market share in commercial goods; copyright protects the economic gains resulting from an exercise of skill and judgment. If trade-mark law does not protect market share in a particular situation, the law of copyright should not be used to provide that protection, if that requires contorting copyright outside its normal sphere of operation. The protection offered by copyright cannot be leveraged to include protection of economic interests that are only tangentially related to the copyrighted work.*[353]

349. Subsection 64(2), *Copyright Act*, S.R.C. 1985, c. C-42.
350. Subsection 64(3), *Copyright Act*, S.R.C. 1985, c. C-42.
351. *See* the opinion of Justice Fish in *Euro-Excellence Inc. v. Kraft Canada Inc.*, [2007] 3 S.C.R. 20, at para. 56.
352. *See* the opinion written by Bastarache, LeBel & Charron JJ. in *Euro-Excellence Inc. v. Kraft Canada Inc*, [2007] 3 S.C.R. 20.
353. *Ibid.*, at para. 83.

Chapter 2. Patents

§1. Sources: Legislation

139. In 1867, the *British North America Act, 1867,*[354] gave to the Federal Parliament the exclusive jurisdiction in matters of 'Patents of Invention and Discovery.'[355]

140. In 1935, a new statute was introduced,[356] which remains the basis of present statutory law.[357] Major changes to the *Act* were brought in 1987,[358] then in 1992[359] and in 1993.[360] In 2001, modifications were made to the *Patent Act* to bring it in line with the rulings of the Dispute Settlement Body of the WTO.[361] In 2004, Canada introduced in the *Patent Act*[362] the legislative framework to enable Canada to respond to the 30 August 2003 decision of the General Council of the WTO on *the Implementation of paragraph 6 of the Doha Declaration on the Agreement on Trade-Related Aspects of Intellectual Property Rights (TRIPs Agreement) and Public Health.*[363]

141. Furthermore, Canada is a party to several multinational conventions. Canada is party to the *Paris Convention for the Protection of Industrial Property* [hereafter named the *Paris Convention*] made on 20 March 1883.[364] Canada has entered into the

354. 1867, 30-31 Vict., c. 3 (UK). The statute was renamed in 1982 the *Constitution Act 1867*, [No. 1 of the Schedule to the *Constitution Act, 1982*, B Schedule to the *Canada Act 1982*, (UK) 1982, c. 11, reproduced in the S.R.C. 1985, appendix II, no. 5.].
355. Section 91(22).
356. 25-26 Geo. V, c. 32.
357. The statute is accompanied by several regulations, the most important ones being the *Patent Rules* (SOR/96-423, amended by SOR/99-291, SOR/2002-120, SOR/2003-208, SOR/2004-67, SOR/2007-90, SOR/2011-61, SOR/2013-212, SOR/2013-231) and the *Patented Medicines (Notice of Compliance) Regulations* (SOR/93-133, amended by SOR/98-166, SOR/99-379, SOR/2006-242, SOR/2008-211, SOR/2011-61).
358. *See* the *Act to amend the Patent Act and to provide for certain matters in relation thereto*, R.C.S., 1985, c. 33, [3rd Supp.].
359. *Patent Act Amendment Act*, 1992, SC 1993, c. 2.
360. *Intellectual Property Law Improvement Act*, SC 1993, c. 15, ss 26–56; *North American Free Trade Agreement Implementation Act*, SC 1993, c. 44, ss 189–200.
361. The Dispute Settlement Body adopted the Report of the Appellate Body, in *Canada – Term of Patent Protection*, WT/DS170/AB/R, 18 Sep. 2000 and the Panel Report in *Canada – Patent Protection of Pharmaceutical Products*, WT/DS114/R, 17 Mar. 2000. *See An Act to amend the Patent Act*, SC 2001, c. 10.
362. An *Act to amend the Patent Act and the Food and Drugs Act (The Jean Chrétien Pledge to Africa)*, SC 2004, c. 23, s. 1.
363. WTO Doc. WT/L/540 and Corr.1.
364. Canada acceded to the Stockholm version on 7 Apr. 1970, and the accession came into force on 7 Jul. 1970; as regards the substantive provisions, Canada acceded to Arts 1–12 at the Stockholm level on 23 Feb. 1996 and the accession became effective on 26 May 1996. *See* WIPO *WIPO-Administered Treaties*, www.wipo.int/treaties/en/.

Agreement Establishing the WTO, which includes the *TRIPs Agreement*.[365] Canada is also party to the *NAFTA* which regroups in a specific chapter on intellectual property, provisions similar to those adopted in the *TRIPs Agreement*.[366] Furthermore, on 30 October 2015, the *EU-Canada Comprehensive Economic and Trade Agreement* (CETA) was signed.[367] As of 1 January 2017, an implementation bill has passed second reading in the House of Commons.[368]

142. Canada is also member to a number of treaties concerning specifically the patent regime, such as the Strasbourg Agreement concerning the International Patent Classification,[369] the Budapest Treaty on the International Recognition of the Deposit of Microorganisms for the Purposes of Patent Procedure.[370] Canada has signed the Patent Law Treaty.[371] In 2015, the Patent Act was amended to allow Canada to ratify the Patent Law Treaty.[372] Canada has also joined the Patent Cooperation Treaty (PCT)[373] and is bound by Chapter I (relating to the international application and international search) and by Chapter II (relating to the international preliminary examination) of the treaty.

§2. Patentable Subject Matter

143. To be patentable, the subject matter must be an invention within the meaning of section 2 of the *Patent Act*, which lists five categories of invention: art (*réalization*), process (*procédé*), machine (*machine*), manufacture (*fabrication*) or composition of

365. The agreement was signed by Canada on 15 Apr. 1994 and ratified on 30 Dec. 1994. It was enacted into domestic law by the *World Trade Organization Agreement Implementation Act*, SC 1994, c. 47.
366. Canada, United States and Mexico, 17 Dec. 1992, Index, *Canada Treaty Series 1994*, 1, 32 I.L.M. 296. The Ch. 17 is the one devoted to intellectual property matters and is reproduced at 32 I.L.M. 670.
367. But as of 1 January 2017, it had not been ratified : *see* Global Affairs Canada, International Trade Minister introduces legislation to Parliament to implement CETA, http://www.international.gc.ca/media/comm/news-communiques/2016/10/31a.aspx?lang=eng .
368. S 61 and ff of Bill C-30 (First Session, Forty-second Parliament, 64-65 Elizabeth II, 2015–2016–2017). *See* the status of the bill in Legisinfo online at http://www.parl.ca/LegisInfo/BillDetails.aspx?Language=en&Mode=1&billId=8549249. Section 131 and ff incorporates some provisions of the *Canada–Korea Economic Growth and Prosperity Act* (SC 2014, c 28) relative to geographical indications.
369. Done in Strasbourg on 24 Mar. 1971, and amended on 28 Sep. 1979. Canada acceded on 11 Jan. 1995 and the accession became effective on 11 Jan. 1996. *See* WIPO *WIPO-Administered Treaties*, www.wipo.int/treaties/en/.
370. Done at Budapest on 28 Apr. 1977, and amended on 26 Sep. 1980 and on 20 Jan. 1981. Canada acceded on 21 Jun. 1996 and the accession became effective on 21 Sep. 1996. *See* WIPO *WIPO-Administered Treaties*, www.wipo.int/treaties/en/.
371. On 21 May 2001. *See* WIPO *WIPO-Administered Treaties*, www.wipo.int/treaties/en/.
372. *Economic Action Plan 2014 Act, No. 2*, SC 2014, c. 30, ss 114–142, still not in force in January 2017.
373. Done at Washington on 16 Jun. 1970, and amended on 2 Oct. 1979, 3 Feb. 1984 and on 2 Oct. 2001. Canada ratified the Treaty on 2 Oct. 1989 and the ratification became effective on 2 Jan. 1990. *See* *Canada Treaty Series 1990*, 22, 22.2, (1991).

matter (*composition de matières*). The list is considered to be exhaustive, which means that a subject matter must fit into one of the enumerated categories.[374] The discovery of a new use for a known compound which is capable of practical application was held to be a new and useful 'art' and patentable subject matter.[375]

144. Section 2 also encompasses any new and useful improvement in any of the five categories of invention. Section 32 confirms that a person who has invented an improvement may obtain a patent, but the patent neither confers to him or her the right of making, vending or using the original invention, nor does the patent for the original invention confer the right of making, vending or using the patented improvement. Are also patentable combinations of known contrivances if the actual combination is new and is not the mere aggregation or a juxtaposition of old elements.[376] In particular, the elements of the combination must have a unitary result.[377]

145. Subsection 27(8) excludes from the range of patentability mere scientific principle or abstract theorem.

146. Other subject matter has been excluded by judicial interpretation of section 2 definitions of 'invention' and section 27(8). Those exclusions concern the fields of computer software, biological invention, professional skill and method of medical treatment.

I. Computer Program

147. The scope of protection for computer programs is presently the subject of great controversy. It is an established principle of Canadian law that a disembodied idea is not per se patentable.[378] At first, it was thought that the use of a computer could not transform mental steps into patentable subject matter. So in 1982 *Schlumberger* case, the Federal Court of Appeal (F.C.A.) held unpatentable a method of collecting measurements in boreholes and transmitting them to a computer programme to make specific calculations.[379] These rulings were consistent with the cases deciding that a patentable subject matter necessarily involves some 'physical effect', some change in the character or condition of material objects.[380] However, in the *Amazon.com* decision, the Federal Court ruled that the 'physical effect' could reside in the use of a computer.[381] So a method for 'one-click' purchasing of products online was held patentable since there is:

374. *Harvard College v. Canada (Commissioner of Patents)*, [2002] 4 S.C.R. 45, 105, para. 120.
375. *Shell Oil Co. v. Canada (Patent Comm.)*, [1982] 2 S.C.R. 536, 549. *See also* for a more recent decision *Calgon Carbon Corporation v. North Bay (City)* (2005), 45 C.P.R. (4th) 241 (F.C.A.).
376. *Canada v. Uhlemann Optical Co.*, [1952] 1 S.C.R. 143, 150.
377. *Domtar Ltd. v. Macmillan Bloedel Packaging Ltd. et al.*, (1977), 33 C.P.R. (2d) 182 (F.C.T.D.), aff'd 41 C.P.R. (2d) 182 (F.C.A.); *Crila Plastic Industries Ltd. v. Ninety-Eight Plastic Trim Ltd.* (1987), 18 C.P.R. (3d) 1 (F.C.A.).
378. *Shell Oil Co. v. Canada (Patent Comm.)*, [1982] 2 S.C.R. 536, 554.
379. *Schlumberger Canada Ltd. v. Commissioner of Patents*, [1982] 1 F.C. 845 (F.C.A.); *Re Application no. 564,175* (1999), 6 C.P.R. (4th) 385 (Patent Comm.).
380. *Lawson v. Commissioner of Patents* (1970), 62 C.P.R. 101 (Ex. Ct.).
381. *Amazon.com, Inc. v. Canada (Attorney General)*, 2010 FC 1011.

> *a practical application of the one-click concept, put into action through the use of cookies, computers, the internet and the customer's own action. ... The 'physical effect', transformation or change of character resides in the customer manipulating their computer and creating an order. It matters not that the 'goods' ordered are not physically changed.*[382]

The Federal Court of Appeal reversed the decision and returned that application to the Commissioner, indicating:

> ... [the]nature of the 'physicality requirement' [...] may change because of advances in knowledge[...]. Nothing in the jurisprudence excludes such a possibility.
>
> [69] However, if it is meant to suggest that this 'physicality requirement' can be met merely by the fact that the claimed invention has a practical application, then I do not agree. The issue, in my view, is similar to the issue raised in the context of the patentability of business methods in that it requires consideration of Schlumberger. The claims in Schlumberger were not saved by the fact that they contemplated the use of a physical tool, a computer, to give the novel mathematical formula a practical application. As explained above, the claims in issue in this case may or may not be distinguishable from the claims in Schlumberger, depending upon how they are construed.[383]

Finally in December 2011, the Canadian Intellectual Property Office (CIPO) issued a notice that it has accepted the patent application and the Office revised in March 2013 the guidance for patent examination practices respecting computer-implemented inventions.[384] CIPO's practice is now summarized in the Manual of Patent Office Practice (MOPOP).[385]

II. Professional Skill and Methods of Medical Treatment

148. The Patent Appeal Board (Pat. App. Bd.) and the courts have stated that exercise of professional skills or judgment is not a subject matter of patent, stressing

382. *Ibid.*, at para. 75.
383. *Canada (Attorney General) v. Amazon.com, Inc.*, 2011 FCA 328, at paras 68–69.
384. Canadian Intellectual Property Office, *Annual Report 2012-2013*, 9. Canadian Intellectual Property Office, *Examination Practice Respecting Computer-Implemented Inventions - PN 2013-03*, available online at http://www.cipo.ic.gc.ca/eic/site/cipointernet-internetopic.nsf/eng/wr03627.html.
385. *See* Ch. 16. The Manual is available online at http://www.cipo.ic.gc.ca/eic/site/cipointernet-internetopic.nsf/eng/h_wr00720.html.

that it is essentially non-economic and unrelated to trade, industry, or commerce.[386] However, the subject matter does not need to be scientific or technological in nature and business methods are not excluded from patentability.[387] The Supreme Court of Canada expressly excluded from patentability methods of medical treatment. In *Tennessee Eastman Co. v. Commissioner of Patents*,[388] a claim for a surgical method for joining the surfaces of incisions by applying certain compounds was held not to be valid. The determination was based on the fact that the then section 41 of the *Patent Act*[389] restricted the scope of patents relating to substances prepared or produced by chemical processes and intended for food or medicine: only process-dependent product claims for those substances were patentable.[390] Since the bonding material could not be patented as product per se, the court felt that the therapeutic use of the compound could not be claimed by a process claim.

149. Although section 41 was abolished in 1987,[391] the courts have continued to declare methods of medical treatment not patentable. For example, a method for cleaning human teeth was held not patentable, even though the method had also cosmetic value.[392] However, in the *Apotex Inc. v. Wellcome Foundation Ltd.* case, the Supreme Court was prepared to draw the distinction between a claim for a new therapeutic use of a known compound and a medical treatment. Justice Binnie explained that:

> The AZT patent does not seek to 'fence in' an area of medical treatment. It seeks the exclusive right to provide AZT as a commercial offering. How and when, if at all, AZT is employed is left to the professional skill and judgment of the medical profession.[393]

---

386. *Lawson v. Commissioner of Patents* (1970), 62 C.P.R. 101 (Ex. Ct.); *Tennessee Eastman Co. et al. v. Commissioner of Patents* (1970), 62 C.P.R. 117 (Ex. Ct.), aff'd [1974] S.C.R. 111; *Shell Oil Co. v. Canada (Patent Comm.)*, [1982] 2 S.C.R. 536, 554.
387. *Canada (Attorney General) v. Amazon.com, Inc.*, 2011 FCA 328.
388. [1974] S.C.R. 111.
389. Section 41. (1) then read: 'In the case of inventions relating to substances prepared or produced by chemical processes and intended for food or medicine, the specification shall not include claims for the substance itself, except when prepared or produced by the methods or processes of manufacture particularly described and claimed or by their obvious chemical equivalents.'
390. That is, substances could not be claimed as an invention except when prepared or produced by methods or processes of manufacture also particularly described and claimed. So there could not be a claim for the product per se except when it resulted from a claimed process.
391. The provision was replaced by one allowing only process-dependent product claims for naturally occurring substances prepared or produced by microbiological processes and intended for food or medicine. This restriction was to last only four years. *See* the *Act to amend the Patent Act and to provide for certain matters in relation thereto*, RSC, 1985, c. 33, [3rd Supp.], subs. 14(1) and *Patent Act Amendment Act, 1992*, SC 1993, c. 2, s. 3.
392. *Imperial Chemical Industries Ltd. v. Commissioner of Patents* (1986), 9 C.P.R. (3d) 289 (F.C.A.). The exclusion was also approved in *Monsanto Canada Inc. v. Schmeiser*, [2004] 1 S.C.R. 902, para. 133.
393. *Apotex Inc. v. Wellcome Foundation Ltd.*, [2002] 4 S.C.R. 153, at para. 50.

So a claim for a vendible compound to be used in a medical treatment is valid, but a claim that encompasses the skill of a medical professional will not be accepted.[394]

III. Biological Inventions

150. The question of patenting of life forms has been the topic of many decisions in Canada. In 1982, the Pat. App. Bd. upheld a claim on a living organism, namely a yeast culture useful in digesting spent sulfite liquor from pulp plants.[395] The Board was careful to put limits on the type of claims it was prepared to accept:

> The organism, to be claimed, should not of course have existed previously in nature, for in that event the 'inventor' did not create it, and his 'invention' is old. It must also be useful, in the sense that it carries out some useful known objective, such as separating oil from sand, producing antibiotics or the like. It cannot be a mere laboratory curiosity whose only possible claim to utility is as a starting material for further research. And it must be sufficiently different from known species that it can be said that its creation involved the necessary element of inventive ingenuity.[396]

The Supreme Court referred to this ruling without questioning its soundness, in three subsequent decisions.[397]

151. In the next case of *Pioneer Hi-Bred Ltd. v. Canada (Commissioner of Patents)*,[398] the claims covered a new soybean variety developed from artificial cross-breeding but cultivated naturally. The court ruled that there was not sufficient disclosure of the soybean variety since the specification was only describing the basic materials used for cross-breeding and that even someone skilled in the art and reading the specification could not arrive at the same result as the inventor without further explanation.[399] The court concluded that, due to this lack of proper disclosure, it was not necessary to decide whether the new soybean variety could be regarded as an invention within the meaning of section 2 of the *Patent Act*. However, the Court did stress the substantial differences between cross-breeding, such as crossing different species or varieties by hybridization, and genetic alteration. In the first case, there is 'human intervention in the reproductive cycle, but intervention which does not alter the actual rules of reproduction, which continues to obey the laws of nature', while in the later case, 'the intervention occurs inside the gene itself. The change made is thus

394. *Novartis Pharmaceuticals Canada Inc v. Cobalt Pharmaceuticals Company*, 2013 FC 985, aff'd *Novartis Pharmaceuticals Canada Inc. v. Cobalt Pharmaceuticals Company*, 2014 FCA 17. *See* also *Cobalt Pharmaceuticals Company c. Bayer Inc.*, 2015 CAF 116.

395. *Re Application of Abitibi Co.* (1982), 62 C.P.R. (2d) 81 (Pat. App. Bd.).

396. *Ibid.*, 91.

397. *Pioneer Hi-Bred Ltd. v. Canada (Commissioner of Patents)*, [1989] 1 S.C.R. 1623, at 1643; *Harvard College v. Canada (Commissioner of Patents)*, [2002] 4 S.C.R. 45, at para. 198; *Monsanto Canada Inc. v. Schmeiser*, [2004] 1 S.C.R. 902, at para. 91.

398. [1989] 1 S.C.R. 1623.

399. *Ibid.*, 1640.

a molecular one and the "new" gene is thus ultimately the result of a chemical reaction, which will in due course lead to a change in the trait controlled by the gene'.[400] Whether patenting should be restricted to the latter is a question that was left open by the court.

152. In the following case of *Harvard College v. Canada (Commissioner of Patents),*[401] the claim concerns the patenting of a mouse that has been genetically altered to increase its susceptibility to cancer. The patent claims extended to all non-human mammals similarly altered. The Court, in a split 5-4 decision, concluded that a higher life form, such as a mouse, was not a 'manufacture' or a 'composition of matter' in the context of the *Patent Act.*[402]

153. Finally, in *Monsanto Canada Inc. v. Schmeiser,*[403] the patent concerned a patented gene which increased the plants' tolerance to herbicides. The claims covered the gene, the cell containing the gene, the vectors and the methods for regenerating a plant from the plant cell containing the chimeric gene. The patentee sued a farmer who had harvested the plants containing the gene from his own fields, had treated it for use as seed and had planted the treated seeds the following year. The court found that the farmer has used the invention in violation of the patentee's rights. The majority distinguished the case from the *Harvard College* decision, stressing that, in the OncoMouse decision, the claims were for the mouse itself. The decision in *Harvard College* did not address the issue of single cells patenting, although the majority suggested in obiter that such a claim could be valid.[404]

§3. Conditions of Patentability

154. Patents must meet the criteria of validity specified in the *Patent Act*. There must be an invention, it must not fall within a subject matter specifically excluded, it must be novel, it must be non-obvious, it must be useful.

I. Novelty

155. The provisions adopted in the 1987 reform,[405] which were proclaimed in force on 1 October 1989,[406] changed the Canadian law from a first-to-invent to a first-to-file regime.

156. The novelty requirement is now set in section 2 of the Act, which provides that an 'invention' means a new invention and section 28.2 which requires that the subject matter of a claim must not have been disclosed prior to the claim date in such a manner that it became available to the public in Canada or elsewhere. Courts apply

400. *Ibid.*, 1632–1633.
401. [2002] 4 S.C.R. 45.
402. *Ibid.*, at para. 155.
403. [2004] 1 S.C.R. 902.
404. *Harvard College v. Canada (Commissioner of Patents)*, [2002] 4 S.C.R. 45, para. 126.
405. *Act to amend the Patent Act and to provide for certain matters in relation thereto*, RSC 1985, c. 33, [3rd Supp.].
406. SI/89-229, *Canada Gazette*, 1989.II.4487.

this condition of novelty by examining whether the claimed invention has been 'anticipated'. The concept of anticipation was considered by the Supreme Court of Canada in *Apotex Inc. v. Sanofi-Synthelabo Canada Inc.*[407] The test is to determine whether the claimed invention has already been disclosed to the public by a single disclosure in such a way as to enable it to be put into practice. The F.C.A. summarized the legal principles:

> *[44] With respect to disclosure, [... a person skilled in the art] reads the particular piece of prior art to understand whether it discloses the second invention. The evidence to be considered is comprised solely of the prior art, as the [person skilled in the art] would understand it. No trial and error or experimentation is permitted.*
>
> [45] Where disclosure is found to exist, the second requirement (enablement) requires the [person skilled in the art] to be able to perform the invention. Enablement is assessed having regard to the particular piece of prior art as a whole. The prior art must provide the [person skilled in the art], using his or her common general knowledge, with enough information to allow the subsequently claimed invention to be performed without undue burden. Where the invention arises in a field of technology where trials and experiments are generally carried out, routine trials are acceptable.[408]

157. Under the current *Patent Act*, the applicant has the benefit of a grace period of one year: a claim will not be anticipated if it was disclosed by him or her or someone deriving knowledge from him or her, in less than one year before the filing date.[409] Finally, a patent will be not be granted if the subject matter was disclosed in an application filed in Canada by a third party which has an earlier filing date or claim date.[410]

158. Also, there is a prohibition against double patenting. As the Supreme Court of Canada has said:

> The inventor is only entitled to 'a' patent for each invention: Patent Act, s. 36(1). If a subsequent patent issues with identical claims, there is an improper extension of the monopoly.[411]

However, courts will accept the validity of a '"selection patent", which is, within the context of pharmaceutical patents, a compound selected from an existing patented class when it is discovered that a new selection of compounds possess unexpected characteristics which could not be predicted before the discovery was made'.[412]

407. 2008 SCC 61, [2008] 3 SCR 265.
408. *Eli Lilly Canada Inc. v. Novopharm Limited*, 2010 FCA 197.
409. Paragraph 28.2(1)(a).
410. Paragraphs 28.2(1)(c)(d).
411. *Whirlpool Corp. v. Camco Inc.*, [2000] 2 S.C.R. 1067, at para. 63.
412. *Apotex Inc. v. Sanofi-Synthelabo Canada Inc.*, 2008 SCC 61, [2008] 3 S.C.R. .265.

159. This condition of novelty is to be distinguished from the criteria for non-obviousness.

II. Non-obviousness

160. This condition, first required by the case law, has been codified in section 28.3 of the *Patent Act* in 1993.[413] This new provision applies only to applications filed on or after 1 October 1989 and to the patents issued on the basis of those applications.[414] For applications made before that date and patents resulting from those applications, one must resort to the judicial determination of inventiveness.

161. The Canadian courts, following the English and American examples, introduced in Canadian law, before the twentieth century, the requirement that an invention must show inventiveness,[415] that is 'a substantial exercise of the inventive power or inventive genius'.[416] For instance, the Ex. C.R. held that could not be patented as a new insulating agent, a material which was nothing more than crushed and grinded gypsum boards, mixed with shredded paper, when the insulating properties of all those elements were well known.[417]

162. The Supreme Court revisited this condition of non-obviousness in its 2008 decision *Apotex Inc. v. Sanofi-Synthelabo Canada Inc.*[418] and stated:

> [67] It will be useful in an obviousness inquiry to follow the four-step approach first outlined by Oliver L.J. in Windsurfing International Inc. v. Tabur Marine (Great Britain) Ltd., [1985] R.P.C. 59 (C.A.). This approach should bring better structure to the obviousness inquiry and more objectivity and clarity to the analysis. The Windsurfing approach was recently updated by Jacob L.J. in Pozzoli SPA v. BDMO SA, [2007] F.S.R. 37 (p. 872), [2007] EWCA Civ 588, at para. 23:
>
> In the result I would restate the Windsurfing questions thus:
>
> *(1)*
>
> *(a) Identify the notional 'person skilled in the art';*

413. *Intellectual Property Law Improvement Act*, SC 1993, c. 15, s. 33.
414. Sections 78.1–78.2.
415. *Ball v. Crompton Corset Co.* (1887), 13 S.C.R. 469; in *Canadian Gypsum Co. Ltd. v. Gypsum, Lime and Alabastine Canada Ltd*, [1931] Ex. C.R. 180, 187.
416. *Canadian General Electric Co. v. Fada Radio Ltd.*, [1930] A.C. 97, 101.
417. *Canadian Gypsum Co. Ltd. v. Gypsum, Lime and Alabastine Canada Ltd.*, [1931] Ex. C.R. 180.
418. 2008 SCC 61, [2008] 3 SCR 265.

(b) Identify the relevant common general knowledge of that person;

(2) Identify the inventive concept of the claim in question or if that cannot readily be done, construe it;

(3) Identify what, if any, differences exist between the matter cited as forming part of the 'state of the art' and the inventive concept of the claim or the claim as construed;

(4) Viewed without any knowledge of the alleged invention as claimed, do those differences constitute steps which would have been obvious to the person skilled in the art or do they require any degree of invention?

It will be at the fourth step of the Windsurfing/Pozzoli approach to obviousness that the issue of 'obvious to try' will arise.

i. When Is the 'Obvious to Try' Test Appropriate?

[68] In areas of endeavour where advances are often won by experimentation, an 'obvious to try' test might be appropriate. In such areas, there may be numerous interrelated variables with which to experiment. For example, some inventions in the pharmaceutical industry might warrant an 'obvious to try' test since there may be many chemically similar structures that can elicit different biological responses and offer the potential for significant therapeutic advances.

ii. 'Obvious to Try' Considerations

[69] If an 'obvious to try' test is warranted, the following factors should be taken into consideration at the fourth step of the obviousness inquiry. As with anticipation, this list is not exhaustive. The factors will apply in accordance with the evidence in each case.

1. Is it more or less self-evident that what is being tried ought to work? Are there a finite number of identified predictable solutions known to persons skilled in the art?

> 2. What is the extent, nature and amount of effort required to achieve the invention? Are routine trials carried out or is the experimentation prolonged and arduous, such that the trials would not be considered routine?
>
> 3. Is there a motive provided in the prior art to find the solution the patent addresses?
>
> [70] Another important factor may arise from considering the actual course of conduct which culminated in the making of the invention. It is true that obviousness is largely concerned with how a skilled worker would have acted in the light of the prior art. But this is no reason to exclude evidence of the history of the invention, particularly where the knowledge of those involved in finding the invention is no lower than what would be expected of the skilled person.
>
> [71] For example, if the inventor and his or her team reached the invention quickly, easily, directly and relatively inexpensively, in light of the prior art and common general knowledge, that may be evidence supporting a finding of obviousness, unless the level at which they worked and their knowledge base was above what should be attributed to the skilled person. Their course of conduct would suggest that a skilled person, using his/her common general knowledge and the prior art, would have acted similarly and come up with the same result. On the other hand, if time, money and effort was expended in research looking for the result the invention ultimately provided before the inventor turned or was instructed to turn to search for the invention, including what turned out to be fruitless 'wild goose chases', that evidence may support a finding of non-obviousness. It would suggest that the skilled person, using his/her common general knowledge and the prior art, would have done no better. Indeed, where those involved including the inventor and his or her team were highly skilled in the particular technology involved, the evidence may suggest that the skilled person would have done a lot worse and would not likely have managed to find the invention. It would not have been obvious to him/her to try the course that led to the invention.

On the test of 'obvious to try', the court also made the following observation:

> [66] For a finding that an invention was 'obvious to try', there must be evidence to convince a judge on a balance of probabilities that it was more or less self-evident to try to obtain the invention. Mere possibility that something might turn up is not enough.

163. In determining obviousness, the courts will review the entire prior art and its cumulative effect. It is thus possible to take the prior art as a mosaic to determine if the invention was obvious to the people skilled in the art.[419] The information to be considered is that prior to the claim date, except for the information disclosed less than a year before the filing date by the applicant, or by a person who obtained knowledge, directly or indirectly, from the applicant. In other words, the applicant has the benefit of a grace period of one year.[420]

164. The notion of obviousness has to be distinguished from the criteria of novelty. In *Beloit Canada Ltd. v. Valmet Oy*,[421] the F.C.A. stated:

> They are, of course, quite different; obviousness is an attack on a patent based on its lack of inventiveness. The attacker says, in effect, 'Any fool could have done that'. Anticipation, or lack of novelty, on the other hand, in effect assumes that there has been an invention but asserts that it has been disclosed to the public prior to the application for the patent. The charge is: 'Your invention, though clever, was already known.'[422]

III. Utility

165. In order to be patentable, a subject matter must be useful. The courts have sometimes given some indication of what is a useful invention. Quoting the third edition of *Halsbury's Laws of England*, late Chief Justice Dickson, in *Consolboard* case,[423] stated:

> It means 'that the invention will not work, either in the sense that it will not operate at all or, more broadly, that it will not do what the specification promises that it will do'. The discussion in Halsbury's Laws of England, [...] continues: ... the practical usefulness of the invention does not matter, nor does its commercial utility, unless the specification promises commercial utility, nor does it matter whether the invention is of any real benefit to the public, or particularly suitable for the purposes suggested. [Footnotes omitted.][424]

And concludes:

> ...it is sufficient utility to support a patent that the invention gives either a new article, or a better article, or a cheaper article, or affords the public a useful choice. [Footnotes omitted.]

419. *Imperial Tobacco Ltd. v. Rothmans, Benson & Hedges Inc.* et al., (1993) 47 C.P.R. (3d) 188 (F.C.A.), 198.
420. Section 28.3.
421. (1986), 8 C.P.R. (3d) 289.
422. *Ibid.*, 293.
423. *Consolboard Inc. v. MacMillan Bloedel (Saskatchewan) Ltd.*, [1981] 1 S.C.R. 504.
424. *Ibid.*, 525.

> Canadian law is to the same effect. In Rodi & Wienenberger A.G. v. Metalliflex Limited [(1959), 19 Fox Pat. C. 49] (affirmed [1961] S.C.R. 117) the Quebec Court of Appeal adopted at p. 53 the following quotation from the case of Unifloc Reagents, Ld. v. Newstead Colliery, Ld. [(1943), 60 R.P.C. (Reports of Patent Cases (U.K.)) 165] at p. 184: 'If when used in accordance with the directions contained in the specification the promised results are obtained, the invention is useful in the sense in which that term is used in patent law. The question to be asked is whether, if you do what the specification tells you to do, you can make or do the thing which the specification says that you can make or do.'[425]

166. The criterion seems therefore easy to meet. As long as the promised result is accomplished, the patent is considered useful.[426] This criterion of utility often serves to invalidate patents that describe inventions too extensively, for example when some material part of the invention claimed will not work or will not produce the promised results.[427] The true cause of invalidity is not that part of the invention had not been tested, but that it was without utility.[428] As the Supreme Court said, 'A specification is addressed to persons skilled in the art and, therefore, is to be construed by the standard of what such a person would understand on reading it.'[429] If a claim covers unsuitable materials, such unsuitability depending on well known properties, the patent will not be held invalid for lack of utility.[430]

167. If the patentee has not completed all the experimentations but can make a sound prediction and draft its claims without going beyond the limits within which the prediction remained sound, the patent will not be open to attack. The doctrine of sound prediction was accepted in *Monsanto Co. v. Commissioner of Patents*,[431] and its components identified in *Apotex Inc. v. Wellcome Foundation Ltd.*:[432]

> *Firstly, as here, there must be a factual basis for the prediction. In Monsanto ([1979] 2 S.C.R. 1108) and Burton Parsons ([1976] 1 S.C.R. 555), the factual basis was supplied by the tested compounds, but other factual underpinnings, depending on the nature of the invention, may suffice. Secondly, the inventor*

---

425. *Ibid.*, 525–526.
426. *Eli Lilly Canada Inc. v. Novopharm Limited*, 2010 FCA 197.
427. *Centre Hospitalier Boehringer Sohn v. Bell-Craig Ltd.*, [1963] S.C.R. 410; *Hoechst Pharmaceuticals of Canada Ltd. v. Gilbert & Co.*, [1966] S.C.R. 189; *Société des usines chimiques Rhône-Poulenc v. Jules R. Gilbert Ltd.*, [1968] S.C.R. 950; *Astrazeneca Canada Inc. c. Apotex Inc.*, 2015 CAF 158. Following some Canadian courts decisions (*Eli Lilly Canada Inc v Novopharm Ltd*, [2010] FCA 197; [2011] FC 1288; *Novopharm Ltd. v. Eli Lilly & Co.*, [2011] FCA 220) invalidating two of its pharmaceutical patents, Eli LilLy brought a claim against the Goverment of Canada under the dispute settlement provisions of NAFTA Chapter 11: Eli Lilly v The Government of Canada, ICSID Case no. UNCT/14/12 : for an update *see* the information on the database ITALAW: http://www.italaw.com/cases/1625.
428. *Monsanto Co. v. Commissioner of Patents*, [1979] 2 S.C.R. 1108, 1113.
429. *Sandoz Patents Limited v. Gilcross Limited*, [1974] S.C.R. 1336, 1347.
430. *Burton Parsons Chemicals, Inc. v. Hewlett-Packard (Canada) Ltd.*, [1976] 1 S.C.R. 555; *Monsanto Co. v. Commissioner of Patents*, [1979] 2 S.C.R. 1108.
431. [1979] 2 S.C.R. 1108.
432. *Apotex Inc. v. Wellcome Foundation Ltd.*, [2002] 4 S.C.R. 153.

must have at the date of the patent application an articulable and 'sound' line of reasoning from which the desired result can be inferred from the factual basis. In Monsanto ([1979] 2 S.C.R. 1108) and Burton Parsons ([1976] 1 S.C.R. 555), the line of reasoning was grounded in the known 'architecture of chemical compounds' [...], but other lines of reasoning, again depending on the subject matter, may be legitimate. Thirdly, there must be proper disclosure. Normally, it is sufficient if the specification provides a full, clear and exact description of the nature of the invention and the manner in which it can be practised: H. G. Fox, The Canadian Law and Practice Relating to Letters Patent for Inventions (4th ed. 1969), at p. 167. It is generally not necessary for an inventor to provide a theory of why the invention works. Practical readers merely want to know that it does work and how to work it. In this sort of case, however, the sound prediction is to some extent the quid pro quo the applicant offers in exchange for the patent monopoly. Precise disclosure requirements in this regard do not arise for decision in this case because both the underlying facts (the test data) and the line of reasoning (the chain terminator effect) were in fact disclosed, and disclosure in this respect did not become an issue between the parties.[433]

§4. Formalities (Procedure for Grant and Obtaining Patent Protection)

168. The formalities for obtaining patent protection begin with the filing of a patent application. In Canada, a patent may be secured either through a Canadian application or by means of an international application under the PCT. The application will be laid open to public inspection eighteen months after the filing date or priority date.[434]

169. A Canadian application must contain a petition and a specification of the invention[435] and the prescribed application fee must be paid.[436] In the specification, the applicant must (a) correctly and fully describe the invention and its operation or use as contemplated by the inventor; (b) set out clearly the various steps in a process, or the method of constructing, making, compounding or using a machine, manufacture or composition of matter, in such full, clear, concise and exact terms as to enable any person skilled in the art or science to which it appertains, or with which it is most closely connected, to make, construct, compound or use it; (c) in the case of a machine, explain the principle thereof and the best mode in which he or she has contemplated the application of that principle; (d) in the case of a process, explain the necessary sequence, if any, of the various steps, so as to distinguish the invention from other

433. *Ibid.*, at para. 70.

434. Section 10.

435. Subsection 27(2). The patent application must include an abstract (s. 79 of the *Patent Rules*). It will normally also include drawings (s. 37 of the *Act*), an appointment of a representative in Canada (s. 78 of the *Patent Rules*), a request for priority (s. 88 of the *Patent Rules*), information about any assignment, a request for examination (s. 35 of the *Act*). Samples or models may be requested by the Commissioner: subs. 38 (1) *Patent Act*.

436. Subsection 27(2).

inventions; and (e) particularly indicate and distinctly claim the part, improvement or combination that he or she claims as his or her invention.[437]

170. This requirement to disclose the invention is said to lie at the heart of the whole patent system.[438] It is part of the bargain between the public and the inventor,[439] as in Canada 'the granting of a patent means the kind of contract between the Crown and the inventor in which the latter receives an exclusive right to exploit his invention for a certain period in exchange for complete disclosure to the public of the invention and the way in which it operates'.[440] So, '[d]isclosure is the quid pro quo for valuable proprietary rights to exclusivity which are entirely the statutory creature of the *Patent Act*'.[441]

171. It follows that the specification must fulfil some conditions. As was said in the *Pioneer* case:

> The applicant must disclose everything that is essential for the invention to function properly.....The description must be such as to enable a person skilled in the art or the field of the invention to produce it using only the instructions contained in the disclosure (Pigeon J. in Burton Parsons Chemicals Inc. v. Hewlett-Packard (Canada) Ltd., [1976] 1 S.C.R. 555, at p. 563; Monsanto Co. v. Commissioner of Patents, [1979] 2 S.C.R. 1108, at p. 1113) and once the monopoly period is over, to use the invention as successfully as the inventor could at the time of his application (Noranda Mines Ltd. v. Minerals Separation North American Corp., [1947] Ex C.R. 306, (1947), 12 C.P.R. 102 (Ex. Ct) [reversed, [1950] S.C.R. 36, (1949), 12 C.P.R. 182 (S.C.C.); affirmed, (1952), 15 C.P.R. 133 (P.C)] at p. 316).[442]

172. The insufficiency of the disclosure, that is a disclosure insufficient to enable a person skilled in the art to make a successful use of the invention, or the ambiguity of the disclosure, affords a ground of invalidity.[443] For instance, in the *Pioneer* case, the invention was a new soybean variety developed from artificial cross-breeding; since an experimenter could only discover the steps involved in the production of the variety by empirical means, the specification was declared inadequate.[444] Also a specification that necessitates the working of a problem will not be adequate.[445] In the *Teva* decision,[446] the Supreme Court of Canada had to deal with 'cascading' patent claims of successively smaller ranges of compounds, ending with two individual

437. Subsections 27(3)(4).
438. *Consolboard Inc. v. MacMillan Bloedel (Saskatchewan) Ltd.*, [1981] 1 S.C.R. 504, at 517.
439. *Free World Trust c. Électro Santé Inc.*, [2000] 2 S.C.R. 1024, para. 13; *Teva Canada Ltd. v. Pfizer Canada Inc.*, 2012 SCC 60, [2012] 3 S.C.R. 625, at para. 32.
440. *Pioneer Hi-Bred Ltd. v. Canada (Commissioner of Patents)*, [1989] 1 S.C.R. 1623, 1636.
441. *Apotex Inc. v. Wellcome Foundation Ltd.*, [2002] 4 S.C.R. 153, para. 37.
442. *Pioneer Hi-Bred Ltd. v. Canada (Commissioner of Patents)*, [1989] 1 S.C.R. 1623, 1638.
443. *Pioneer Hi-Bred Ltd. v. Canada (Commissioner of Patents)*, [1989] 1 S.C.R. 1623, 1638; *Apotex Inc. v. Wellcome Foundation Ltd.*, [2002] 4 S.C.R. 153, 192; *TRW Inc. v. Walbar of Canada Inc.* (1991), 39 C.P.R. (3d) 176 (F.C.A.), 195.
444. *Pioneer Hi-Bred Ltd. v. Canada (Commissioner of Patents)*, [1989] 1 S.C.R. 1623, 1641.
445. *Ibid.*
446. *Teva Canada Ltd. v. Pfizer Canada Inc.*, 2012 SCC 60, [2012] 3 S.C.R. 625.

compounds, used for the treatment of erectile dysfunction. Only one of the two individual compounds had been shown to be effective. The court considered the patent to be invalid for lack of proper disclosure,[447] stating:

> [79] Whether or not a specification is sufficient depends on what a skilled person would consider to be sufficient [...]. Expert evidence in this case reveals that there was no basis for a skilled person to determine which of Claim 6 and Claim 7 contained the useful compound. [The patent holder]'s own expert witness admitted that a person skilled in the art who read the patent would not know which compound was shown by the study to be useful in treating ED [...].
>
> [80] I would not make too much of the fact that Claim 1 included over 260 quintillion compounds. The practice of cascading claims - although it may, as in this case, result in claims that are overly broad - is a common one that does not necessarily interfere in every case with the public's right to disclosure. The skilled reader knows that, when a patent contains cascading claims, the useful claim will usually be the one at the end concerning an individual compound. The compounds that do not work are simply deemed invalid. In accordance with s. 58, any valid claim - in this case, Claim 7 - survives despite the existence of invalid claims. However, the public's right to proper disclosure was denied in this case, since the claims ended with two individually claimed compounds, thereby obscuring the true invention. The disclosure failed to state in clear terms what the invention was. [The patent holder] gained a benefit from the Act - exclusive monopoly rights - while withholding disclosure in spite of its disclosure obligations under the Act. As a matter of policy and sound statutory interpretation, patentees cannot be allowed to 'game' the system in this way. This, in my view, is the key issue in this appeal. It must be resolved against [the patent holder].

173. In *Minerals Separation North American Corp. v. Noranda Mines Ltd.*, the court stated that ' ... the inventor must act *uberrima fide* and give all information known to him that will enable the invention to be carried out to its best effect as contemplated by him'.[448] This duty to act in good faith seems to imply a duty to disclose not only one method to work the invention, but in fact the best method known to the inventor. In case of a machine, the *Patent Act* expressly requires that the applicant states the principle and the best mode in which he or she has contemplated the application of the principle.[449] The current *Patent Rules* ask that the applicant sets forth at least one mode contemplated by the inventor for carrying of the invention.[450]

447. Few months later, the F.C.A. confirmed the Federal Court decision declaring the patent invalid: *Pfizer Ireland Pharmaceuticals v. Apotex Inc.*, 2014 FCA 13.

448. *Minerals Separation North American Corp. v. Noranda Mines Ltd.*, [1947] Ex. C.R. 306 at 317, reversed, (1949), [1950] S.C.R. 36, (S.C.C.), affirmed (1952), 15 C.P.R. 133, 143–148 (P.C.).But for an example of a contrary opinion, *see Pfizer Canada Inc. v. Apotex Inc.*, 2014 FC 314.

449. Paragraph 27(3)(c).

450. *Patent Rules*, para. 80(1)(f).

174. The *Patent Act* was modified to allow applicants to refer to a deposit of biological material to supplement the written description of an invention.[451] A reference to a deposit of biological material in a specification does not create a presumption that the deposit was required for an adequate disclosure.[452] The *Patent Rules* indicate that the deposit must be made by the applicant with an international depositary authority[453] on or before the filing date of the application. The *Patent Rules* also provide for the possibility to restrict access to samples of deposited material until either a patent has been issued on the basis of the application or the application is refused, or is abandoned and no longer subject to reinstatement, or is withdrawn.[454]

175. Subsection 27(4) prescribes that the specification must end with a claim or claims defining distinctly and in explicit terms the subject matter of the invention for which an exclusive privilege or property is claimed. In *Free World Trust v. Électro Santé Inc.*,[455] the Court stressed that patent claims are frequently analogized to "fences" and "boundaries", giving the "fields" of the monopoly a comfortable pretence of bright line demarcation.[456] Consequently, the claims must be clear and precise. In *Minerals Separation North American Corp. v. Noranda Mines, Ltd.*,[457] the Ex. C.R. explained:

> By his claims the inventor puts fences around the fields of his monopoly and warns the public against trespassing on his property. His fences must be clearly placed in order to give the necessary warning and he must not fence in any property that is not his own. The terms of a claim must be free from avoidable ambiguity or obscurity and must not be flexible; they must be clear and precise so that the public will be able to know not only where it must not trespass but also where it may safely go.

176. However, the task of the inventor is far from simple:

> It is stressed in many cases that an inventor is free to make his claims as narrow as he sees fit in order to protect himself from the invalidity which will ensue if he makes them too broad. From a practical point of view, this freedom is really quite limited because if, in order to guard against possible invalidity, some area is left open between what is the invention as disclosed and what is covered by the claims, the patent may be just as worthless as if it was invalid. Everybody

451. Subsection 38.1(1).
452. Subsection 38.1(2).
453. *See* ss 103–104 of the *Patent Rules*. Canada is a member of the *Budapest Treaty on the International Recognition of the Deposit of Microorganisms for the Purposes of Patent Procedure*, which deals with the depositing of microorganisms in culture collections for patent purposes and set the framework under which culture collections entities are recognized as 'international depositary authorities'. In Canada the recognized authority is the International Depositary Authority of Canada (IDAC) of the Public Health Agency of Canada www.nml-lnm.gc.ca/IDAC-ADI/index-eng.htm.
454. Subsection 104(4) of the *Patent Rules*.
455. *Free World Trust c. Électro Santé Inc.*, [2000] 2 S.C.R. 1024, 1035, para. 14.
456. *Free World Trust c. Électro Santé Inc.*, [2000] 2 S.C.R. 1024, 1036, para. 14.
457. [1947] Ex. C.R. 306, 352, as quoted in *Free World Trust c. Électro Santé Inc.*, [2000] 2 S.C.R. 1024, 1035–1036.

will be free to use the invention in the unfenced area. It does not seem to me that inventors are to be looked upon as Shylock claiming his pound of flesh.[458]

This reasoning lead the courts to take a purposive approach when construing patent claims, looking at the description and the drawings for the proper interpretation and taking into account that the addressee is s a person skilled in the art.[459]

177. As stated in section 53 of the *Patent Act*, a patent can be void if any material allegation in the petition is untrue, or if the specification and drawings contain more or less than is necessary for obtaining the end for which they purport to be made, and the omission or addition is wilfully made for the purpose of misleading. If the omission or addition was an involuntary error, the remainder part of the patent can be held valid. It has been said that the non-material facts are those respecting anything other than the subject matter of the claims.

178. A patent application may claim a priority date, called the 'claim date', based on the filing date of an earlier patent application made in the previous twelve months in a country member of the *Paris Convention*, or a member of the *WTO*, or a country with which Canada has a special arrangement.[460]

179. The application will be laid open to public inspection eighteen months after the filing date or priority date.[461]

180. The framework for an international application is set by the *PCT Treaty* and the Canadian *Patent Act*. It starts with an international application sent to the local patent office, called the receiving office, which checks the application and grants the international filing date. The international application is then sent to the International Bureau of the World Intellectual Property Organization and to an International Searching Authority for an international search and later, if that step is chosen, to an International Preliminary Examining Authority for an international preliminary examination. In Canada, the Canadian Intellectual Property Office can act as the International Searching Authority and the International Preliminary Examining Authority for applications filed by Canadian applicants with the Canadian receiving office or the International Bureau. After completion of the international phase, the application begins the national phase, where it is examined in each of the designated states. Each state can decide to grant or not patent protection, following its own national criteria.

181. The *Canadian Intellectual Property Office* examines if an applicant has met all the requirements for the issuance of a patent under the *Act*.[462] The application will be refused if the examiner is satisfied that an applicant is not by law entitled to

458. *Burton Parsons Chemicals Inc. v. Hewlett-Packard (Canada) Ltd.*, [1976] 1 S.C.R. 555, 565.
459. *Whirlpool Corp. v. Camco Inc.*, [2000] 2 S.C.R. 1067; *Free World Trust v. Électro Santé Inc.*, [2000] 2 S.C.R. 1024.
460. Sections 28.1 and 28.2.
461. Section 10.
462. Section 27.

be granted a patent.[463] There is a possibility to defer a substantive examination of the petition for up to five years.[464]

182. When delivered, the patent certificate bears on its face the filing date of the application for the patent, the date on which the application became open to public inspection under section 10, the date on which the patent is granted and issued and any prescribed information.[465] It is a prima facie proof of the patent validity.[466]

§5. Ownership and Transfer (Assignment: Licences)

I. The Right to Grant

183. The *Patent Act* confers normally to the inventor the right to apply for a patent.[467]

184. On the issue of of ownership of patent rights in inventions made during the course of employment, the F.C.A. has recently stated :

> Given the silence of the Patent Act on this issue in the context of a private employment relationship, the existence of an employee-employer relationship will not necessarily disqualify an employee from patenting an invention discovered in the course of employment. The employer can nevertheless seek ownership of the intellectual property rights if it can demonstrate that: (i) there is formal agreement between the employer and the employee to the effect that the employer retains ownership of the intellectual patent rights; or, (ii) the employee was hired for the express purpose of inventing (Comstock Canada v. Electec Ltd., [1991] F.C.J. No. 987, 45 F.T.R. (Federal Trial Reports) 241 (QL)).[468]

II. Assignment

185. The *Patent Act* states that every patent is assignable in law, either as to the whole interest or as to any part thereof.[469] One can also assign a pending application.[470] Assignments should be put in writing[471] and registered.[472]

---

463. Section 40.
464. Section 96 *Patent Rules* (for applications filed on or after 1 Oct. 1996).
465. Section 43.
466. Subsection 43(2).
467. Sections 2 (definition of applicant) and 27. On the notion of inventor, *see* *Apotex Inc. v. Wellcome Foundation Ltd.*, [2002] 4 S.C.R. 153.
468. Brown v. Canada, 2016 FCA 37 . For an example of the latter case, *see* G.D. Searle & Co. v. Novopharm Ltd., 2007 FCA 173, [2008] 1 FCR 529.
469. Subsection 50(1).
470. Section 49. Immanuel Goldsmith, *Patents of Invention* ss 296–297 147 (Carswell 1981.
471. Subsection 50(1).
472. Subsection 50(2).

III. Licences

186. An exclusive licence must be in writing.[473] Most scholars caution that all licences should be in writing,[474] although there is no legal requirement as such for non-exclusive licences.

IV. The Right to Sue

187. In Common Law, the rule was simple: the licensee, having no interest in the patent, has no right to sue for infringement. The rule was followed by the Supreme Court of Canada in 1933.[475] In 1935, the legislator intervened by enacting a disposition which became subsection 55(1) of the *Patent Act*:

> A person who infringes a patent is liable to the patentee and to all persons claiming under the patentee for all damage sustained by the patentee or by any such person, after the grant of the patent, by reason of the infringement. [...]

188. The expression 'persons claiming under the patentee' was interpreted as including an exclusive licensee[476] and a non-exclusive licensee.[477] It also encompasses the purchaser of a patented article,[478] since a purchaser has a licence, composed of the right to use the article and the right to sell it, together with the same 'right of use', to another person and 'so on *ad infinitum*'.[479] When such a person claiming under the patentee starts a proceeding, the patentee must be made a party to the action.[480]

V. Registration

189. Every assignment of a patent, and every grant of any exclusive right must be registered.[481] No formalities are prescribed for non-exclusive rights.

190. It seems that failure to register an assignment or an exclusive licence does not affect the capacity of the assignee or the licensee to sue for infringement.[482]

473. Subsection 50(2).
474. Harold G. Fox, *Canadian Patent Law and Practice* 286 (4th ed., Carswell 1969); Immanuel Goldsmith, *Patents of Invention* s. 300 148 (Carswell 1981).
475. *Electric Chain Co. of Canada Ltd. v. Art Metal Works Inc.*, [1933] S.C.R. 581.
476. *Spun Rock Wools Ltd., v. Fiberglas Canada Ltd.*, [1943] S.C.R. 547, aff'd [1947] A.C. 313.
477. *Armstrong Cork Canada Ltd. v. Domco Industries Ltd.*, [1982] 1 S.C.R. 907; *Apotex Inc. v. Wellcome Foundation Ltd.* (2000), 10 C.P.R (4th) 65 (F.C.A.), aff'd [2002] 4 S.C.R. 153.
478. *Signalisation de Montréal Inc. v. Services de Béton Universels Ltée*, [1993] 1 F.C. 341 (F.C.A.).
479. *Ibid.*, at para. 20. Since s. 42 of the *Patent Act* grants to the patentee the exclusive right to sell the invention, a supplier of a patented article must have a licence to be able to sell the good.
480. Subsection 55(3).
481. Subsection 50(2).
482. Harold G. Fox, *Canadian Patent Law and Practice* 286 (4th ed., Carswell 1969; Gordon Henderson, 'Problems involved in the Assignment of Patents and Patent Rights', (1970) 60 C.P.R. 237, 251; David Vaver, *Intellectual Property Law* 590 (2nd ed., Irwin Law 2011).

191. Registration is important for determining the rights enforceable against subsequent assignees. Section 51 provides:

> Every assignment affecting a patent for invention, whether it is one referred to in section 49 or 50, is void against any subsequent assignee, unless the assignment is registered as prescribed by those sections, before the registration of the instrument under which the subsequent assignee claims.

So registered assignments take priority in order of registration.

§6. Scope of Exclusive Rights

192. Section 42 of the *Patent Act* defines the exclusive rights granted to the patent holder: he or she has the 'privilege and liberty of making, constructing, using the invention and selling it to others to be used'. This raises two types of questions: (I) has the defendant taken the invention?, (II) has the defendant performed one of the restricted activities? There is also some protection available through the regime established by the *Patented Medicines (Notice of Compliance) Regulations.*[483]

I. The Taking of the Invention

193. A patent can include product claims and process claims. A claim to a product is infringed at the moment when a product is made which contains all the elements claimed. A claim to a process is infringed when the complete process has been carried out. In an action for infringement of a patent granted for a process for obtaining a new product, there is a presumption that any product that is the same as the new product had been produced by the patented process.[484]

194. To determine whether the defendant has taken the invention, one must read the claims in an informed and purposive way, although the '*Patent Act* promotes adherence to the language of the claims', which should be given primacy.[485] According to two recent Supreme Court decisions, this purposive approach 'does away with the first step of purely literal interpretation but disciplines the scope of "substantive" claims

483. The regime was introduced in 1993: *Patent Act Amendment Act, 1992*, SC 1993, c. 2 and the *Patented Medicines (Notice of Compliance) Regulations*, (the *PM(NOC) Regulations*), SOR/93-133, amended by SOR/98-166, SOR/99-379, SOR/2006-242, err. (E), Vol. 140, No. 23, SOR/2008-211, SOR/2010-212, SOR/2011-89, s. 1.

484. Section 55.1.

485. *Free World Trust v. Électro Santé Inc.*, [2000] 2 S.C.R. 1024, 1048. The Court made the following statement at 1053–1054: ' The words chosen by the inventor will be read in the sense the inventor is presumed to have intended, and in a way that is sympathetic to accomplishment of the inventor's purpose expressed or implicit in the text of the claims. However, if the inventor has misspoken or otherwise created an unnecessary or troublesome limitation in the claims, it is a self-inflicted wound. The public is entitled to rely on the words used provided the words used are interpreted fairly and knowledgeably.'

construction in the interest of fairness to both the patentee and the public'.[486] As indicated in a summary provided by the F.C.A.,[487] the test put forward by the Supreme Court involves the identification of the essential and non-essential elements of the patented invention:

> Thus the elements of the invention are identified as either essential elements (where substitution of another element or omission takes the device outside the monopoly), or non-essential elements (where substitution or omission is not necessarily fatal to an allegation of infringement). For an element to be considered non-essential and thus substitutable, it must be shown either (i) that on a purposive construction of the words of the claim it was clearly not intended to be essential, or (ii) that at the date of publication of the patent, the skilled addressees would have appreciated that a particular element could be substituted without affecting the working of the invention, i.e., had the skilled worker at that time been told of both the element specified in the claim and the variant and 'asked whether the variant would obviously work in the same way', the answer would be yes: ... In this context, I think 'work in the same way' should be taken for our purposes as meaning that the variant (or component) would perform substantially the same function in substantially the same way to obtain substantially the same result.[488]

The formulation of the test is as follows:

> [...] (e) the claims language will, on a purposive construction, show that some elements of the claimed invention are essential while others are non-essential. This allocation will be made in the following manner:

- *on the basis of the common knowledge of the worker skilled in the art to which the patent relates [...]*
- *what constitutes an 'essential' element is to be interpreted in light of the knowledge of the art at the date of the publication of the patent specification [...]*
- *regard is to be had to whether it was obvious at the time the patent was published that substitution of a different variant would make a difference to the way in which the invention works [...]*
- *according to the intent of the inventor expressed or inferred from the claims of the patent [...]*
- *based on the patent specification itself without resort to extrinsic evidence [...]*[489]

> [The Court also] referred to a 'series of three concise questions' that were drawn by Hoffman J. (as he then was) in Improver Corp. v. Remington Consumer Products Limited, [1990] F.S.R. 181 from Lord Diplock's analysis in Catnic, [Catnic Components Ltd. v. Hill & Smith Ltd., [1982] R.P.C. 183]. Binnie J.

486. *Free World Trust v. Électro Santé Inc.*, [2000] 2 S.C.R. 1024, 1053. *See also Whirlpool Corp. c. Camco Inc.*, [2000] 2 S.C.R. 1067, 1092–1093.
487. *Canamould Extrusions Ltd. v. Driangle Inc.*, (2004) 30 C.P.R. (4th) 129 (F.C.A.), 141–144.
488. *Ibid.*, 141.
489. *Ibid.*, 142.

added that these questions, although not exhaustive, 'encapsulate the heart of Lord Diplock's analysis'. The questions posed by Hoffman J., as they appear at page 189, are:

(1) *Does the variant have a material effect upon the way the invention works? If yes, the variant is outside the claim. If no –*
(2) *Would this (i.e., that the variant had no material effect) have been obvious at the date of publication of the patent to a reader skilled in the art. If no, the variant is outside the claim. If yes –*
(3) *Would the reader skilled in the art nevertheless have understood from the language of the claim that the patentee intended that strict compliance with the primary meaning was an essential requirement of the invention. If yes, the variant is outside the claim.*[490]

The Federal Court of Appeal has also given an account of the guiding principles in reading patent claims:

> [39] The principles set forth by the Supreme Court in Whirlpool [Whirlpool Corp. v. Camco Inc., [2000] 2 S.C.R. 1067], and Free World [Free World Trust v. Électro Santé Inc., [2000] 2 S.C.R. 1024], can be summarized as follows:
>
> **The task of the Court is to construe the claims of the patent with the aid of expert witnesses (Whirlpool at paragraphs 43, 45 and 57).*
>
> **Construction of the claims is not to be a result-oriented exercise and must be conducted by the Court prior to its consideration of the issue of infringement (Whirlpool at paragraphs 43 and 49(a)).*
>
> **The claims are to be construed as of the publication date of the patent (Whirlpool at paragraph 42; Free World at paragraph 44).*
>
> **In construing the claims of the patent, the Court is called upon to determine, on an objective basis, what a skilled reader would have understood the inventor to mean (Whirlpool, at paragraph 48; Free World at paragraph 51).*
>
> **The claim of the patent which is to be construed by the Court must be read in the context of the rest of the specification. I would add to this, however, that reference to the rest of the specification cannot be used to expand the patentee's monopoly as expressed in the claim (Whirlpool at paragraphs 48, 49(f) and 52).*

490. *Ibid.*, 142–143.

**The expert witnesses are there to help the Court understand the invention and its context, as well as the meaning of the terms used in the patent. Needless to say, it is the Court's duty to construe the claims and not that of the experts (Whirlpool at paragraphs 45 and 57).*

**In construing the claims, the Court is to keep in mind that the patent is addressed to the 'ordinary person skilled in the art', i.e. a hypothetical person possessing the ordinary skill and knowledge of the particular art to which the invention relates, and a mind willing to understand a specification that is addressed to him (Whirlpool at paragraphs 53, 70, 71 and 74).*

**The 'disclosure' found in the patent must describe the invention in a sufficiently complete and accurate manner so to allow the person skilled in the art to construct or use the invention when the period of monopoly has expired (Whirlpool at paragraph 42). The resulting construction of the claims should be one which is 'in the interest of fairness both to the patentee and the public' (Free World at paragraph 50). As a result, the construction of the claim may lead to an expansion or limitation of the text of the claim. As Binnie J. said in Free World at paragraph 51:*

51. The involvement in claims construction of the skilled addressee holds out to the patentee the comfort that the claims will be read in light of the knowledge provided to the Court by expert evidence on the technical meaning of the terms and concepts used in the claims. The words chosen by the inventor will be read in the sense the inventor is presumed to have intended and in a way that is sympathetic to accomplishment of the inventor's purpose express or implicit in the text of the claims. However, if the inventor has misspoken or otherwise created an unnecessary or troublesome limitation in the claims, it is a self-inflicted wound. The public is entitled to rely on the words used provided the words used are interpreted fairly and knowledgeably.[491]

II. Types of Exclusive Rights

195. Section 42 defines the types of exclusive rights: making, constructing, using and selling it to others to be used the invention. The purpose of the section is to prevent 'any act that interferes with the full enjoyment of the monopoly granted to the patentee'.[492] A broad interpretation of the exclusive right to use the invention has the potential to encompass all the other rights (of making, constructing or selling the invention). As the Supreme Court of Canada puts it:

491. *Pfizer Canada Inc. v. Canada (Health)*, 2007 FCA 209, at para. 39.
492. *Monsanto Canada Inc. v. Schmeiser*, [2004] 1 S.C.R. 902, para. 34, quoting Harold G. Fox, *Canadian Patent Law and Practice* 349 (4th ed., Carswell 1969).

> Applied to 'use', the question becomes: did the defendant's activity deprive the inventor in whole or in part, directly or indirectly, of full enjoyment of the monopoly conferred by law?[493]

The intention to infringe is immaterial;[494] the question is whether the defendant appropriated the patented invention.[495]

196. A commercial activity involving the use of the invention and its utilization to make profits or further financial interests will be particularly likely to constitute an infringing use, but even in the absence of commercial exploitation by the defendant, the patent holder will have a recourse.[496] Of course, if the patentee seeks an account of profit, the court may conclude that, because the infringer made no financial gain from the use of the invention, the patentee is entitled to nothing.[497] The infringing activity may consist in the making or construction, the selling, or the utilization of the invention.

A. Making or Constructing the Invention

197. Making in Canada, for whatever purpose, the invention is normally an infringement,[498] unless the defendant can claim a recognized or legal exception. Making an invention seems to require some inferring with the laws of nature: simply letting a plant which contains a patented cell and gene, reproduce itself is not necessarily the equivalent of making the intention. However, saving and planting the seeds, then harvesting and selling the resultant plants would be considered using the invention within the meaning of section 42.[499]

B. Selling or Importing the Invention

198. The sale of the invention is also an infringement. There is however an implicit right to resell patented articles: the sale of a patented article is presumed to give the purchaser the right to use or sell or deal with the goods as the purchaser pleases,[500] so on *ad infinitum*.[501]

493. *Monsanto Canada Inc. v. Schmeiser*, [2004] 1 S.C.R. 902, para. 35.
494. Harold G. Fox, *Canadian Patent Law and Practice* 381 (4th ed., Carswell 1969); *Monsanto Canada Inc. v. Schmeiser*, [2004] 1 S.C.R. 902, para. 49.
495. *Monsanto Canada Inc. v. Schmeiser*, [2004] 1 S.C.R. 902, para. 49.
496. *Monsanto Canada Inc. v. Schmeiser*, [2004] 1 S.C.R. 902, paras 36–38.
497. *Monsanto Canada Inc. v. Schmeiser*, [2004] 1 S.C.R. 902, paras 104–105.
498. Harold G. Fox, *Canadian Patent Law and Practice* 383 (4th ed., Carswell 1969).
499. *Monsanto Canada Inc. v. Schmeiser*, [2004] 1 S.C.R. 902, paras 26–69.
500. *Eli Lilly & Co. v. Novopharm Ltd.*, [1998] 2 S.C.R. 129, para. 100.
501. *Signalisation de Montréal Inc. v. Services de Béton Universels Ltée*, [1993] 1 F.C. 341 (F.C.A.), para. 20.

C. *Use of the Invention*

199. Use of the invention will often occur when the invention is contained or incorporated in a broader structure or process. If the patented invention is significant or important to the defendant's activities that involve the unpatented structure, the use will be within the scope of the patent.[502] Use will also cover the output of the invention. For example, the Supreme Court[503] approved the ruling of a 1936 decision[504] according to which zippers made by a patented process and a patented machine were infringing goods, even if the zippers themselves were unpatented.[505] Plaintiff was entitled to damages for loss sustained by reason of defendant's sales of the zippers. Section 42 is also interpreted to cover the importation into Canada of items produced abroad but that if made in Canada would have infringed a Canadian patent.[506]

200. Possession can also amount to infringement, even if the patented object is not actively used. A potential value, combined with possession, can constitute use; such is the case of a fire extinguisher or a pump on a ship.[507] The Supreme Court summarized the rules in the following manner:

> *– Possession of a patented object or an object incorporating a patented feature may constitute 'use' of the object's stand-by or insurance utility and thus constitute infringement. – Possession, at least in commercial circumstances, raises a rebuttable presumption of 'use' – While intention is generally irrelevant to determining whether there has been 'use' and hence infringement, the absence of intention to employ or gain any advantage from the invention may be relevant to rebutting the presumption of use raised by possession.*[508]

D. *Inducing Violation*

201. The courts have acknowledged that a third party may be liable for inducing others to infringe. Such is the case of the seller of all the unassembled parts of a patented sailboard, which could be used only for the construction of the invention.[509] The courts have identified the following conditions for an infringement by inducement:

502. *Monsanto Canada Inc. v. Schmeiser*, [2004] 1 S.C.R. 902. *See* the propositions identified by the Court at para. 58.
503. *Monsanto Canada Inc. v. Schmeiser*, [2004] 1 S.C.R. 902, para. 41.
504. *Colonial Fastener Co. v. Lighting Fastener Co.*, [1937] S.C.R. 36.
505. The Court quotes the monograph of David Vaver, *Intellectual Property Law* 152 (Irwin Law 1997).
506. David Vaver, *Intellectual Property Law* 380 (2d ed., Irwin Law 2011).
507. *Monsanto Canada Inc. v. Schmeiser*, [2004] 1 S.C.R. 902, paras 47–51.
508. *Monsanto Canada Inc. v. Schmeiser*, [2004] 1 S.C.R. 902, para. 58.
509. *Windsurfing International Inc., v. Trilantic Corp.* (1985), 8 C.P.R. (3d) 241 (F.C.A.); however, there must be something in the conduct of the defendant inciting others to infringe. Such is the case of the defendant who provides instructions on how to use the part he sells, with the rest of the patented kit: *MacLennan c. Produits Gilbert Inc.* 2008 FAC 35, at paras 38–40. As the F.C.A. stated, 'The test is a difficult one to meet.': *Corlac Inc. v. Weatherford Canada Inc.*, 2011 FCA 228, para. 162.

(1) *That the act of infringement was completed by the direct infringer.*
(2) *Completion of the act of infringement was influenced by the acts of the inducer. Without said influence, infringement would not otherwise take place.*
(3) *The influence must knowingly be exercised by the seller, that is, the seller knows his or her influence will result in the completion of the act of infringement.*[510]

III. Protection Through the Regime Established by the Patented Medicines (Notice of Compliance) Regulations

202. As Parliament was abolishing the compulsory licensing regime in 1993, it reshaped the *Patent Act* to achieve a new balance between the rights of patent holders and the interests of Canadian consumers.[511] In particular, it created in favour of generic industry an exemption for stockpiling of patented medicines for sale after expiry of patent (the stockpiling exception) and an exception concerning the use of a patent for the purposes of developing and submitting samples of a competing version of a patented product to regulatory authorities for their review (the regulatory review exception). It also created a link between the patent protection and the granting of marketing approval for medicinal products in the *Patented Medicines (Notice of Compliance) Regulations*. In *Merck Frosst Canada Inc. v. (Minister of National Health and Welfare)*,[512] Iacobucci J. identified the purpose of the *Regulations*:

> simply to prevent patent infringement by delaying the issuance of NOCs until such time as their implementation would not result in such infringement.[513]

203. Under the *Food and Drugs Act*,[514] a new drug may not be marketed in Canada without the regulatory approval of the Minister of Health. A manufacturer of a new pharmaceutical must file a submission to obtain a Notice of Compliance (NOC) which will authorize the marketing of the drug in Canada. If the Minister is satisfied that the drug is safe, effective and otherwise complies with the regulations, a NOC will be issued to the manufacturer. Under the *PM(NOC) Regulations*, a first person, the patentee or an exclusive licensee, may submit a patent list in respect of a drug covered by a submission or by a NOC.[515]

204. When a generic company (the second person) seeks a NOC with respect to another drug, it can make a comparison with or refer to a drug for which a NOC has already been issued and concerning which the innovator has filed a patent list with

510. *Dableh v. Ontario Hydro*, [1996] 3 F.C. 751 (F.C.A.), at para. 43, reproducing the conditions enunciated in *Warner-Lambert Co. v. Wilkinson Sword Canada Inc.* (1988), 19 C.P.R. (3d) 402 (F.C.T.D.).
511. SOR/93-133, amended by SOR/98-166, SOR/99-379, SOR/2006-242, err. (E), Vol. 140, No. 23, SOR/2008-211, SOR/2010-212, SOR/2011-89, s. 1.
512. [1998] 2 S.C.R. 193.
513. *Ibid.* at para. 30.
514. RSC, 1985, c. F-27.
515. Section 4 of the *PM(NOC) Regulations*.

the Minister,[516] but then his or her submission must contain one or the other of two prescribed statements: (i) a statement that the generic manufacturer accepts that the NOC will not issue until the relevant listed patent expires; or (ii) an allegation that the innovator is not the owner or the exclusive licensee of the patent, that the patent has expired, that the patent is not valid, or that the generic manufacturer's marketing of the drug would not infringe any claim for the patented medicine itself or any claim for the dosage form or use of the patented medicine.[517] In case of an allegation described in section (ii), the first person (the patentee) must be notified.[518]

205. According to section 6, the patentee can then apply to the Court for an order prohibiting the Minister of Health and Welfare from issuing a NOC to the second person. The Minister may not issue the NOC during the twenty-four-month period following receipt of the first person's notice of application,[519] unless the stay is terminated earlier by the expiry of the patent, by a declaration by the court that the patent is not valid or that a non-infringement allegation is justified, or by the withdrawal, discontinuance or dismissal of the prohibition proceedings.[520] Some have described the stay order as 'draconian because it permits a patent holder to delay the entry of competitors into the market without having to establish even a prima facie case of patent infringement'.[521] If the patentee's application is ultimately unsuccessful, under section 8, the generic drug manufacturer can claim compensation for the sales lost during the prohibition order period.[522]

516. The generic presents what is called an abbreviated new drug submission (ANDS) which compares its drug to another drug (the 'Canadian reference product'). However, according to the *Food and Drug Regulations* (CRC, c 870), the generic company faces a six-year ban on the filing of the ANDS after the date of the first Notice of Compliance (NOC) issued to the innovator's drug; and (2) an eight-year ban on the issuance of an NOC to a generic product after the date of the first NOC issued to the innovative drug. An additional six-month extension is available for some results of clinical trials concerning the use of the drug in paediatric populations. *See* section C.08.004.1of the Regulations.

517. Section 5 of the *Patented Medicines (Notice of Compliance) Regulations*, (the *PM(NOC) Regulations*).

518. Subsection 5(3) of the *PM(NOC) Regulations*.

519. As originally promulgated, the *Regulations* prohibited the Minister from issuing the Notice of Compliance for a period of thirty months, but that period was reduced to twenty-four months by an amendment in 1998 (SOR/98-166).

520. Subsections 7(1)(e) and 7(2)(4) of the *PM(NOC)Regulations*.

521. *Bristol-Myers Squibb Canada Inc. v. Canada (Attorney General)* (2001), 11 C.P.R. (4th) 539 (F.C.A.), 541–542.

522. The methods to calculate those damages have been discussed by the courts: *see* notably *Apotex Inc. v. Sanofi-Aventis*, 2014 FCA 68, confirmed by the Supreme Court of Canada (*Sanofi-Aventis v. Apotex Inc.*, 2015 SCC 20) and *Teva Canada Limited v. Sanofi-Aventis Canada Inc.*, 2014 FCA 67.

§7. Limitations and Exceptions to the Scope of Patent Protection: Compulsory Licences

206. The *Patent Act* provides a number of limitations to the patent holder's rights. These include the exception concerning the use of a patent for the purposes of developing and submitting samples of a competing version of a patented product to regulatory authorities for their review (the regulatory review exception), an exception in favour of a previous purchaser of the invention, limitations in case of abuse of rights and control of patented medicines prices, and a regime of compulsory licences to benefit certain developing and least-developed countries. The courts have also recognized some users' rights to use inventions for experiments and research and the buyer's rights to repair. Finally, the Canadian *Competition Act*[523] may impose some limits to a patentee's rights.

I. The Regulatory Review Exception

207. In 1993, Parliament, while reinforcing the patent holders' rights, introduced in the *Patent Act* two exceptions intended to benefit the generic industry: an exemption for stockpiling of patented medicines for sale after expiry of patent (the stockpiling exception) and an exception concerning the use of a patent for the purposes of developing and submitting samples of a competing version of a patented product to regulatory authorities for their review (the regulatory review exception).[524] However, in 2001, the Dispute Settlement Body of the WTO ruled that the stockpiling exception was not consistent with Canada's obligations under Article 28.1 of the *TRIPs Agreement* and did not satisfy all the conditions of Article 30 that authorizes exceptions to the exclusionary patent rights laid down in Article 28.[525] On the other hand, the regulatory review exception was said to satisfy all three conditions of Article 30, and thus was not ruled inconsistent with Canada's obligations under Article 28.1 of the *TRIPs Agreement*.[526] The stockpiling exception was therefore abrogated in 2001,[527] leaving only the regulatory review exception in the legislative scheme.[528]

II. Acquired Rights of a Previous Purchaser or User

208. Section 56 protects the rights of the person who, before the claim date of a claim in a patent has purchased, constructed or acquired the subject matter defined by the claim. That person has the right to use and sell to others the specific article

523. RSC 1985, c. C-34.
524. *Patent Act Amendment Act*, 1992, SC 1993, c. 2, s. 4.
525. The Dispute Settlement Body adopted the Report of the Appellate Body, in *Canada – Term of Patent Protection*, WT/DS170/AB/R, 18 Sep. 2000 and the Panel Report in *Canada – Patent Protection of Pharmaceutical Products*, WT/DS114/R, 17 Mar. 2000.
526. *Ibid.*
527. *See An Act to amend the Patent Act*, SC 2001, c. 10, s. 2.
528. Section 55.2.

patented, constructed or acquired without being liable to the patentee.[529] The right to use an invention protected by section 56 has been interpreted to include the right to use and sell things produced with the patented machine. Thus, said the F.C.A., the purchaser of a subsequently patented piece of cloth would have the right to make the cloth into a suit.[530]

III. Control of Patented Medicines Prices

209. From 1923 to 1987, the *Patent Act* provided for the compulsory licensing for the manufacture, use and sale, and later import, of food and drugs made by patented processes. In 1987, the regime was changed. It prescribed certain periods during which the compulsory licences were differed and established the Patented Medicines Price Review Board, whose function was to ensure that patentees of medicines did not charge excessive prices during the deferral periods.[531]

210. In 1993, the regime of compulsory licensing was completely abolished and the powers of the Board were increased.[532] The Board has now the mandate to report on major pharmaceutical trends and to protect the consumers' interests by ensuring that patented drug prices are not excessive. If the Board finds that a patentee of an invention pertaining to a medicine is selling the medicine in any market in Canada[533] at an excessive price, the Board may order that the price be reduced to a non-excessive level, or may take measures to offset the excessive revenues derived from excessive pricing.[534] If there has been a policy to sell at excessive pricing, the measures can be directed to offset up to twice the amount of excessive revenues.[535] The factors to determine if a price is excessive are set out in the *Patent Act*[536] and the *PMPRB's Guidelines.*[537]

---

529. Section 56 has been modified several times over the years. The various versions are applicable depending on the application filing date of the patents. *See* subss 56(3)(4).
530. *Merck & Co. v. Apotex Inc.*, [1995] 2 F.C. 723 (F.C.A.).
531. *See* the legislative history in *ICN Pharmaceuticals, Inc. v. Canada (Staff of the Patented Medicine Prices Review Board)*, [1997] 1 F.C. 32 (F.C.A.).
532. *Patent Act Amendment Act, 1992*, SC 1993, c. 2.
533. The provisions apply even when the drugs are sold through the Special Access Programme set up to provide access to drugs needed for the treatment of serious or life-threatening conditions, that are not otherwise available on the market: *Celgene Corp. v. Canada (Attorney General)*, 2011 SCC 1, [2011] 1 SCR 3.
534. Section 83.
535. Subsection 83(4).
536. Section 85.
537. *See* the *Compendium of Policies, Guidelines and Procedures*, available on the website of the Patented Medicines Price Review Board: www.pmprb-cepmb.gc.ca.

IV. Compulsory Licences to the Benefit of Certain Developing and Least-Developed Countries

211. Following the Decision of the General Council of 30 August 2003[538] to waive some of the obligations set out in Article 31 of the *TRIPs Agreement* with respect to pharmaceutical products, Canada modified the *Patent Act* in 2004. It introduced a regime of compulsory licences authorizing Canadian firms to manufacture in Canada specific patented pharmaceutical products for export to certain developing and least-developed countries.[539] In 2007, Canada made a first application of the mechanism set up by the WTO by issuing a compulsory licence allowing a generic firm to manufacture and export some HIV/AIDS drugs to Rwanda.[540]

V. Limitations in Case of Abuse of Rights

212. If the patent holder is abusing the legal monopoly, the Attorney General of Canada or an interested party may apply for a series of relief, such as a licence or even revocation of the patent.[541] Such abuse can be considered only three years after grant.[542] Abuse can happen when (1) the demand is not being met to an adequate extent and on reasonable terms; (2) the trade or industry in Canada has suffered a prejudice because of the refusal of the patentee to grant a licence (if such a licence is in the public interest), or because the patentee attached unreasonable conditions to such a licence;[543] (3) the production, use or sale of a non-patented product has been unfairly prejudiced by the use of a process patent.[544]

213. In setting the terms of the licence, the Commissioner must try to ensure the widest possible use of the invention in Canada, maximum advantage to the patentee, reasonable profit for the licensee and equality among licensees.[545] He or she may refuse to grant a licence if he or she is of the opinion that the goals of sections 65–66 would be best served by a refusal.[546] The decision by the Commissioner on abuse is subject to appeal to the Federal Court of Canada (F.C.).[547]

538. *Implementation of paragraph 6 of the Doha Declaration on the TRIPS Agreement and Public Health*, WT/L/540, 1 Sep. 2003.
539. *An Act to Amend the Patent Act and the Food and Drugs Act (The Jean Chrétien Pledge to Africa),* SC 2004, c.23, s. 1.
540. *See* the *Notification under para 2(c) of the Decision of 30 Aug. 2003 on the Implementation of para. 6 of the Doha Declaration on the TRIPs Agreement and Public Health*, Doc. IP/N/10/CAN/1 (8 Oct. 2007).
541. Section 66.
542. Subsection 65(1).
543. *See* for instance *International Cone Co. Ltd. v. Consolidated Wafer Co.*, [1926] Ex. C.R. 143; 1927 S.C.R. 300, where it was found that the patentee had failed to supply the patented article on reasonable terms.
544. Subsection 65(2).
545. Subsection 66(4).
546. Paragraph 66(1)(e).
547. Section 71.

VI. Experiment and Research

214. There are just a few Canadian decisions accepting that research and experiments are not infringing activities. The Supreme Court of Canada did decide that an experimental user seeking a compulsory licence, which conducts bona fide experiments with the patented article to determine if it could manufacture a quality product, is not infringing the exclusive right of the patentee: this right to experiment is the logical result of the right to apply for a compulsory licence.[548] The F.C.A. went even further, accepting that there is a general exception for the mere making of the invention for the purpose of experiment, as long as there is neither using nor vending for profit and stating that the mere making for the purpose of experiment, and not for a fraudulent purpose, ought not to be considered within the meaning of the prohibition, and if it were, it is certainly not the subject for an injunction.[549]

VII. Repairs

215. As seen previously, the sale of a patented article is presumed to give the purchaser the right 'to use or sell or deal with the goods as the purchaser pleases'.[550] Similarly, a purchaser of a patented article may carry out repairs to it without infringement.[551]

VIII. Limitations Imposed by the Competition Act[552]

216. The *Competition Act* seeks to maintain and encourage competition in Canada.[553] As intellectual property rights can be used in anti-competitive conducts that inappropriately create, enhance or maintain market power or are likely to substantially lessen or prevent competition among firms, the exercise of intellectual property rights is subject to the *Competition Act* provisions. The *Act* itself prescribes that if a right is used to restrain trade, the Federal Court can make an order to void an agreement, stop its execution, grant a licence or may order any measure necessary to prevent the anti-competitive use.[554] Also an agreement involving intellectual property rights can

548. *Smith Kline & French Inter-American Corp. v. MicroChemicals Ltd.*, [1972] S.C.R. 506.
549. *Dableh v. Ontario Hydro*, [1996] 3 F.C. 751 (F.C.A.), para. 44. *See also Apotex Inc. v. Merck & Co.*, 2006 FCA 323, at para. 109.
550. *Eli Lilly & Co. v. Novopharm Ltd.*, [1998] 2 S.C.R. 129, para. 100.
551. But the buyer's right to repair does not cover a remaking or reconstruction of the patented article. David Vaver, *Intellectual Property Law* 405–406 (2d ed., Irwin Law, 2011).
552. RSC 1985, c. C-34.
553. Section 1.1, *Competition Act*.
554. Section 32, *Competition Act*.

constitute a criminal offence of the *Competition Act*[555] or a reviewable (civil) matter.[556] The Competition Bureau of Canada has published the *Intellectual Property Enforcement Guidelines*,[557] in which it indicates when it will consider that a conduct involving intellectual property may raise an issue under the *Competition Act*.

§8. Duration of Protection: Maintaining and Termination of Patent Protection

217. The *Patent Act* provides for the expiration of the term of a patent by the passage of time (section 45) or the failure to pay fees (section 46), and for the reissue (section 47) and for the disclaimer (section 48), but it is silent about terminating patent rights by dedicating the patent to the public. The courts however have studied the impact of this practice.

I. Duration

218. As mentioned earlier, the patent certificate bears on its face the filing date of the application for the patent, the date on which the application became open to public inspection under section 10, the date on which the patent is granted and issued and any prescribed information.[558] It is a prima facie proof of the patent validity.[559]

219. The patents issued on the basis of an application filed on or after 1 October 1989 have a term of twenty years from the filing date.[560] For the other patents, the *Act* now provides a term of seventeen years from the date on which the patent is issued, or twenty years from the filing date, whichever term expires later.[561] The CETA implementation bill will allow for the grant of certificates of supplementary protection

555. They include conspiracy (s. 45), bid-rigging (s. 47), false or misleading representations and other deceptive marketing practices in telemarketing, multi-level marketing plan, pyramid selling and contests (ss. 52–55.1).
556. Reviewable matters include deceptive marketing practices (s. 74.01), refusal to deal (s. 75), price maintenance (s. 76), exclusive dealing, tied selling and market restriction (s. 77), abuse of dominant position (s. 79), mergers (s. 92), and anti-competitive agreements (s. 90.1).
557. They were issued in 2000, revised in 2016, and are available on the Competition Bureau website www. competitionbureau.gc.ca.
558. Section 43. *See* no. 184 of this monograph.
559. Subsection 43(2).
560. Section 44.
561. Section 45. In 2000, the United States claimed that the term of seventeen years from grant, which was the norm for pre-1989 patent was inconsistent with Canada's obligations under Arts 33 and 70 of the *TRIPs Agreement*. On 12 Oct. 2000, the Dispute Settlement Body of the WTO concluded that s. 45 was inconsistent with Art. 33 of the *TRIPS Agreement* and Canada was requested to amend the *Patent Act* (*Canada – Term of Patent Protection*, WT DS170). It did so in June 2001 (*An Act to amend the Patent Act*, SC 2001, c. 10, s. 1.).

for pharmaceutical products that suffered from delay in getting their marketing authorization.[562]

II. Failure to Pay Fees

220. Section 46 prescribed that maintenance fees must be paid to maintain patents in good standing.[563] Those fees are governed by sections 100, 155, 182 of the *Patent Rules* and listed in Items 31, 32 of Schedule II.

III. Reissue, Re-examination, Disclaimer

221. If within four years of issuance, a patent is believed to be defective or inoperative by reason of insufficient description and specification, or by reason of the patentee's claiming more or less than he or she had a right to claim as new, a reissue examination may be requested.[564] The purpose of the procedure is to correct deficiencies in the description or claims, not to alter the subject matter of the patent;[565] it should not be used if an inventor has failed to claim protection for an invention he or she did not know or believe to be patentable[566] or if the patent does not meet the legal requirements.[567] Failure by the first patent attorney to fully comprehend and describe the invention is a proper case to apply the reissue procedure.[568] The commissioner can deliver a new patent that takes effect for the remaining part of the term, if the error which was made arose from inadvertence, accident or mistake, without any fraudulent or deceptive intention.

222. In 1989, the legislator also introduced a procedure for requesting a re-examination of any claim by filing prior art.[569] The re-examination is performed by a board constituted in the Patent Office.[570] If the patent is found null, it is reputed to never have existed. If only some of the claims are found void, the patent is deemed to have been issued in the corrected form. If a new or amended claim is allowed, the claim is effective from the date of the certificate.[571]

562. S 59 and ff of Bill C-30 (First Session, Forty-second Parliament, 64-65 Elizabeth II, 2015–2016–2017). *See* the status of the bill in Legisinfo online at http://www.parl.ca/LegisInfo/BillDetails.aspx?Language=en&Mode=1&billId=8549249.
563. Note that 'maintenance fees' are also required at specified times to maintain an application. *See* s. 27.1.
564. Section 47.
565. *Hoffmann-La Roche Ltd. v. Apotex Inc.* (1989), 24 C.P.R. (3d) 289 (F.C.A.).
566. *Northern Electric Co. v. Photo Sound Corp.*, [1936] S.C.R. 649.
567. *Farbwerke Hoechst Aktiengesellschaft Vormals Meister & Bruning v. Canada (Commissioner of Patents)*, [1966] S.C.R. 604.
568. *Curl-Master Manufacturing Co. v. Atlas Brush Ltd.*, [1967] S.C.R. 514.
569. *See* the *Act to amend the Patent Act and to provide for certain matters in relation thereto*, S.C.R. 1985, c. 33, [3rd Supp.], s.18.
570. Section 48.2.
571. Section 48.4.

223. The patentee may also make a disclaimer of parts of the patent if he or she has drafted his or her patent specification too broadly by reason of an accident, a mistake or inadvertence, without any wilful intent to defraud or mislead the public.[572]

IV. Dedication

224. In *Parke-Davis Division v. Canada (Minister of Health)*,[573] the F.C.A. indicated that practice by which Canadian patent holders dedicated their patent to the public should be legal.

§9. Infringement and Remedies

225. Provincial courts and the F.C. have concurrent jurisdiction to entertain actions for infringement of patent.[574] Section 55.01 provides with a six-year limitation period for infringement action. Remedies for infringement of a patent are regulated by sections 55 and 57 of the *Act*. They include: damages, account of profit, injunction and delivery up.

I. Damages

226. Damages aim at compensating the patentee for the harm caused by the infringement, which may include the patent holder's lost profits from sales or lost royalty payments.[575] The Federal Court has identified the following principles:

> Damages for infringement of a patent differ according to whether the patentee would itself manufacture the invention for profit or merely allow others to use the invention in return for royalties. In the first instance the basis for damages is the lost manufacturing profits. In the second instance the basis for damages is the loss of royalties [… and …] the plaintiff's damages are limited to the amount that the defendant would have had to pay for a license. […] This is a matter of evidence to be directed to ascertaining what a willing licensee would pay to a willing licensor for the use of the patents.[576]

227. When damages are based on lost profits, they are not restricted to the loss of profits on the patented article itself, but may extend to the loss of profits on articles

572. Section 48; *Hershkovitz v. Tytco Safety Products Canada Ltd.*, 2010 FCA 190.
573. [2003] 2 F.C. 514 (F.C.A.), 547.
574. Section 54.
575. *Monsanto Canada Inc. v. Schmeiser*, [2004] 1 S.C.R. 902, para. 100.
576. *Consolboard Inc. v. MacMillan Bloedel (Saskatchewan) Ltd.* (1982), 63 C.P.R. (2d) 1 (F.C.T.D.), 7.

accompanying normally the patented article.[577] Exemplary damages may be awarded in the proper circumstances.[578]

II. Account of Profits

228. The plaintiff can elect for an accounting of profits.[579] An accounting of profits, by contrast with damages, deals with the profits made by the infringer: its goal is not to punish the defendant, 'but to prevent his unjust enrichment by compelling him to surrender those profits that were improperly made as a result of the infringement'.[580]

III. Injunction

229. A successful plaintiff can normally obtain a permanent injunction.[581] Interlocutory injunctions are also possible as long as the plaintiff can satisfy the test established by the courts.[582] Courts have also on occasion granted Anton Piller orders[583] and Mareva injunctions.[584]

230. Delivery up orders are also possible: the ordinary order let the infringer make the choice between destruction and delivery up.[585] If, by removing a part, an article can be rendered non-infringing, the order can be modified to so allow.[586]

§10. Overlapping and Relation to Other Intellectual Property Laws

231. In principle, there is no reason why several intellectual property rights may not attach to the same article. As long as the respective conditions of protection are met, the intellectual property rights must be enforced by the courts. Thus the Federal Court clearly stated that the 'disclosure of an idea in a patent does not prevent copyright

577. *Colonial Fastener Co. v. Lightning Fastener Co.*, [1937] S.C.R. 36; *Monsanto Canada Inc. v. Schmeiser*, [2004] 1 S.C.R. 902, para. 41.
578. *See* for instance *Lubrizol Corp v. Imperial Oil Ltd.* (1992), 45 C.P.R. (3d) 449 (F.C.A.).
579. *Beloit Canada Ltd. v. Valmet-Dominion Inc.*, [1997] 3 F.C. 497 (F.C.A.).
580. *Reading & Bates Construction Co. v. Baker Energy Resources Corp.*, [1995] 1 F.C. 483 (C.A.). para. 12; *Lubrizol Corp. v. Imperial Oil Ltd.*, (1992), 45 C.P.R. (3d) 449 (F.C.A.).
581. Immanuel Goldsmith, *Patents of Invention* s. 532 231 (Carswell, 1981).
582. *See* for example the F.C.A.'s decision in *Cutter Ltd. v. Baxter Travenol Laboratories of Canada Ltd.* (1980), 47 C.P.R. (2d) 53.
583. *Nintendo of America, Inc. v. Coinex Video Games Inc.*, [1983] 2 F.C. 189, at 197–99.
584. *Reading & Bates Horizontal Drilling Co. v. Spie, Horizontal Drilling Co. Inc.* (1986), 13 C.P.R. (3d) 37 (F.C.T.D.).
585. *Baxter Laboratories of Canada Ltd. v. Cutter (Canada) Ltd.* (1983), 68 C.P.R. (2d) 179 (F.C.A.).
586. *Baxter Laboratories of Canada Ltd. v. Cutter (Canada) Ltd.* (1983), 68 C.P.R. (2d) 179 (F.C.A.).

attaching to a work which uses that idea, but which is independently a proper subject matter for copyright'.[587]

232. The courts will try to identify what is the proper subject matter of each right and restrict the protection accordingly. Thus a patentee may not claim trademarks rights (passing off or rights attached to a registered trademark) on the shape of its invention when that shape is an essential element of the invention.[588] Correlatively, patent laws are said to be concerned with processes belonging to a useful art as distinct from a fine art.[589] The *Copyright Act* indicates that copyright protection will not extend to utilitarian features of a work.[590] The *Industrial Design Act* stipulates that no protection afforded by its provisions shall extend to features applied to a useful article that are dictated solely by a utilitarian function of the article, or extend to any method or principle of manufacture or construction.[591]

233. As far as plant breeders' rights are concerned, nothing in either Acts precludes a cumulative protection for a plant, by way of a patent and a breeder's rights certificate. In the *Harvard College v. Canada (Commissioner of Patents)*,[592] the majority thought that the enactment of the *Plant Breeders' Rights Act* was an element showing that the *Patent Act* was not tailored to protect plants. It was a factor leading to the conclusion that the Parliament had not intended higher life forms to be patentable. However in *Monsanto Canada Inc. v. Schmeiser*,[593] the Court upheld a patent on a gene which increased the plants' tolerance to herbicides. Arguably, patent protection is now available for plants as long as not the plant itself, but the genes and the plant cells are targeted in the claims.

---

587. *DRG Inc. v. Datafile Ltd.* [1988] 2 F.C. 243, 259, aff'd on other grounds (1991) 35 C.P.R. (3d) 243 (F.C.A.).
588. Courts will have recourse to the doctrine of functionality: *Kirkbi AG v. Gestions Ritvik Inc.*, [2005] 3 S.C.R. 302.
589. *Tennessee Eastman Co.* et al. *v. Commissioner of Patents* (1970), 62 C.P.R. 117 (Ex. Ct.), 154–155, aff'd [1974] S.C.R. 111.
590. Section 64.1, *Copyright Act*, RSC 1985, c. C-42.
591. Section 5.1, *Industrial Design Act*, RSC 1985, c. I-9.
592. [2002] 4 S.C.R. 45.
593. [2004] 1 S.C.R. 902.

Chapter 3. Utility Models

§1. Sources: Legislation

234. Canada does not have a utility model regime.

§2. The Protection of Utility Models

235. In Canada, utility models can be protected if they meet the requirements of the patent legislation or they may be kept as trade secrets.[594]

594. *See* c. 9 of this monograph.

Chapter 4. Trademarks

§1. Sources: Legislation

236. In Canada, trademarks are protected by the provincial common law (either by the provisions of the *Civil Code of Québec* in Québec, or by the rules of the common law and equity in the other provinces and territories), as well as by the federal statute entitled to the *Trademarks Act*.[595] In 1867, the *British North America Act, 1867*,[596] (renamed in 1982 the *Constitution Act, 1867*)[597] granted legislative powers to the Federal Parliament and the provincial legislatures.[598] However, there is no statutory allocation of powers concerning trademarks. The courts have indicated that an obvious

595. RSC 1985, c. T-13.
596. (1867) 30-31 Vict., c. 3 (U.K.).
597. *See* No. 1 of the Schedule to the *Constitution Act, 1982*, being Sch. B of the *Canada Act 1982*, (U.K.) 1982, c.11.
598. Sections 91–92.

source of authority for the Federal Parliament is the second head of section 91 of the *Constitution Act, 1867*[599] dealing with 'The Regulation of Trade and Commerce.'[600]

599. *Supra* n. 593.
600. In *Kirkbi AG v. Ritvik Holdings Inc.*, [2005] 3 S.C.R. 302, the Supreme Court of Canada explained: '15. The grant of legislative authority to the Parliament of Canada listed in s. 91 of the Constitution Act, 1867 does not specify that trademarks are a component of the federal government's power to legislate. Patents and copyrights are explicitly allocated to federal legislative power (subss 91(22) and (23)). Pursuant to subs. 91(2), the Federal Government has exclusive jurisdiction in relation to trade and commerce. In *Citizens Insurance Co. of Canada v. Parsons* (1881), 7 App. Cas. 96, the Judicial Committee of the Privy Council (P.C.) distinguished two branches of federal power under subs. 91(2): (1) the power over international and interprovincial trade and commerce; and (2) the power over general trade and commerce affecting Canada as a whole ('general trade and commerce'). [...] 16. The 'general trade and commerce' category requires an assessment of the relative importance of an activity to the national economy as well as an inquiry into whether an activity should be regulated by Parliament as opposed to the provinces. To determine whether a particular issue requires national rather than local regulation, this Court has set out five criteria to be considered. These criteria are integrated into an assessment of whether federal legislation can be supported on the basis of Parliament's authority over general trade and commerce. [...] 17. The jurisprudence of our Court now recognizes that the following factors are hallmarks of a valid exercise of Parliament's general trade and commerce power: (i) the impugned legislation must be part of a regulatory scheme; (ii) the scheme must be monitored by the continuing oversight of a regulatory agency; (iii) the legislation must be concerned with trade as a whole rather than with a particular industry; (iv) the legislation should be of a nature that provinces jointly or severally would be constitutionally incapable of enacting; and (v) the failure to include one or more provinces or localities in a legislative scheme would jeopardize the successful operation of the scheme in other parts of the country (*General Motors of Canada Ltd. v. City National Leasing*, [1989] 1 S.C.R. 641, at pp. 662-63). These factors are not exhaustive and, to be valid, it is not necessary for federal legislation to satisfy all five criteria. [...] 18. The federal government's power to legislate with respect to trademarks has never been the target of a direct constitutional challenge. The issue was raised in the Privy Council in a 1937 decision examining the constitutionality of federal trademark legislation. The Privy Council judgment relies, albeit implicitly, on the second branch of the trade and commerce powers under s. 91(2) to confirm Parliament's jurisdiction to enact trademark legislation: *Attorney-General for Ontario v. Attorney-General for Canada*, [1937] A.C. 405.' Lord Atkin for the P.C. commented as follows (at p. 417): 'No one has challenged the competence of the Dominion to pass such legislation. If challenged one obvious source of authority would appear to be the class of subjects enumerated in subs. 91(2), the Regulation of trade and commerce, referred to by the Chief Justice. There could hardly be a more appropriate form of the exercise of this power than the creation and regulation of a uniform law of trade marks'.

Provisions dealing with unregistered trademarks were said to be within the legislative power of the Parliament of Canada, because they round out the federal trademark scheme.[601]

However a provision creating a civil cause of action for acts of unfair competition beyond the domain of patents and trademarks was held unconstitutional.[602] In 1953, the Federal Parliament adopted the *Trademarks Act*[603] which is still the governing legislation in Canada.[604]

237. Furthermore, Canada is a party to several multinational conventions. Canada is party to the *Paris Convention for the Protection of Industrial Property* made on 20 March 1883.[605] Canada has entered into the *Agreement Establishing the WTO*, which includes the *Agreement on Trade-Related Aspects of Intellectual Property Rights* (*TRIPs Agreement*).[606] Canada is also a party to the *NAFTA*, which regroups in a specific chapter on intellectual property, provisions similar to those adopted in the *TRIPs*

601. *See Kirkbi AG v. Ritvik Holdings Inc.*, [2005] 3 S.C.R. 302 at para. 33: As outlined above, subs. 7(b) of the Act only minimally intrudes into provincial jurisdiction over property and civil rights. It is a remedial provision limited to trademarks as defined in the Act (ss. 2 and 6). As this Court observed in *MacDonald v. Vapor Canada Ltd.*, [1977] 2 S.C.R. 134 and the F.C.A. held in *Asbjorn Horgard A/S v. Gibbs/Nortac Industries Ltd.* (1986), 8 C.I.P.R. 232 (F.C.T.D.), rev'd in part [1987] 3 F.C. 544 (C.A.), s. 7(b) 'rounds out' the federal trademarks scheme. In this regard subs. 7(b) is, in its pith and substance, directly connected to the enforcement of trademarks and trade names in Canada because it is directed at avoiding confusion through the use of trademarks.
602. *McDonald* et al. *v. Vapor Canada Ltd.*, [1977] 2 S.C.R. 134; *Bousquet also known as Jean Cacharel*, et al. *v. Barmish Inc.* (1993), 46 C.P.R. (3d) 510 (F.C.A.) Therefore, in the absence of a trademark, the Federal Court has no jurisdiction to hear a passing off action *Dumont Vins & Spiritueux Inc. v. Celliers du Monde Inc.* (1992), 42 C.P.R. (3d) 197 (F.C.A.)
603. RSC 1985, c. T-13.
604. The statute is accompanied by the *Trade-marks Regulations*, SOR/96-195, amended by SOR/99-292; SOR/2003-209; SOR/2007-91.
605. The Paris Convention was signed on 20 Mar. 1883, and was revised at Brussels in 1900, at Washington in 1911, at the Hague in 1925, at London in 1934, at Lisbon in 1958 and at Stockholm in 1967 and amended on 28 Sep. 1979. Canada ratified the Convention as revised at Brussels and Washington on 1 Sep. 1923; *See Canada Treaty Information*, DFAIT www.treaty-accord.gc.ca and H. G. FOX, *Canadian Patent Law and Practice* 561 (4th ed., Carswell, 1969). Canada signed the Hague revision on November 1925: the instrument of accession was deposited on 1 May 1928: *Canada Treaty Series 1928*, 3, (1929). The London revision was signed on 2 Jun. 1934: the instrument of accession was deposited on 26 Jun. 1951 and the ratification was in force on 30 Jul. 1951: *Canada Treaty Series 1951*, 10, (1952) and H. G. FOX, *Canadian Law of TradeMarks* 28 (2d ed., Carswell 1956). Canada was not a party to the Lisbon version of 1958. Canada acceded to the Stockholm version on 7 Apr. 1970, and the accession came in force on 7 Jul. 1970; as regards the substantive provisions, Canada acceded to Arts 1–12 at the Stockholm level on 23 Feb. 1996 and the accession became effective on 26 May 1996. *Treaties with Canada* (Carswell Thomson Professional Publishing 2001 1967).
606. The agreement was signed by Canada on 15 Apr. 1994 and ratified on 30 Dec. 1994. It was enacted into domestic law by the *World Trade Organization Agreement Implementation Act*, SC 1994, c. 47.

Agreement.[607] On 19 June 2014, the *Economic Action Plan 2014 Act, No. 1*[608] received royal assent.[609] As expressed in its Legislative Summary, the statute amends the *Trademarks Act* 'to, among other things, make that *Act* consistent with the *Singapore Treaty on the Law of Trademarks* and add the authority to make regulations for carrying into effect the *Protocol Relating to the Madrid Agreement Concerning the International Registration of Marks*'.[610] The statute also adopts the classification established by the *Nice Agreement Concerning the International Classification of Goods and Services for the Purposes of the Registration of Marks.*[611] Another legislation, the *Combating Counterfeit Products Act*[612] was also enacted in 2014, containing overlapping provisions with the *Economic Action Plan 2014 Act, No. 1*[613].

§2. Subject Matter of Protection

238. The *Trademarks Act*[614] formerly defined a trademark as 'a mark that is used by a person for the purpose of distinguishing or so as to distinguish wares or services manufactured, sold, leased, hired or performed by him from those manufactured, sold, leased, hired or performed by others'. The new regime introduced in 2014, adopts the following definition: 'a sign or combination of signs that is used or proposed to be used by a person for the purpose of distinguishing or so as to distinguish their goods or services from those of others'.[615] It is therefore necessary to identify the signs which may serve as trademarks.

607. 32 I.LM. 296. The c. 17 is the one devoted to intellectual property matters and is reproduced at 32 I.L.M. 670. The agreement was signed on 17 Dec. 1992 by the governments of the United States, Mexico and Canada. It came into force on 1 Jan. 1994. *See* Index, *Canada Treaty Series 1994* 1 , (1998). Its goal is to create a free trade zone between the three countries. It was enacted into Canadian domestic law by the *North American Free Trade Agreement Implementation Act*, SC 1993, c. 44.

608. SC 2014, c. 20.

609. The provisions will come into force when the necessary regulatory changes will have been made. The Canadian Intellectual Property Office will announce the regulatory amendments on its website : https://www.ic.gc.ca/eic/site/cipointernet-internetopic.nsf/eng/home.

610. The *Legislative Summary* is available on the Parliament of Canada website http://www.parl.gc.ca/legisinfo/BillDetails.aspx?Language=E&Mode=1&billId=6483626&View=8. *See also* s. 65.1 of the *Economic Action Plan 2014 Act, No. 1*, SC 2014, c. 20.

611. *See* the *Legislative Summary* available on the Parliament of Canada website http://www.parl.gc.ca/legisinfo/BillDetails.aspx?Language=E&Mode=1&billId=6483626&View=8.

612. SC 2014 c 32.

613. As of 1 January 2017, some provisions from those two statutes were still not in force and some will probably never take effect : *see* on this issue Teresa Scassa, *Canadian Trademark Law* p 693 and ff (2d ed., LexisNexis Canada).

614. Section 2.

615. Subsection 319(4) of the *Economic Action Plan 2014 Act, No. 1*, SC 2014, c. 20.

I. Signs Which May Serve as Trademarks According to the Trademarks Act

239. Before 2014, the *Act* did not specify what a mark was. It seems that the omission was intentional: it was felt that by not providing a definition, a possibly restrictive interpretation would be avoided.[616] The following signs were accepted as registrable trademarks: existing or coined words, trade names[617] or personal names, letters, initials, numbers, even a phone number,[618] logos or designs, pictures. Shape or packaging of wares could also form a trademark and they were known as 'distinguishing guises'.[619] The 2014 amendments introduced a definition of sign as including: ' a word, a personal name, a design, a letter, a numeral, a colour, a figurative element, a three-dimensional shape, a hologram, a moving image, a mode of packaging goods, a sound, a scent, a taste, a texture and the positioning of a sign'.[620]

II. Different Categories of Marks

240. The definition provided in section 2 of the *Trademarks Act* specifies that trademark is not only a mark used or intended to distinguish as explained in section 2-I, but can also be a certification mark, a distinguishing guise and a proposed trademark. This last category is really a mean to create an exception to the use requirement, which will be explained in section 3. Thus we can deduce that the *Act* recognizes at least three categories of trademarks: certification marks, ordinary marks and special marks (including distinguishing guises). The *Act* also grants some to official marks, which we shall deal with at the end of this section. The *Trademark Act* also contains a protective scheme for geographical indications, which is explained in Chapter 10 of this monograph.

A. *Certification Marks*

241. Section 2 defines a certification mark as:

> 'certification mark' means a sign or combination of signs that is used or proposed to be used for the purpose of distinguishing or so as to distinguish goods or services that are of a defined standard from those that are not of that defined standard, with respect to (a) the character or quality of the goods or services, (b) the working conditions under which the goods are produced or the services performed, (c) the class of persons by whom the goods are produced or the

616. William L. Hayhurst, *'What is a Trade-mark? The Development of Trade-mark Law'* in *Trademarks Law of Canada* 68 (Gordon F. Henderson ed, Carswell 1993).
617. *Dubiner v. Cheerio Toys and Games Ltd.*, [1965] 1 Ex. C.R. 524, aff'd [1966] S.C.R. 206.
618. *Pizza Pizza Ltd., v. Canada (Reg. of Trade-marks)*, [1989] 3 F.C. 379 (F.C.A.).
619. *See* the definition of distinguishing guise in s. 2 abrogated in 2014; *see* subs. 319(1) of the *Economic Action Plan 2014 Act, No. 1*, S.C. 2014, c. 20.
620. Subsection 319(5) of the *Economic Action Plan 2014 Act, No. 1*, SC 2014, c. 20.

services performed, or (d) the area within which the goods are produced or the services performed;.

As the Federal Court has stated:

It is tantamount to the conferment of a seal of approval and would naturally enhance the sale in accordance with the good repute acquired by the certification mark.

The purpose of the certification mark is to distinguish the wares so marked from those which are not of the defined standard with respect to the matters specified in the definition in s. 2.

By virtue of s. 23 a certification mark can be adopted and registered only by a person or association not engaged in dealing in the wares with which the mark is associated. Therefore a registered owner of a certification cannot be the user thereof in the ordinarily accepted sense. The registered owner may license others to use the trade mark when satisfied that the licensee deals in wares which meet the defined standards.[621]

B. *Ordinary Trademarks*

242. The definition of the word 'trademark' found in the *Trademarks Act*[622] requires that the trademark be 'used by a person for the purpose of distinguishing or so as to distinguish goods or services'. In *Tommy Hilfiger Licensing, Inc. v. International Clothiers Inc.*,[623] the owner of retail clothing stores had been selling shirts and shorts featuring a crest design similar to that of the plaintiffs' crest design trademarks. In its defence, the retailer argued that it did not infringe the plaintiffs' interests because it did not use its crest as a trademark but rather as mere ornamentation. The F.C.A. had thus to decide the meaning of the words 'used [...] for the purpose of distinguishing or so as to distinguish'. The court concluded that the retailer had used its crest design mark as a trademark. Quoting *Fox on Canadian Law of Trademarks and Unfair Competition*,[624] it ruled that:

621. *Wool Bureau of Canada Ltd v. Queenswear (Canada) Ltd.* (1980), 47 C.P.R. (2d) 11 (F.C.T.D.) at 15.

622. Section 2.

623. (2004), [2005] 1 F.C.R. 148 (F.C.A.).

624. A.Kelly Gill, *Fox on Canadian Law of Trade-marks and Unfair Competition* 3–12, 3–13 and 3–14 (4th ed Carswell 2002).

> [t]he nature of the use sufficient to fulfil the definition of a trademark is not to be considered in any restrictive sense. Both the intention of the user and recognition by the public are relevant facts and either may be sufficient to show that there has been trademark use: it is not necessary that there should be both, but at least one must be present.[625]

As the trial judge had concluded that there was confusion between the parties' crests, the Court of Appeal ruled that it was a proof that the appellants' crest design would be recognized by the public as a trademark.[626]

C. Special Signs (Including Distinguishing Guises)

243. As mentioned earlier, a distinguishing guise was formerly expressly included in the concept of trademark.[627] A distinguishing guise was the shape of wares or their containers, or a mode of wrapping or packaging wares, which is used for the purpose of distinguishing or so as to distinguish wares or services.[628] It was registrable only if it has been so used in Canada as to have become distinctive.[629] In the 2014 reform scheme, a distinguishing guise is just one of the many signs[630] for which, at the request of the Registrar, an applicant must furnish evidence of distinctiveness at the filing date of an application for registration.[631] The same rule applies to sounds, scents, tastes, textures and any other prescribed signs.[632]

If a registration is likely to unreasonably limit the development of any art or industry, it may be expunged by the Federal Court.[633] Furthermore, the registration of a distinguishing guise must not interfere with the use of any utilitarian feature embodied in the distinguishing guise.[634]

D. Official Marks

244. There are some official marks which are protected through some special regimes. Such is the case of the marks related to the Olympic Games and the Paralympic

625. At para. 36.
626. At paras 44–45.
627. Section 2, definition of 'trademark'.
628. Section 2, definition of 'distinguishing guise'.
629. Subsection 13(1)(a).
630. It is now one type of signs included in the definition of s. 2 and which can constitute a trademark.
631. *See* 32 of the *Trademark Act*, as introduced by s. 339 of the *Economic Action Plan 2014 Act, No. 1*, SC 2014, c. 20.
632. *See* 32 of the *Trademark Act*, as introduced by s. 339 of the *Economic Action Plan 2014 Act, No. 1*, SC 2014, c. 20.
633. The rule, previously expressed in subs. 13(3) has been moved to s.18(1) by s. 326 of of the *Economic Action Plan 2014 Act, No. 1*, SC 2014, c. 20.
634. Subsection 13(2). The rule, previously enunciated in subs. 13(3), is now expressed in s 12(2) and s. 20 (1.1) of the *Trademark Act*, as introduced by s. 326 and s. 332 of the *Economic Action Plan 2014 Act, No. 1*, SC 2014, c. 20.

Games, whose sponsorship rights are granted by the *Olympic and Paralympic Marks Act.*[635]

245. Public authorities may also register official marks under subparagraph 9(1)(n)(iii) of the *Trademarks Act.*[636] The procedure starts when a public authority presents a request to the Registrar to give public notice of its adoption and use[637]. It has been said that:

> [o]nce public notice has been given with respect to the adoption and use of an official mark, the mark is ' hardly and virtually unexpungeable':[638]
>
> The purpose of section 9 is to remove all the kinds of marks as listed above from the field of trade or business. It is to preclude any person from capitalizing on any well known, respected public symbols and adopting it for his or her own wares or services. These emblems, badges or crests are associated with public institutions, not involved in trade or business, but which nevertheless are deemed to be invested with respectability, credibility and other civic virtues. Section 9, in a sense, ensures that these symbols do not become pawns of trade or proprietorship.[639]

246. There are important advantages attached to the registration of an official mark, compared to that of an ordinary trademark. The F.C.A. summarized those advantages in *Ontario Assn. of Architects v. Assn. of Architectural Technologists of Ontario:*[640]

> An important effect of the giving of public notice under paragraph 9(1)(n)(iii) is that, from that date, other persons are prevented from using any mark 'as a trade-mark or otherwise' that is likely to be mistaken for the official mark (section 11), except in connection with goods or services with which the mark was used before public notice was given of the official mark [...] Moreover, the Registrar may not refuse to give public notice of the adoption and use of a mark as an official mark for wares or services on the ground that it is merely descriptive, is not distinctive of the public authority's wares or services, or is liable to be confused with another's mark. Indeed, the Registrar has virtually no discretion to refuse to give notice of the adoption and use of a mark as an official mark,

635. SC 2007, c. 25.

636. A similar regime exists for the arms, crest or flag adopted and used at any time by any federal, provincial or municipal corporation in Canada: *see* para. 9(1)(e).

637. The entity must present evidence of public authority status : *see* Canadian Intellectual Property Office, Practice Notice: Official Marks pursuant Sub-paragraph 9(1)(n)(iii) , available at https://www.ic.gc.ca/eic/site/cipointernet-internetopic.nsf/eng/home

638. *Mihaljevic v. British Columbia* (1988), 23 C.P.R. (3d) 80 (F.C.T.D.), at 89; *Ontario Association of Architects v. Association of Architectural Technologists of Ontario* (2002), [2003] 1 F.C. 331 (F.C.A.) at para. 63.

639. *Techniquip Ltd. v. Canadian Olympic Assn*, (1998), 80 C.P.R. (3d) 225 (F.C.T.D.), aff'd. (1999), 3 C.P.R. (4th) 298 (F.C.A.), at 233.

640. (2002), [2003] 1 F.C. 331 (F.C.A.).

once the body making the request establishes that the statutory criteria have been met. [...][641]

247. For an official mark to be protected under subparagraph 9(1)(n)(iii) of the Act, an entity qualifying as a public authority must have adopted and used the mark in Canada prior to the publication of the public notice. Internal use is not enough to conclude that there has been adoption and use of the official mark,[642] but displaying a mark on a public website was considered sufficient.[643] The official mark does not have to distinguish goods or services[644] and it is protected against the use of any resembling mark likely to be mistaken for it, in connection with a business.[645]

248. What is a public authority? At first, it was suggested that a three-part test be used to determine what a public authority is: (1) there must be a duty to the public; (2) there must be a significant degree of governmental control; and (3) any profit earned must be for the benefit of the public and not for private benefit.[646] The F.C.A. opted for a two-part test of government control and public benefit,[647] but stressed that a duty to the public may still be considered:

> As most subsequent cases have recognized, in Registrar of Trade Marks v. Canadian Olympic Association, [[1983] 1 F.C. 692], this Court regarded the public duty test as inappropriate in the context of subparagraph 9(1)(n)(iii), at least in the way that it had been applied in some cases dealing with public authorities and short limitation periods. I see no reason for departing from the two-part test of government control and public benefit. However, in determining whether a body's functions are sufficiently for the public benefit, a court may consider its objects, duties and powers, including the distribution of its assets. In this context, a duty to do something that is of benefit to the public is relevant as an element of 'public benefit', even though it is not a 'public duty' in the sense

641. *Ibid.*, at para. 34. The Court noted at para. 35, other important differences between the regime concerning official marks and ordinary trademarks: 'Nonetheless, section 56 imposes no duty on the Registrar to give prior notice of a request made under subparagraph 9(1) (n)(iii) and no provision is made for an objector to be heard before the Registrar grants the request, perhaps because of the limited range of issues that the Registrar has to decide. This is, of course, quite unlike the registration of a trademark, which is preceded by public notice of the application and a determination by the trademarks opposition board based on the submissions of the applicant for the registration of a trademark and of any opponents [...]'.

642. *You In-Canadian Athletes Fund Corp. v. Canadian Olympic Committee*, 2008 FCA 124; Teresa Scassa, *Canadian Trademark Law* 157 (LexisNexis, 2010).

643. *FileNet Corp v. Canada (Registrar of Trade-marks)*, 2001 FCT 865 at para. 65 (aff'd 2002 FCA 418); *Insurance Corporation of British Columbia v. Stainton Ventures Ltd.*, 2014 BCCA 296.

644. *Ontario Association of Architects v. Association of Architectural Technologists of Ontario* (2002), [2003] 1 F.C. 331 (F.C.A.), at para. 63.

645. *Canadian Olympic Assn. v. Konica Canada Inc.*, [1992] 1 F.C. 797 (F.C.A.) at para. 34.

646. *Registrar of TradeMarks v. Canadian Olympic Association*, [1983] 1 F.C. 692 (F.C.A.) at 699.

647. *See* Canadian Intellectual Property Office, Practice Notice: Official Marks pursuant Subparagraph 9(1)(n)(iii) , available at https://www.ic.gc.ca/eic/site/cipointernet-internetopic.nsf/eng/home.

of being legally enforceable by a public law remedy, such as an order of mandamus or its equivalent.[648]

249. The governmental control test is satisfied when the government exercises a degree of ongoing influence in the body's governance and decision-making process: it is not enough that the legislature may change the body's statutory objects or powers by enacting from time to time a new legislation[649] or that the organization as a charity is obliged to comply with some specific laws generally relating to charities, including taxation laws.[650] The F.C.A. also concluded that the government exercising the control must be a public authority in Canada.[651]

§3. Conditions of Protection

250. In order to secure registration of a trademark, an applicant must meet the appropriate distinctiveness standard and must indicate on which basis his or her application rests.

I. The Distinctiveness Standard

251. Section 2 of the *Trademarks Act* provides a definition of what is a distinctive trademark:

> distinctive, in relation to a trademark, means 'a trade-mark that actually distinguishes the goods or services in association with which it is used by its owner from the goods or services of others or is adapted so to distinguish them.

So a trademark is distinctive if it 'actually distinguishes' the goods and services of one trader from those of others or if it is 'adapted so to distinguish them'. A coined or invented word is normally a word adapted to distinguish. However, a laudatory epithet or a word descriptive of the character of quality of the ware has no inherent distinctiveness[652] and it must have been used so as to actually distinguish the goods or services to become registrable. Finally, there are some terms which may never serve as registrable trademarks.

252. The *Trademarks Act* follows in large those principles: for instance, by virtue of sections 12 and 13, a trademark is not registrable if it is the name or the

648. *Ontario Assn. of Architects v. Assn. of Architectural Technologists of Ontario* (2002), [2003] 1 F.C. 331 (F.C.A.) at para. 52.
649. *Ontario Association of Architects v. Association of Architectural Technologists of Ontario* (2002), [2003] 1 F.C. 331 (F.C.A.), at para. 62.
650. *Chosen People Ministries Inc. v. Canadian Jewish Congress*, 2003 FCA 272 at para. 4.
651. *United States Postal Service v. Canada Post Corp.*, [2006] 3 F.C.R. 28 (F.C.T.D.), aff'd 2007 FCA 10.
652. *Standard Coil Products (Canada) Ltd v. Standard Radio Corp.*, [1971] F.C. 106 (F.C.T.D.), at para. 39.

surname of an individual, or a term clearly descriptive or deceptively misdescriptive of the character or quality of the goods, or a distinguishing guise, but it may become registrable if it was used by the owner so as to have become 'distinctive'. Sections 9–12 prohibit the adoption or use of certain words. It is therefore necessary to distinguish between three categories of expressions: the prohibited expressions, expressions registrable upon proof of acquired distinctiveness and all other expressions.

A. Prohibited Expressions

253. The list is given in part in section 9. For instance, no person shall adopt in connection with a business, as a trademark or otherwise, any mark consisting of, or so nearly resembling as to be likely to be mistaken for the arms or crest of any member of the Royal Family or of the Governor General of Canada,[653] the flags, arms and crests of a country party to the *Paris Convention* or member of the WTO following a proper communication and public notification, and some international organization names or signs.[654] Are also excluded from adoption and registrability any scandalous, obscene or immoral word or device, any matter that may falsely suggest a connection with any living individual, the portrait or signature of any individual who is living or has died within the preceding thirty years.[655] Section 10 also bars the adoption of any mark who has, by ordinary and bona fide commercial usage, become recognized in Canada as designating the kind, quality, quantity, destination, value, place of origin or date of production of any goods or services. Finally, section 12 prohibits the registration of a mark:

- if it is the name in any language of any of the goods or services with which the mark is used or proposed to be used;[656]
- if it is confusing with a registered trademark;[657]
- if its adoption is prohibited by another provision of the *Act*;[658]
- if it is in whole or in part a protected geographical indication, where the trademark is to be registered in association with a wine or a spirit not originating in a territory indicated by the geographical indication;[659]
- if its adoption is prohibited by the *Olympic and Paralympic Marks Act*[660] and it is not covered by an exception provided by the same statute;[661]

653. Paragraphs 9(1)(a)(b)(c). The prohibition extends to any word or symbol likely to lead to the belief that the wares or services are under royal governmental patronage. *See* para. 9(1)(d) as modified by s. 323 of the *Economic Action Plan 2014 Act, No. 1*, SC 2014, c. 20.
654. Paragraphs 9(1)(f)–(h.1), (i)–(i.3) and (m), as modified by s. 323 of the *Economic Action Plan 2014 Act, No. 1*, SC 2014, c. 20.
655. Paragraphs 9(1)(j)(k)(l).
656. Paragraph 12(1)(c).
657. Paragraph 12(1)(d).
658. Paragraphs (12 (1)(e)(f) referring to ss 9–10.1.
659. Paragraphs 12(1)(g)(h).
660. S.C. 2007, c. 25, s. 3.
661. *Ibid.*, subss 3(3)(4).

– if, in relation to the goods or services in association with which it is used or proposed to be used, its features are dictated primarily by a utilitarian function.[662]

B. *Expressions Registrable upon Proof of Acquired Distinctiveness*

254. Those are names and descriptive words, distinguishing guises, and marks lacking inherent distinctiveness.

1. Names and Descriptive Words

255. Under paragraphs 12(1)(a)(b), and 13, surnames and names, descriptive words (and before the 2014 reform, distinguishing guises) are in principle barred from registration, but subsection 12(2), renumbered subsection 12(3) in the 2014 reform[663] provide an exception to non-registrability. If it can be shown that, by long use of the mark in association with the goods, the mark have become distinctive of the applicant's goods at the date of application for registration, it may gain registrability.[664] The court will consider if, through use, the mark, although an ordinary word, has acquired a dominant secondary or distinctive meaning in relation to the goods or services of the applicant.[665] The onus of proof is said to be a heavy one.[666]

256. Also under the former section 14, foreign registered trademarks which are not inherently distinctive could overcome an argument of non-distinctiveness if the applicant could provide evidence that the mark was not without distinctive character, having regard to all the circumstances of the case including the length of time during which it has been used in any country. This was a less demanding test than distinctiveness (although some use of the mark in Canada seemed necessary[667]) which was eliminated in the 2014 legislative reform.[668]

257. But what are the words covered by the provisions of subsections 12 (1)(a) and (b)? Subsection 12(1)(a) deals with a word that is *primarily merely* the name or the surname of an individual who is living or has died within the preceding thirty years. Thus, the fact that the word is the surname of few individuals in Canada will not bar registration if the general public of Canada would rather read it as a coined

662. Subsection 12(2) of the *Trademark Act*, as replaced by s. subsection 326 (4) of the of the *Economic Action Plan 2014 Act, No. 1*, SC 2014, c. 20.

663. *See* subs 326(4) of the *Economic Action Plan 2014 Act, No. 1*, SC 2014, c. 20. For the distinguishing guises, s. 13 (2) prescribed the same rule before the 2014. Now, s. 32, as amended by s. 339 of the *Economic Action Plan 2014 Act, No. 1*, indicates that, at the request of the Registrar, an applicant must furnish evidence of distinctiveness at the filing date of an application for registration.

664. Under subs. 32(2). Registration may be restricted to the territorial area where the mark has acquired secondary meaning: *see* e.g., *Home Juice Co. v. Orange Maison Ltée*, [1970] S.C.R. 942.

665. *Molson Breweries v. John Labatt Ltd.*, [2000] 3 F.C. 145 (F.C.A.), at para. 30.

666. *Ibid.*

667. *Boston Pizza International Inc. c. Boston Chicken, Inc.*, 2003 FAC 120; 24 C.P.R. (4th) 150 (F.C.A.), at paras 12–13.

668. Section 328 of the *Economic Action Plan 2014 Act, No. 1*, SC 2014, c. 20.

word.[669] Adoption of the name of a fictitious person is not precluded from registration, provided it does not coincide with the name of a living person or one who has died recently.[670]

Section 12(1)(b) concerns words which, whether depicted, written or sounded, are either clearly descriptive or deceptively misdescriptive[671] in the English or French language of the character or quality of the goods or services in association with which they are used or proposed to be used or of the conditions of or the persons employed in their production or of their place of origin. The purpose of the provision is to prevent the monopolization by a single trader of a term that is clearly descriptive or common to the trade.[672] For a trademark to be objectionable under subsection 12(1)(b), the word must be clearly descriptive, and not merely suggestive of the character or quality of the goods or services in association with which it is used or proposed to be used, even in the case where a word used skilfully alludes to a quality of the goods. It is also to be noted that section 35 allows for the disclaimer of a portion of the trademark. Furthermore, to be considered clearly descriptive, the words must go to the material composition of the goods or services or refer to an obvious intrinsic quality of the goods or services.[673] In case of a mark consisting of a geographic name, the F.C.A. draws a distinction between clearly descriptive and deceptively misdescriptive cases:

> [65] If the wares or services originate in the place referred to by the trade-mark, then the trade-mark is clearly descriptive of place of origin. There is no ambiguity when the trade-mark is the name of the place of origin that would invite further inquiry: referring to the place of origin by its name is the pinnacle of clarity. This is why the perspective of the ordinary consumer of the wares or services is unnecessary. As stated earlier, when filing an application for registration of a trade-mark referring to a geographical place, an applicant should not be allowed to benefit from the consumer's lack of knowledge in geography. [...]
>
> [66] On the other hand, if the trade-mark refers to a geographic place that is not the actual place of origin of the goods or services, then it cannot be clearly descriptive of place of origin. It is misdescriptive, and further analysis is required to determine whether it is deceptively so[;] the perspective of the ordinary consumer [...] is only meaningfully relevant when there is ambiguity whether the trade-mark actually refers to a place...[674]

669. *Standard Oil Co v. Canada (Registrar of TradeMarks) (Fior Case)*, [1968] 2 Ex.C.R. 523.
670. *Gerhard Horn Investments Ltd v. Canada (Registrar of TradeMarks)*, [1983] 2 F.C. 878 (F.C.T.D.).
671. *See* for instance the decision *Ron Matusalem & Matusa of Florida Inc. v. Havana Club Holding Inc., S.A.*, 2011 FCA 244, where the F.C.A confirmed that the mark 'The Spirit of Cuba' was deceptively misdescriptive when used in association with rum produced in the Dominican Republic.
672. *General Motors Corp. v. Bellows*, [1949] S.C.R. 678.
673. *Jordan & Ste-Michelle Cellars Ltd. v. T.G. Bright & Co., Limited*, [1984] 1 F.C. 964 (F.C.A.).
674. *MC Imports Inc. v. AFOD Ltd.*, 2016 FCA 60.

2. Special Signs (Including Distinguishing Guises)

258. Before the 2014 reform, specific provisions applied to distinguishing guises. It was registrable only if it has been so used in Canada as to have become distinctive.[675] In the 2014 reform scheme, a distinguishing guise is just one of the many signs[676] for which, at the request of the Registrar, an applicant must furnish evidence of distinctiveness at the filing date of an application for registration.[677] The same rule applies to sounds, scents, tastes, textures and any other prescribed signs.[678]

3. Marks Lacking Inherent Distinctiveness

259. Before 2014, marks that did not offend section 12 or 13 of the *Act* were registrable, even if they were not inherently distinctive. In the 2014 reform, it is stipulated that if the Registrar's preliminary view is that the trademark is not inherently distinctive, he may require evidence establishing that the trademark is distinctive at the filing date of the application.[679] The issue can also be raised in opposition proceedings.[680]

C. Other Expressions

260. Marks that are coined words[681] or original designs[682] will be considered inherently distinctive and registrable. Words that do not relate to something material in the composition of the product will also not face objection.[683]

---

675. Former subs. 13(1)(a).
676. It is now one type of signs included in the definition of s. 2 and which can constitute a trademark.
677. *See* 32 of the *Trademark Act*, as introduced by subs. 339 of the *Economic Action Plan 2014 Act, No. 1*, SC 2014, c. 20.
678. *See* 32 of the *Trademark Act*, as introduced by s. 339 of the *Economic Action Plan 2014 Act, No. 1*, SC 2014, c. 20.
679. *See* 32 of the *Trademark Act*, as introduced by s. 339 of the *Economic Action Plan 2014 Act, No. 1*, SC 2014, c. 20.
680. *See* subs. 38(2)(d).
681. *AstraZeneca AB v. Novopharm Ltd.*, 2003 FCA 57, 24 C.P.R. (4th) 326 (F.C.A.) at para. 16.
682. *Choice Hotels International Inc. v. Hotels Confortel Inc.* (1996), 67 C.P.R. (3d) 340 (F.C.T.D.) at para. 21, aff'd 12 C.P.R. (4th) 101 (F.C.A.).
683. In *Eastman Photographic Materials Company v. Comptroller General of Patents, Designs and TradeMarks*, (1898) A.C. 571, Lord Herschell said at 580:

[...] any word in the English language may serve as a trademark – the commonest word in the language might be employed. In these circumstances it would obviously have been out of the question to permit a person by registering a trademark in respect of a particular class of goods to obtain a monopoly of the use of a word having reference to the character or quality of these goods. The vocabulary of the English language is common property: it belongs alike to all; and no one ought to be permitted to prevent the other members of the community from using for purposes of description a word which has reference to the character or quality of goods. If, then, the use of every word in the language was to be permitted as a trademark, it was surely essential to prevent its use as a trademark where such use would deprive the rest of the community of the right which they possessed to employ that word for the purpose of describing the character or quality of goods.

Are also acceptable as subject matter for a trademark, letters[684] and numbers,[685] provided they are not referring to the quality or character of the products. They will be given a narrow ambit of protection, unless some design features grant them greater distinctiveness.[686]

II. The Basis of the Application

261. According to section 3, a trademark is deemed to have been adopted by a person 'when that person or his predecessor in title commenced to use it in Canada or to make it known in Canada or, if that person or his predecessor had not previously so used it or made it known, when that person or his predecessor filed an application for its registration in Canada'. Previously, the persons entitled to registration were determined accordingly. Section 16 provided four grounds on which one could claim the right to register: use of the mark in Canada, making the mark known in Canada, use and registration of the mark in another country, and the mark proposed use. Under the 2014 legislative reform, an applicant is not required to specify in the application the basis of the application or the date of first use of the trademark in Canada.[687]

A. Use in Canada

262. Subsection 30(1) of *Act* as amended by the *Economic Action Plan 2014 Act, No. 1*,[688] states that persons may file an application for the registration of a trademark if 'they are using or propose to use, and are entitled to use, the trademark in Canada'. To be registered, the mark must not be confusing with another trademark previously used or made known or a trademark in respect of which an application for registration had been previously filed or a trade name that had been previously used.[689]

263. Subsections 4(1) and (2) provide the definitions of use of a trademark in association with goods or services. A trademark is used in association with goods:

> if, at the time of the transfer of the property in or possession of the goods, in the normal course of trade, it is marked on the goods themselves or on the packages in which they are distributed or it is in any other manner so associated with the

684. In Lake *Ontario Cement Ltd. v. Canada (Registrar of TradeMarks)* (1976), 31 C.P.R. (2d) 103 at para. 7, (F.C.T.D.), the Federal Court stressed that: 'the Canadian TradeMarks Act contains no provision denying registration to letters and initials and numerous registrations have been made of trademarks consisting only of initials.' In *ITV Technologies Inc. v. WIC Television Ltd.*, 2003 FC 1056 at par 123 (aff'd 2005 FCA 96), the Federal Court added : ' … trade-marks formed purely of letters of the alphabet are generally considered weak marks entitled to a small ambit of protection.'
685. *Pizza Pizza Ltd. v. Canada (Registrar of Trade-marks)*, [1989] 3 C.F. 379 (F.C.A.).
686. *Cochrane-Dunlop Hardware Ltd. v. Capital Diversified Industries Ltd.* (1976), 30 C.P.R. (2d) 176 (Ont. C.A.), at para. 18.
687. *See* s. 16 and 30 of the Trademark Act as amended by s. 330 and 339 of the *Economic Action Plan 2014 Act, No. 1*, SC 2014, c. 20.
688. SC 2014, c. 20.
689. Section 16 of the *Act*.

goods that notice of the association is then given to the person to whom the property or possession is transferred.

The courts have drawn the conclusion that:

[section] 4 contemplates the normal course of trade as beginning with the manufacturer, ending with the consumer and with a wholesaler and retailer or one of them as intermediary. When the applicant sold to the retailer and the retailer sold to the public, the public came to associate [the] mark with the [product]; s. 4 contemplates that the use between the retailer and the public enures to the benefit of the manufacturer and its use in Canada. In other words – if any part of the chain takes place in Canada, this is 'use' in Canada within the meaning of s. 4.[690]

264. Three conditions must exist to establish use of the mark:

(1) *the mark must be a trademark as defined in section 2 [of the Trademarks Act], that is, used for the purpose of distinguishing goods;*
(2) *the mark must be associated with the goods so that notice of the association is given; and*
(3) *the transfer of the property or possession therein must occur in the normal course of trade.*[691]

265. Use in association with services is governed by subsection 4(2), which states:

A trade-mark is deemed to be used in association with services if it is used or displayed in the performance or advertising of those services.

So, contrary to the concept of use in association with goods, the display of a mark in the advertising of a service may constitute use in association with that service.[692] However, the service that is advertised must also be performed in Canada.[693]

690. *Manhattan Industries Inc. v. Princeton Manufacturing Ltd.* (1971), 4 C.P.R. (2d) 6 (F.C.T.D.), at para. 40.
691. *J.C. Penney Co. v. Gaberdine Clothing Co.* (2001), 2001 FCT 1333, 16 C.P.R. (4th) 151 (F.C.T.D.), at para. 72 quoting *White Consolidated Industries Inc. v. Beam of Canada Inc.* (1991), 39 C.P.R. (3d) 94 (F.C.T.D.), at 108–109.
692. *Eye Masters Ltd v. Ross King Holdings Ltd.*, [1992] 3 F.C. 625 (F.C.T.D.).
693. *Porter v. Don the Beachcomber*, [1966] Ex.C.R. 982; *Marineland Inc. v. Marine Wonderland and Animal Park Ltd.*, (1974) 16 C.P.R. (2d) 97 (F.C.T.D.); *Motel 6 Inc. v. No. 6 Motel Ltd et al.* (1981), [1982] 1 F.C. 638 (F.C.T.D.), at 651–652.

B. *Making Known in Canada*

266. Subsection 16(1), before the 2014 reform, allowed the registration of a mark on the basis that the applicant or its predecessor had made its mark known in Canada within the meaning of section 5 of the *Act.*[694] Section 5 sets forth the restrictive means by which a trademark may be made known and indicates that the mark, to qualify, must have already been used in a country of the Paris Union or a WTO member and have become well known in Canada.

267. If the mark is registered abroad, an applicant member of a Union country[695] can also claim a priority date, if the Canadian application concerns the same or substantially the same mark, for use in association with the same kind of goods, and the foreign application was filed in or for a county of the Union no more than six months before the Canadian filing date.[696]

C. *Use and Registration of the Mark in Another Country*

*268. Before the 2014 reform, a*n application could be filed on the basis of registration and use abroad.[697]

D. *Proposed Use*

269. Before the 2014 reform, an application for registration could be based on intended use of a trademark in Canada.[698] Section 30 still allows an application based on intended use but it is no longer required to state such intent as the *basis* of the application. Simply the application concerning a proposed trademark must include a statement that the applicant, by itself or through a licensee, intends to use the trademark in Canada.[699]

§4. Formalities (Procedure for Obtaining Protection, Establishing and Maintaining Trademarks)

270. The procedure for obtaining protection starts with the filing of an application which must comply with the formal requirements set out in section 30. Divisional

---

694. It seems that this basis for trademark registration was incorporated in the Canadian *Act* because it was believed that it was required by the *Paris Convention*, notably by Arts 6 and 6*bis* of the *Convention*. Doubts have been cast on this interpretation of the *Paris Convention*. *See* Alan Troicuk, *Legal and Technical Implications of Canadian Adherence to the Madrid Protocol*, (2002/1/25) available at http://strategis.gc.ca/sc_mrksv/cipo/tm/madrid_index-e.html, at 21 and 36.
695. Union country includes, according to s. 2, any country that is a member of the *Union for the Protection of Industrial Property* constituted under the *Paris Convention*, or any WTO Member.
696. Section 34.
697. *See* former subs. 16(2) of the *Act*.
698. *See* subs. 16(3) of the *Act*.
699. Subsection 30 (e).

applications are permitted in the 2014 reform;[700] the procedure will allow non-problematic portions of an application to proceed separately from the objectionable part.

271. The Registrar, (in reality an examiner of the Canadian Intellectual Property Office), then examines the application for compliance with the requirements of the *Trademarks Act* and *Regulations*. For example, by virtue of section 12, a mark may be refused because it consists only of a name or descriptive words without secondary meaning, or because it comes into conflict with any other registered trademark. If the mark is confusing with a mark that is the subject matter of a pending application on the day on which the applicant's application is advertised under subsection 37(1), the application will also be rejected.[701] The 2014 reform is granting additional powers to the Registrar, who may require any evidence establishing that the trademark is distinctive at the filing date of the application if:

- the applicant claims that the trademark is registrable under new subsection 12(3) of the *Trademarks Act*;
- the Registrar's preliminary view is that the trademark is not inherently distinctive;
- the trademark consists exclusively of a single colour or of a combination of colours without delineated contours;
- the trademark consists exclusively or primarily of one or more of the following: the three-dimensional shape of any of the goods specified in the application, or of an integral part or the packaging of any of those goods, a mode of packaging goods, a sound, a scent, a taste, a texture or any other prescribed sign.[702] The registration may then be restricted to the defined territorial area in Canada in which the trademark is shown to be distinctive.[703]

272. When the Registrar is satisfied that the application satisfies the legal requirements, he or she publishes the application in the Trademarks Journal.[704] Within two months after the advertisement of the application, any person may file a statement of opposition with the Registrar. Grounds for opposition are: (a) that the application does not conform to the requirements of section 30; (b) that the trademark is not registrable; (c) that the applicant is not the person entitled to registration of the trademark; or (d) that the trademark is not distinctive, (e) that the applicant is not using and does not propose to use the trademark in Canada, (f) that the applicant is not entitled to use the trademark in Canada.[705] After considering the evidence and representations filed by either or both parties, the Registrar decides whether to refuse

700. Section 39 of the Act as replaced by s. 344 of the *Economic Action Plan 2014 Act, No. 1*, SC 2014, c. 20.
701. Section 16 (2) as amended by subs. 330(1) of the *Economic Action Plan 2014 Act, No. 1*, SC 2014, c. 20.
702. Section 32 as replaced by s. 339 of the *Economic Action Plan 2014 Act, No. 1*, SC 2014, c. 20.
703. Subsection 32 (2) as replaced by s. 339 of the *Economic Action Plan 2014 Act, No. 1*, SC 2014, c. 20.
704. Subsection 37(1) *in fine*.
705. Subsection 38(2).

the application or reject the opposition.[706] If no opposition is filed, the application is allowed.[707] Upon payment of the prescribed fees, a certificate of registration is issued.[708] Section 19 establishes a presumption of validity of the registration.

§5. Ownership and Transfer (Assignment: Licences)

273. As seen in section 3-II, after the 2014 reform, the right to register can be based upon use or proposed use of the mark in Canada. The *Act* provides in sections 48 and 50 that registration (or the right to register) may be assigned and that a mark may be licensed. However, it is important that no deception or confusion of the public in the message conveyed by the trademark should occur as a result of those transactions and the parties' behaviour.

I. Assignment

274. The common law principle was that, since a trademark was indicative of origin, it could be assigned only along with the business or the goodwill of the assignor.[709] In 1953,[710] subsection 48(1) of the Canadian *Trademarks Act* was enacted in the following terms:

> 48. (1) A trade mark, whether registered or unregistered, is transferable, and deemed always to have been transferable, either in connection with or separately from the goodwill of the business and in respect of either all or some of the goods or services in association with which it has been used.

275. This right to transfer a mark was interpreted as being subject to the requirements of subsections 18(1)(b) and of the definition of 'distinctiveness' given in section 2. Consequently, after transfer, the transferee should not allow the trademark to be used in a deceiving or confusing way.[711] Failing to maintain the trademark distinctiveness, for instance by selling in Canada, after the assignment of the trademark, products manufactured by the assignor and still bearing the assigned mark, will result in the trademark invalidity.[712]

706. Subsection 38(3–12), as amended by subs 343(3) of the *Economic Action Plan 2014 Act, No. 1*, SC 2014, c 20.

707. Section 40.

708. Section 40.

709. *See Pinto v. Badman*, (1891) 8 R.P.C. 181, per Fry, L.J. at 194–195, as referred to in *Wilkinson Sword (Canada) Ltd. v. Juda (c.o.b. Continental Watch Import Co.)*, [1968] 2 Ex. C.R. 137, at n. 32.

710. *Trademarks Act*, SC 1952–1953, c. 49.

711. *Wilkinson Sword (Canada) Ltd. v. Juda (c.o.b. Continental Watch Import Co.)*, [1968] 2 Ex. C.R. 137, at 170–171; *Magder v. Breck's Sporting Goods Co.*, [1976] 1 S.C.R. 527, at para. 12.

712. *Wilkinson Sword (Canada) Ltd. v. Juda (c.o.b. Continental Watch Import Co.)* [1968] 2 Ex. C.R. 137, at 172.

II. Licensing

276. In common law, licensing of the trademark in gross vitiated the mark, because use by another trader lead to public deception.[713] In 1953, the *Trademarks Act* was modified to allow for trademark licensing. Licences could be granted but the owner had to register them; the licensee became a registered user and the *Act* deemed that use by a registered user had the same effect as use by the owner.[714] In 1993, the *Act* was changed again,[715] repealing the 'registered user' provisions and substituting a new section. The current section 50[716] also provides that the owner of a trademark may allow another person to use his or her trademark and such licensed use is deemed to be used by the owner. Two conditions are laid down: (1) there must be a licence agreement; and (2) there must be a certain control over the character and the quality of the goods. Under subsection 50(2), a public notice of use under a licence and of the identity of the owner leads to a presumption of the required control.

§6. Scope of Exclusive Rights

277. Sections 19, 20 and 22 determine the scope of protection of registered trademarks. Section 19 gives to the owner the exclusive right to the use of the trademark throughout Canada. Section 20 protects the trademark from likely confusion in the marketplace and section 22 from likely depreciation of the value of the goodwill. Thus

713. *Wilkinson Sword (Canada) Ltd. v. Juda (c.o.b. Continental Watch Import Co.)*, [1968] 2 Ex. C.R. 137, at 167–168.

714. Section 50 read as follows:
- (1)A person other than the owner of a registered trademark may be registered as a registered user thereof for all or any of the wares or services for which it is registered.
- The use of a registered trademark by a registered user thereof in accordance with the terms of his or her registration as such in association with wares or services manufactured, sold, leased, hired or performed by him or her, or the use of a proposed trademark as provided in subs. 40(2) by a person approved as a registered user thereof, is in this section referred to as the 'permitted use' of the trademark.
- The permitted use of a trademark has the same effect for all purposes of this Act as a use thereof by the registered owner.

715. *An Act to amend the Copyright Act, the Industrial Design Act, the Integrated Circuit Topography Act, the Patent Act, the Trademarks Act and other Acts in consequence thereof*, SC 1993, c. 15, s. 69.

716. Section. 50 now reads:
- (1)For the purpose of this Act, if an entity is licensed by or with the authority of the owner of a trademark to use the trademark in a country and the owner has, under the licence, direct or indirect control of the character or quality of the wares or services, then the use, advertisement, or display of the trademark in that country as or in a trademark, trade name or otherwise by that entity has, and is deemed always to have had, the same effect as such a use, advertisement or display of the trademark in that country by the owner.
- For the purposes of this Act, to the extent that public notice is given of the fact that use of a trademark is a licensed use and of the identify of the owner, it shall be presumed, unless the contrary is proven, that the use is licensed by the owner of the trademark and the character or quality of the wares or services is under the control of the owner.

a registered owner can sue for infringement under sections 19 and 20, and for depreciation of goodwill in respect to its trademark contrary to section 22 of the *Trademarks Act*. He or she can also claim that the defendant's use of the trademark constitutes passing off and violates its rights contrary to paragraph 7(b) of the *Act*. In Québec, he or she can argue that the defendant's conduct is an act of unfair competition.

I. Passing Off and Protection under Paragraph 7(B) of the Trademarks Act

278. To succeed in an action for passing off, the plaintiff must prove three components:

> existence of goodwill, deception of the public due to a misrepresentation and actual or potential damage to the plaintiff.[717]

279. Paragraph 7(b) of the *Act* prohibits a person from directing public attention to his or her wares, services or business in such a way as to cause or be likely to cause confusion, at the time he or she commenced the activity in question, with the goods, services or business of another. Paragraph 7(b) of the *Act* is said to be a codification of the common law tort of passing off.[718] It includes three requirements:

> [...] no person shall (1) direct public attention to his goods, services or business (2) in such a way as to cause or be likely to cause confusion in Canada (3) at the time he commenced so to direct attention to them, between his goods, services or business and the goods, services or business of another. What is deemed to cause confusion is explained in s. 6.[719]

II. Unfair Competition

280. In Québec, any act or practice contrary to honest practices that causes damages will constitute an act of unfair competition and will be sanctioned as part of the general tort law. Section 1457 of the *Civil Code of Québec*[720] will allow the aggrieved

717. *Ciba-Geigy Canada Ltd. v. Apotex Inc.*, [1992] 3 S.C.R. 120, at para. 33. The Supreme Court of Canada also refers at times to the wider formulation of the passing off doctrine formulated by Lord Diplock in *Erven Warnink B.V. v. J. Townend & Sons (Hull) Ltd.*, [1979] A.C. 731, at 742, where five elements were held necessary to create a valid cause of action: '(1) a misrepresentation; (2) made by a trader in the course of trade; (3) to his customers or to ultimate consumers of his product; (4) which may, in a reasonably foreseeable way, injure the business or goodwill of a competitor and (5) which causes actual damage'. *See Consumers Distributing Co. c. Seiko Time Canada*, [1984] 1 R.C.S. 583, at 608; *Ciba-Geigy Canada Ltd. c. Apotex Inc.*, [1992] 3 S.C.R. 120, at para. 31; *Kirkbi AG v. Ritvik Holdings Inc.*, [2005] 3 S.C.R. 302, at para. 65.

718. *Kirkbi AG v. Ritvik Holdings Inc.*, [2005] 3 S.C.R. 302, at para. 23.

719. *Asbjorn Horgard A/S v. Gibbs/Nortac Industries Ltd.*, [1987] 3 F.C. 544 (F.C.A.), at para. 40.

720. Online www3.publicationsduquebec.gouv.qc.ca/loisreglements/loisrefondues.en.html.

party to sue for damages or ask for an injunction. So causing confusion with respect to another's enterprise or its activities, in particular, with respect to the products or services offered by such enterprise, by using a confusing trademark, constitutes an act of unfair competition.[721]

281. The French doctrine of 'parasitism', that is benefiting from the goodwill attached to another creation or from the work of another, in order to make profit out of it, has been recently accepted by the Quebec Court of Appeal (QCCA).[722]

III. Exclusive Right to Use in Canada

282. Section 19 provides that, subject to sections 21, 32 and 67, the registration of a trademark, unless shown to be invalid, gives to the owner the exclusive right to the use of the mark throughout Canada. The provision applies only if the defendant is using an identical trademark[723] in respect of goods or services defined in the registration.

283. The F.C.A. has also determined that a licensee, even one who has been granted an exclusive licence, cannot invoke the *Trademarks Act* to stop the grey marketing of the goods, that is the parallel importation of goods manufactured and put on the market by the trademark owner or by an affiliate or subsidiary of the trademark owner.[724] The court explained:

> Smith & Nephew, as Canadian licensee and importer of goods bearing BDF's trade-marks, cannot complain of the sale in Canada of other goods which are also manufactured by or under license from BDF and bear the same trade-marks. There can be no deception as to the origin of the goods, which are exactly what they purport to be, Nivea facial cream and soap whose quality and character is controlled by BDF. If the respondent is distressed that the goods imported by appellants are different in quality or character from those which it imports and obtains from BDF, or that they are in the Canadian marketplace at lower prices in direct competition with it, its complaint must surely be with BDF itself. There is no evidence that the appellants have obtained the goods illegally and they have no obligation either in contract or under the provisions of the Trade-marks Act not to compete with the respondent in the Canadian market.[725]

Some commentators argue that, in case of importation of goods of an inferior or different quality, the *Trademarks Act* could provide a right of action.[726]

721. *Boulangerie Canada Bread ltée c. Boulangerie St-Méthode Inc.*, 2013 QCCA 1503.
722. *Groupe Pages jaunes cie c. 4143868 Canada Inc.*, 2011 QCCA 960; 9213-1705 Québec Inc. c. Geitzen, 2016 QCCA 71.
723. *Mr Submarine Ltd. v. Amandista Investments Ltd.* (1987), 19 C.P.R. (3d) 3 (F.C.A.).
724. *Smith & Nephew Inc. v. Glen Oak Inc.*, [1996] 3 F.C. 565 (F.C.A.).
725. *Ibid.*, at para. 14.
726. D. Gervais & E. Judge, *Intellectual Property: the Law in Canada* 535 (2d ed., Carswell 2011).

IV. Likely Confusion

284. Paragraph 20(1)a) provides that the right of the owner of a registered trademark to its exclusive use shall be deemed to be infringed by a person who sells, distributes or advertises goods or services in association with a confusing trademark or trade name. Although the provision does not expressly require a use within the meaning of section 4, it has sometimes been decided that infringement under section 20 is also dependent upon 'use' of the registered mark as defined in section 4.[727] In 2014, the *Combating Counterfeit Products Act*[728] added new causes of action against any person who :

(a) *manufactures, causes to be manufactured, possesses, imports, exports or attempts to export any goods in association with a confusing trademark or trade name, for the purpose of their sale or distribution;*
(b) *sells, offers for sale or distributes any label or packaging, in any form, bearing a trademark or trade name, if (i) the person knows or ought to know that the label or packaging is intended to be associated with goods or services that are not those of the owner of the registered trademark, and (ii) the sale, distribution or advertisement of the goods or services in association with the label or packaging would be a sale, distribution or advertisement in association with a confusing trademark or trade name; or*
(c) *manufactures, causes to be manufactured, possesses, imports, exports or attempts to export any label or packaging, in any form, bearing a trademark or trade name, for the purpose of its sale or distribution or for the purpose of the sale, distribution or advertisement of goods or services in association with it, if (i) the person knows or ought to know that the label or packaging is intended to be associated with goods or services that are not those of the owner of the registered trademark, and (ii) the sale, distribution or advertisement of the goods or services in association with the label or packaging would be a sale, distribution or advertisement in association with a confusing trademark or trade name.*[729]

285. Section 20 applies when trademarks are used in the market place in a confusing manner. The *Act* provides a definition of 'confusion' in subsection 6(2):

> the use of a trade-mark creates confusion with another trade-mark if the use of both trade-marks in the same area would be likely to lead the inference that the wares or services associated with those trade-marks are manufactured, sold, leased, hired or performed by the same person whether or not the wares or services are of the same general class.

---

727. *Pro-C Ltd. v. Computer City Inc.* (2001), 55 O.R. (3d) 577, 14 C.P.R. (4th) 441 (Ont. C.A.); *Red Label Vacations Inc. (Redtag.ca) v. 411 Travel Buys Limited (411 Travel Buys Limited)*, 2015 FCA 290.
728. SC 2014, c 32, s. 22.
729. Par 20(1) b) c) and d).

The 2014 amendments change the provision by referring to 'goods or services' and indicate that the confusion may exist 'whether or not the goods or services are of the same general class or appear in the same class of the Nice Classification'.[730]

The Supreme Court of Canada has specified that the test:

> to be applied is a matter of first impression in the mind of a casual consumer somewhat in a hurry who sees the [word] on the respondent's storefront or invoice, at a time when he or she has no more than an imperfect recollection of the [mark], and does not pause to give the matter any detailed consideration or scrutiny, nor to examine closely the similarities and differences between the marks.[731]

Furthermore, one must not discount the likelihood of confusion by considering what actions the consumer might take after encountering a mark in the marketplace. As the Court explained:

> [72]... It is confusion when they encounter the trade-marks that is relevant. Careful research which may later remedy confusion does not mean that no confusion ever existed or that it will not continue to exist in the minds of consumers who did not carry out that research.
>
> [73] Indeed, before source confusion is remedied, it may lead a consumer to seek out, consider or purchase the wares or services from a source they previously had no awareness of or interest in. Such diversion diminishes the value of the goodwill associated with the trade-mark and business the consumer initially thought he or she was encountering in seeing the trade-mark. Leading consumers astray in this way is one of the evils that trade-mark law seeks to remedy.[732]

The test is 'based upon the hypothetical assumption that both trade names and trademarks are used 'in the same area', irrespective of whether this is actually the case'.[733] So the location where the marks were actually used does not matter.

286. Subsection 6(5) enumerates a non-exhaustive list of circumstances to consider while determining whether the trademarks are confusing:

(a) *the inherent distinctiveness of the trademarks or trade names and the extent to which they have become known;*
(b) *the length of time the trademarks or trade names have been in use;*
(c) *the nature of the wares, services or business;*
(d) *the nature of the trade; and*

---

730. Subsection 321(1) of the of the *Economic Action Plan 2014 Act, No. 1*, SC 2014, c. 20.
731. *Veuve Clicquot Ponsardin v. Boutiques Cliquot Ltée*, [2006] 1 S.C.R. 824, at para. 20.
732. *Masterpiece Inc. v. Alavida Lifestyles Inc.*, 2011 SCC 27, [2011] 2 S.C.R. 387, at paras 72–73.
733. *Masterpiece Inc. v. Alavida Lifestyles Inc.*, 2011 SCC 27, [2011] 2 S.C.R. 387, at para. 30.

(e) *the degree of resemblance between the trademarks or trade names in appearance or sound or in the ideas suggested by them.*

The confusion must be assessed given all the potential uses that the registered owner may adopt within the scope of the registration, and should not be restricted to his or her actual use at the time of the proceedings.[734]

287. In 2006, the factors enumerated in subsection 6(5) were closely examined by the Supreme Court of Canada in two cases involving famous marks: the VEUVE CLICQUOT trademark[735] and the BARBIE trademark.[736] The court underlined that, as specified in section 6(2), confusion may occur 'whether or not the goods or services are of the same general class'. Thus section 20 does not require a 'resemblance' a 'connection' or a 'similarity' between the respective goods and services. However, if a difference in goods or services does not necessarily negate confusion, the use of a famous trademark does automatically mean likelihood of confusion when the mark is used on products different than those defined in the registration. The court concluded that each situation must be judged in its full factual context and approved in the lower courts decisions that there was no likelihood of confusion.

V. Likelihood of Depreciation of the Value of Goodwill

288. Subsection 22(1) provides that no person shall use a trademark registered by another person in a manner that is likely to have the effect of depreciating the value of the goodwill attaching thereto. In 2006, the Supreme Court of Canada enumerated the four necessary elements in the section 22 depreciation claim:

> [...]Firstly, that a claimant's registered trade-mark was used by the defendant in connection with wares or services – whether or not such wares and services are competitive with those of the claimant. Secondly, that the claimant's registered trade-mark is sufficiently well known to have significant goodwill attached to it. Section 22 does not require the mark to be well known or famous (in contrast to the analogous European and U.S. laws), but a defendant cannot depreciate the value of the goodwill that does not exist. Thirdly, the claimant's mark was used in a manner likely to have an effect on that goodwill (i.e. linkage) and fourthly that the likely effect would be to depreciate the value of its goodwill (i.e. damage).[737]

289. The court refused to interpret section 22 as requiring that the defendant had used a mark identical to the one registered.[738] Preferring a purposive interpretation

734. *Masterpiece Inc. v. Alavida Lifestyles Inc.*, 2011 SCC 27, [2011] 2 S.C.R. 387, at paras 56–59.
735. *Veuve Clicquot Ponsardin v. Boutiques Cliquot Ltée*, [2006] 1 S.C.R. 824.
736. *Mattel, Inc. v. 3894207 Canada Inc.*, [2006] 1 S.C.R. 772.
737. *Veuve Clicquot Ponsardin v. Boutiques Cliquot Ltée*, [2006] 1 S.C.R. 824, at para. 46.
738. *Veuve Clicquot Ponsardin v. Boutiques Cliquot Ltée*, [2006] 1 S.C.R. 824, at para. 48.

of section 22, it said that if the casual observer would recognize the mark used by the respondents as the mark of the appellant, it would suffice.[739]

290. As goodwill is not defined in the *Act*, the Supreme Court, in the VEUVE CLICQUOT case,[740] referred to judicial definitions:

> In ordinary commercial use, it connotes the positive association that attracts customers towards its owner's wares or services rather than those of its competitors. In Manitoba Fisheries Ltd. v. The Queen, [1979] 1 S.C.R. 101, at p. 108, this Court adopted the following definition of 'goodwill'
>
> 'Goodwill' is a word sometimes used to indicate a ready formed connection of customers whose custom is of value because it is likely to continue. But in its commercial sense the word may connote much more than this. It is, as Lord Macnaghten observed in Inland Revenue Commissioners v. Muller & Co.'s Margarine Ltd., [1901] A.C. (Law Reports, Appeal Cases (U.K.)) 217, 224, 'the attractive force which brings in custom,' and it may reside, not only in trade connections, but in many other quarters, such as particular premises, long experience in some specialised sphere, or the good repute associated with a name or mark. It is something generated by effort that adds to the value of the business. [...]
>
> In Clairol International Corp. v. Thomas Supply & Equipment Co., [1968] 2 Ex. C.R. 552, Thurlow J. adopted the following definition of goodwill attaching to a trade-mark at p. 573:
>
> [T]he goodwill attaching to a trade mark is I think that portion of the goodwill of the business of its owner which consists of the whole advantage, whatever it may be, of the reputation and connection, which may have been built up by years of honest work or gained by lavish expenditure of money and which is identified with the goods distributed by the owner in association with the trade mark.[741]

As the Court failed to find evidence that consumers who saw the word 'Cliquot' used in the defendants' stores would make any link or connection to the plaintiff's mark, it concluded that without such a link, connection or mental association between the respondents' display and the VEUVE CLICQUOT mark, there could be no depreciation. The section 22 claim was rejected.

---

739. *Ibid.*

740. *Veuve Clicquot Ponsardin v. Boutiques Cliquot Ltée*, [2006] 1 S.C.R. 824.

741. *Ibid.*, paras 50–52.

§7. Limitations of the Scope of Trademark Protection

291. The *Act* itself provides for limitation of the scope of trademark protection. Section 20 indicates that no registration of a trademark prevents a person from making (a) any bona fide use of his or her personal name as a trade name; or (b) any bona fide use, other than as a trademark: (i) of the geographical name of his or her place of business; or (ii) of any accurate description of the character or quality of his or her goods or services, in such a manner as is not likely to have the effect of depreciating the value of the goodwill attaching to the trademark.[742] Furthermore, no registration of a trademark prevents a person from making use of generic names for the wines or spirits listed in subsections 11.18(3) and 11.18(4).[743] The new subsection 20 (1.1) specifies that the registration of a trademark does not prevent a person from using any utilitarian feature embodied in the trademark.

§8. Use Requirements

292. An applicant is entitled to secure registration of a trademark even if it has not used the trademark in Canada.[744] Subsection 30(1) of *Act* as amended by of the *Economic Action Plan 2014 Act, No. 1*,[745] expressly states that persons may file application for the registration of a trademark if 'they are using or propose to use, and are entitled to use, the trademark in Canada'.

§9. Duration of Protection: Renewal – Termination

293. Registration lasts for a period of fifteen years from the day of the registration and is subject to renewals.[746] After the coming into force of the *Economic Action Plan 2014 Act, No. 1*, the registration will last for ten years.[747] Section 19 establishes a presumption of validity of the registration. Errors in the register may be corrected by the Registrar[748]

294. There are several ways to attack a registration. Section 45 of the Act provides a summary procedure for clearing the Register of trademark registrations that are obsolete or outdated. As summarized by the F.C.A.,

> [55] The purpose of section 45 proceedings is to remove registrations which have fallen into disuse. The burden of proof on the registered owner is not a heavy one. In Locke v. Osler, Hoskin & Harcourt LLP, 2011 FC 1390 (CanLII),

742. For a recent application, *see Osmose-Pentox Inc. v. Société Laurentides Inc.*, 2014 FCA 146.
743. Subsection 20(2).
744. *See* paras 273–280 of this monograph.
745. SC 2014, c. 20.
746. Section 46.
747. *See* s. 350 and 359 of the *Economic Action Plan 2014 Act, No. 1*, SC 2014, c. 20.
748. Subsection 41(3) as introduced by s. 346 of the *Economic Action Plan 2014 Act, No. 1*, SC 2014, c. 20.

> 98 C.P.R. (4th) 357, O'Keefe J. stated at paragraph 23 that "[t]he threshold to establish use is relatively low and it is sufficient if the applicant establishes a prima facie case of use". It has also been said that the purpose of section 45 of the Act is to remove deadwood from the Register (see Eclipse International Fashions Canada Inc. v. Shapiro Cohen, 2005 CAF 64 (CanLII), 2005 FCA 64, 348 N.R. 86, at paragraph 6). In Dart Industries Inc. v. Baker & Mckenzie LLP, 2013 FC 97 (CanLII), 426 F.T.R. 98, at paragraph 13, O'Keefe J. commented that "[p]roceedings under section 45 of the Act are summary and administrative in nature".[749]

The procedure can be set in motion by the Registrar at any time[750] and by any person who presents a written request to the Registrar after three years from the date of the registration.[751]

295. The Registrar gives notice requiring the registered owner to furnish within three months an affidavit or a statutory declaration showing, with respect to each of the goods or services specified in the registration, use of the trademark in Canada during the three-year period immediately preceding the date of the notice.[752] The declaration or affidavit must provide some evidence of use.

296. If the trademark had not been used during the three-year period immediately preceding the date of notice, the registered owner may invoke that there were special circumstances excusing the non-use.[753] To evaluate those special circumstances, the courts will take into account 'the length of non-use, whether the non-use was due to circumstances beyond the registered owner's control and whether there was an intention to resume use of the mark in the near term'.[754]

297. Registration can also be attacked under subsection 18(1) of the *Act*. The onus of proof is then on the person seeking expungement to establish the invalidity of the registration, since a registered trademark is presumed to be valid.[755] The grounds for expungement are set out in subsection 18(1) and section 18.1, as introduced by the *Economic Action Plan 2014 Act, No. 1*:[756] (a) the registration is likely to unreasonably limit the development of any art or industry, (b) the trademark was not registrable at the date of registration, (c) the trademark is not distinctive at the time proceedings

---

749. Sport Maska Inc. v. Bauer Hockey Corp., 2016 FCA 44, at para. 55.
750. The 2014 reform will require a three-years period of non-use before the Registrar can initate the procedure: *see* section 349 of the *Economic Action Plan 2014 Act, No. 1*, SC 2014, c. 20.
751. Section 45.
752. *Ibid.*
753. Such would be the case if the marketing was delayed to satisfy legal requirements or to adapt the product to local quality and promotional standards: *Spirits International N.V. v. Canada (Registrar of TradeMarks)*, 2006 FC 520, 49 C.P.R. (4th) 196 (F.C.T.D.). But *see Canada (Registrar of TradeMarks) v. Harris Knitting Mills Ltd.* (1985), 4 C.P.R. (3d) 488 (F.C.A.), where changes in market demand for sweaters and knitted suits were held not to be special circumstances excusing absence of use.
754. *Scott Paper Ltd. v. Smart & Biggar*, 2008 FCA 129, at para. 9; *see also Canada (Registrar of TradeMarks) c. Harris Knitting Mills Ltd.*, (1985), 4 C.P.R. (3d) 488 (F.C.A.).
755. *General Motors of Canada v. Décarie Motors Inc. / Les Moteurs Décarie Inc.*, [2001] 1 F.C. 665 (F.C.A.) at para. 31.
756. SC 2014, c. 20.

bringing the validity of the registration into question are commenced, or (d) the trademark has been abandoned, and (e) subject to section 17, the applicant for registration was not the person entitled to secure the registration.

298. This last ground of invalidity can only be invoked by someone who had adopted the mark before the registered owner did. According to subsection 17(2), the proceedings for expungement must be initiated within a five-year period of the registration against an owner who registered the mark in good faith. Only a registration obtained by a person who had knowledge of the previous use or making known may be attacked at any time. When the five-year period has lapsed and the registration is protected by subsection 17(2), the first user may ask for a concurrent right to use the mark under section 21 of the *Act*: if the court considers that it is not contrary to the public interest, it may allow the continued use of the confusing trademark in a defined territorial area and with some distinction from the registered trademark.

§10. Infringement and Remedies

299. Both the Federal Court and the superior courts (C.S.) of provinces have jurisdiction to hear and determine actions for the infringement of trademarks. They may make any order considered appropriate in the circumstances, including injunctions, (as well as interlocutory injunctions), awards of damages, account of profit, order for the destruction, exportation or other disposition of any offending goods, packages, labels and advertising material or related dies.[757] Under sections 53 and 53.1 of the *Trademarks Act*, if the court finds that the importation or distribution of goods is or would be contrary to the *Act*, it may authorize the seizure of the goods[758] and may make an order prohibiting future importation.[759]

300. There are also some criminal remedies. According to section 407 of the *Criminal Code*,[760] a person who, with the intent to deceive or defraud the public or any person, whether ascertained or not, forges a trademark, commits an offence. It is also a criminal offence to remove marks without authority.[761] Other offences in relation to trademarks are sanctioned in the *Criminal Code*.[762]

757. Section 53.2.
758. The Court makes the order considered appropriate under the circumstances, including the goods be destroyed, exported or delivered to the applicant.
759. Then under s. 136 of the *Customs Tariff*, L.C. 1997, c. 36, the articles bearing the trademark become prohibited goods classified under tariff item No. 9897.00.00 of the List set out in the schedule to the *Customs Tariff*. The *Tariff* is administered by the Canada Border Services Agency (CBSA) and is available at the CBSA website www.cbsa.gc.ca/trade-commerce/tariff-tarif/menu-eng.html. It should be noted that the court may not, other than in exceptional circumstances, order that the goods bearing the infringing trademark should be exported with the infringing trademark intact: *see* . s. 53.3.
760. RSC 1985, c. C-46.
761. Section 417 of the *Criminal Code*, RSC 1985, c. C-46.
762. *See* ss 408–417 of the *Criminal Code*, RSC 1985, c. C-46.

§11. Overlapping and Relation to Other Intellectual Property Laws

301. As mentioned earlier, in principle, there is no reason why several intellectual property rights may not attach to the same article. As long as the respective conditions of protection are met, the intellectual property rights must be enforced by the courts. Even the *Copyright Act* restores the full copyright protection to a design used for the manufacture of multiple copies of a useful article, when the work is a trademark or a label.[763]

302. However, the courts will try to identify what is the proper subject matter of each right and restrict the protection accordingly. Thus a patentee may not use trademarks protection to perpetuate a patent monopoly.[764] For instance, a toy maker may not claim trademarks rights (passing off or rights attached to a registered trademark) on the shape of its invention when that shape is an element essential of the invention.[765] As the Supreme Court of Canada said, if 'what is sought to be registered as a trade mark has a functional use or [a] characteristic, it cannot be the subject of a trade mark'.[766]

303. Likewise, if a design is solely ornamental, was not selected or used at any time as a distinguishing feature, nor has it acquired a secondary meaning in the market, then it may not be registered as a trademark.[767] As the court warned, one cannot 'convert what is merely ornamental design into a trade mark'.[768] But the restriction applies only if the design is merely or solely ornamental.[769]

763. Subsection 64(3) of the *Copyright Act*, RSC 1985, c. C-42.
764. *Kirkbi AG v. Ritvik Holdings Inc.*, [2005] 3 S.C.R. 302, at paras 52–53.
765. Courts will have recourse to the doctrine of functionality: *Ibid.*
766. *Parke, Davis & Co. v. Empire Laboratories Ltd.*, [1964] S.C.R. 351, at 354.
767. *W.J. Hughes & Sons 'Corn Flower' Ltd v. Morawiec*, (1970) 62 C.P.R. 21 (Ex. Ct.); *Adidas (Canada) Ltd v. Colins Inc.*, (1979) 38 C.P.R. (2d) 145 (F.C.T.D.); but *see Tommy Hilfiger Licensing, Inc. c. International Clothiers Inc.*, [2005] 1 F.C.R. 148 (F.C.A.), where, given the evidence, it was accepted that a crest design was recognized by the public as a trademark.
768. *Adidas (Canada) Ltd v. Colins Inc.*, (1979) 38 C.P.R. (2d) 145 (F.C.T.D.), at 169.
769. *Canada's Royal Gold Pinetree Manufacturing Co. v. Samann*, (1986) 9 C.P.R. (3d) 223 (F.C.A.), at 231.

Chapter 5. Trade Names

§1. Sources: Legislation

304. In Canada, the rules governing trade names, their availability and legal protection, are either part of the general principles of the common law (in the common law provinces) and of the civil law (in Québec), or to be found in the statutes dealing with corporate and cooperative law, or in more specific statutes governing business names.

305. Indeed all Canadian jurisdictions, federal and provincial, regulate the registration of corporate and cooperative names. In each case, the rules are scattered in several statutes.

306. At the federal level, the statutory provisions are to be found in:

- the *Canada Business Corporations Act*[770] and associated regulations[771] (for the corporate names of federally incorporated businesses);
- the *Canada Not-for-Profit Corporations Act*[772] and associated regulations,[773] (for the names of federal non-profit corporations); and
- the *Canada Cooperatives Act*[774] and associated regulations[775] (for the federal non-financial cooperatives).

307. Similar legislation and regulation have been enacted by the provincial legislatures.

308. In Prince Edward Island, the main legal provisions are to be found in:

- the *Companies Act*;[776]
- the *Limited Partnerships Act*;[777] and
- the *Partnership Act*.[778]

309. In British Columbia, they are:

- the *Business Corporations Act*;[779]

770. RSC 1985, c. C-44, ss 6, 10–13.
771. *Canada Business Corporations Regulations*, 2001, SOR/2001-512, ss 17–32.
772. SC 2009, c 23, ss 7, 11-14.
773. *Canada Not-for-profit Corporations Regulations, SOR/2011-223, ss 42–58.*
774. SC 1998, c. 1, ss 11, 20–25.
775. *Canada Cooperatives Regulations*, SOR/99-256, ss 8–23.
776. R.S.P.E.I. 1988, c. C-14, ss 6, 12, and 16.
777. R.S.P.E.I. 1988, c. L-13, ss 3, 5, 18.
778. R.S.P.E.I. 1988, c. P-1, ss 6, 50–54.
779. S.B.C. 2002, c. 57, ss 21–29, 51.21; 382 and 383. *Business Corporations Regulation*, B.C. Reg. 65/2004, ss 7–10.

- the *Partnership Act*;[780] and
- the *Cooperative Association Act*.[781]

310. In Alberta, they are:

- the *Business Corporations Act*;[782]
- the *Cooperatives Act*;[783] and
- the *Partnership Act*.[784]

311. In Saskatchewan, they are:

- the *Business Corporations Act*;[785]
- the *Cooperatives Act, 1996*;[786]
- the *Business Names Registration Act*;[787] and
- the *Partnership Act*.[788]

312. In Manitoba, they are:

- the *Business Names Registration Act*;[789]
- the *Corporations Act*;[790]
- the *Cooperatives Act*;[791] and
- the *Partnership Act*.[792]

313. In Ontario, they are:

780. R.S.B.C. 1996, c. 348, ss 51, 53, 70, 89, 100.
781. R.S.B.C. 1999, c. 28, ss 22–26, 68–69.
782. R.S.A. 2000, c. B-9, ss 10–14, 15.4 and; *Business Corporations Regulation*, Alta. Reg. 118/2000, ss 2, 4–18.
783. R.S.A. 2001, c. C-28.1, ss 5, 16–21, 387, 413 and 423; *Cooperatives Regulation*, Alta. Reg. 55/2002, ss 2–16.
784. R.S.A. 2000, c. P-3, ss 52, 54, 70, 81, 82, 91, 109, 110; *Partnership Regulation*, Alta. Reg. 105/2009, s. 5, 13, 14, 20, 24, 32.
785. R.S.S. 1978, c. B-10, ss 6, 10–13, 167, 282, 292–298, 299; *Business Corporations Regulations*, R.R.S. c. B-10 Reg. 1, ss 8–10.9.
786. S.S. 1996, c. C-37.3, ss 7, 12–19, 144, 198, 213, 230, 245 and 260; *Co-operatives Regulations, 1998*, RRS c C-37.3 Reg 1, ss 3–3.52; *Business Names Registration (Designated Extraprovincial Limited Partnerships) Regulations*, RRS c B-11 Reg 2.
787. R.S.S. 1978, c. B-11; *Business Names Registration Regulations*, R.R.S. c. B-11 Reg. 1.
788. R.S.S. 1978, c. P-3, ss 6, 53, 86, 95 and 98; *Partnership Regulations*, RRS c P-3 Reg 3, ss 4,5, 10 and 11.
789. C.C.S.M. c. B110; *Business Names Registration Regulation*, Man. Reg. 381/87 R.
790. C.C.S.M. c. C225, ss 6, 10–13, 167, 174.1 and 191; *Corporations Regulation*, Man. Reg. 385/87 R, ss 2.2 and 6.
791. C.C.S.M. c. C223, ss 9, 17–21, 276, 297 and 378; *Cooperatives Regulation*, Man. Reg. 95/99, ss 2–4.
792. C.C.S.M. c. P30, ss 6, 58 and 74.

- the *Business Names Act*;[793]
- the *Business Corporations Act*;[794]
- the *Co-operative Corporations Act*;[795]
- the *Partnerships Act*;[796] and
- the *Limited Partnerships Act*.[797]

314. In Québec, they are:

- the *An Act Respecting the Legal Publicity of Enterprises;*[798]
- the *Charter of the French Language*;[799]
- the *Business Corporations Act;*[800]
- the *Companies Act* (for the names of Quebec non-profit corporations)*;*[801] and
- the *Cooperatives Act.*[802]

315. In New Brunswick, the main legal provisions are:

- the *Business Corporations Act*;[803]
- the *Co-operative Associations Act*;[804]
- the *Partnerships and Business Names Registration Act*;[805] and
- the *Limited Partnership Act*.[806]

316. In Nova Scotia, they are:

793. R.S.O. 1990, c. B.17; *General*, O. Reg. 121/91; *Restrictions Respecting Names*, O. Reg. 122/91; *Refund of Fee for Electronic Application for New Registration*, O Reg 18/07.
794. R.S.O. 1990, c. B.16, ss 3.2, 8–12, 168 and 171; *General*, R.R.O. 1990, Reg. 62, ss 1–22.1.
795. R.S.O. 1990, c. C.35, ss 5, 7–12, 151 and 153; *General*, RRO 1990, Reg 178, ss 4–10.
796. R.S.O. 1990, c. P.5, ss 5, 44.3–44.4.
797. R.S.O. 1990, c. L.16, ss 6 and 19; *General*, RRO 1990, Reg 713.
798. CQLR, c P-44.1; *Regulation respecting the Application of the Act respecting the Legal Publicity of enterprises, CQLR c P-44.1, r 1.*
799. CQLR c C-11, ss 63–68, 71; *Regulation respecting the language of commerce and business*, CQLR c C-11, r 9, s. 27.
800. CQLR, c S-31.1, ss 5, 8, 16–28, 243; *Regulation respecting names of companies governed by Part I of the Companies Act*, CQLR c S-31.1, r 1.01; *Regulation respecting names of companies governed by Part IA of the Companies Act*, CQLR c S-31.1, r 1.02.
801. CQLR c C-38, ss 9.1–10, 18.1–21, 34.1, 219 and 221.1; *Regulation respecting the names of Legal Persons or associations governed by Part III of the Companies Act*, CQLR c C-38, r 2.
802. CQLR c C-67.2, ss 15–20, 221.6.1–221.8, 226.2 and 231; *Regulation under the Co-operatives Act*, CQLR c C-67.2, r 1, ss 1–3.
803. S.N.B. 1981, c. B-9.1, ss 4, 8–11, 113 and 171; *General Regulation*, N.B. Reg. 81-147, ss 10–11.
804. S.N.B. 1978, c. C-22.1, ss 6, 10–12 and 17.
805. R.S.N.B. 1973, c. P-5; *Partnerships and Business Names Registration Regulationt*, N.B. Reg. 81-35.
806. S.N.B. 1984, c. L-9.1, ss 3–4, 6–10 and 23; *General Regulation – Limited Partnership Act*, N.B. Reg. 84-196, s. 3.

- the *Companies Act*;[807]
- the *Co-operative Associations Act*;[808]
- the *Partnerships and Business Names Registration Act;*[809]
- the *Partnership Act*;[810] and
- the *Limited Partnerships Act.*[811]

317. In Newfoundland and Labrador, they are:

- the *Corporations Act*;[812]
- the *Co-operatives Act*;[813]
- the *Partnership Act;*[814] and
- the *Limited Partnerships Act.*[815]

318. In Yukon, they are:

- the *Business Corporations Act*;[816]
- the *Societies Act;*[817]
- the *Partnership and Business Names Act*;[818]
- the *Cooperative Associations Act.*[819]

319. In Northwest Territories, they are:

- the *Business Corporations Act*;[820]
- the *Partnership Act;*[821] and
- the *Co-operative Associations Act.*[822]

320. In Nunavut:

807. R.S.N.S. 1989, c. 81, ss 10–12, 15–18 and 80–82.
808. R.S.N.S. 1989, c. 98, ss 7–8, 11, 13 and 19.
809. R.S.N.S. 1989, c. 335; *Partnerships and Business Names Registration Act Regulations*, NS Reg 52/92.
810. R.S.N.S. 1989, c 334, ss 7 and 56.
811. R.S.N.S. 1989, c 259, ss 5 and 7; *Firm Names Regulations*, NS Reg 1/86.
812. R.S.N.L. 1990, c. C-36, ss 12, 17–25, 279, 377, 403–405, 423, 438, 451, 469 and 500–501; *Corporations Regulations*, C.N.L.R. 750/96, ss 4–13.
813. S.N.L. 1998, c. C-35.1, ss 7–8, 12 and 99; *Cooperative Societies Regulations*, CNLR 956/96, ss 14–15.
814. R.S.N.L. 1990, c. P-3, ss 5, 55, 60, 65, 71 and 78.
815. R.S.N.L. 1990, c. L-17, ss 4, 6 and 22.
816. R.S.Y. 2002, c. 20, ss 8, 9, 12–16, 175, 179, 248 and 279; *Naming Regulation,* YOIC 2015/07.
817. RSY 2002, c 206, ss 10–10.3, 24, 25, 29–30; *Naming Regulation*, YOIC 2015/07.
818. R.S.Y. 2002, c. 166; *Partnership and Business Names Regulation*, YOIC 2015/11.
819. R.S.Y. 2002, c. 43, ss 3, 7 and 8; *Naming Regulation*, YOIC 2015/07.
820. S.N.W.T. 1996, C. 19, ss 6, 10–13, 176, 179, 248 and 283–286; *Business Corporations Regulations*, NWT Reg 018-98, ss 11–30.
821. R.S.N.W.T. 1988, c. P-1, ss 47–50.3, 58, 60, 76, 102.9–102.10 and 102.18.
822. R.S.N.W.T. 1988, c. C-19, ss 3 and 6.

- the *Business Corporations Act;*[823]
- the *Partnership Act;*[824]
- Co-operative Associations Act.[825]

321. In all provinces and territories, registration is mandatory. The federal and provincial provisions will specify conditions for the eligibility of a corporate name. The regimes vary from one another and they are in general quite detailed.[826] The legislation and accompanying regulations will normally prohibit the use of certain terms or expressions which connote governmental association or professional connections, or of words solely descriptive of the business or of the goods and services of the corporation. They will also typically require that the name includes at the end a legal element such as Limited, Incorporated or Corporation, or contractions of these, such as Ltd., Inc. or Corp. Usually the name of a company must be in an English form, or in a French form, or in both of these forms. In Quebec, all enterprises doing business in the province, even foreign corporations, must register and use a French version of their business name, which must comply with the *Charter of the French Language.*[827]

§2. Protection of Trade Names

322. In Canada, trade names are protected, by the provincial common law (either by the provisions of the *Civil Code of Québec* in Québec,[828] or the rules of the common law relating to passing off in the other provinces and territories), as well as by section 7(b) of the *Trademarks Act.*[829] There are also *Criminal Code* provisions relating to passing off and forgery of trade names.[830]

323. Corporate laws and cooperatives law will also provide some protection. They preclude organizations from adopting as their names words that are confusing

823. SNWT (Nu) 1996, c 19, ss 6, 10–13, 176, 179 and 248; *Business Corporations Regulations*, NWT Reg (Nu) 018-98, ss 11–30.
824. R.S.N.W.T. (Nu) 1988, c. P-1, ss 47–50.2, 58.
825. RSNWT (Nu) 1988, c C-19, ss 3 and 6.
826. *See* for instance the federal regulation with a long set of conditions: *Canada Business Corporations Regulations*, 2001, SOR/2001-512, ss 17–32.
827. Section 63 of the *Charter of the French Language (CQLR c C-11)* prescribes that the name of an enterprise must be in French and s. 64 states that, to obtain juridical personality, it is necessary to have a name in French. However s. 67 provides that family names, place names, expressions formed by the artificial combination of letters, syllables or figures, and expressions taken from other languages may appear in the distinctive element of business names. Section 68 allows for the name of an enterprise to be accompanied with a version in a language other than French provided that, when used, the French version of the name appears at least as prominently as the other version.
828. Section 1457 of the *Civil Code of Québec*. *See* for example *Kisber & Co. Ltd. c. Ray Kisber & Associates Inc.*, [1998] R.J.Q. 1342, J.E. 98-1001 (Qué. C.A.).
829. RSC 1985, c. T-13.
830. *See* e.g., ss 408–412 of the *Criminal Code*, RSC 1985, c. C-46.

with an existing trade name or trademark.[831] So for a provincial or federal incorporation, a corporate name search report is required. Similarly, the *Trademarks Act*[832] specifies that a person is not entitled to secure the registration of a trademark confusing with a trade name already in use.[833] If a confusing trade name has been granted, the officer in charge of the registry will normally have the power to order a name change. The decision is, in most jurisdictions, subject to a judicial control.

324. To determine if trade names are confusing, the statutes adopt different tests. Some will consider signs confusing if the use of the name 'is likely to lead to the inference that the business carried on or intended to be carried on under the corporate name and the business connected [with the existing mark or name] are one business'.[834] Others will prohibit a name 'if the use of that name would be likely to deceive'.[835] Some will specify that 'a name must not resemble the name of a company, [...] to such an extent that, in the opinion of the registrar, the name is likely to confuse or mislead'.[836] In Québec, on the other hand, the legislator enacted a prohibition to adopt a name which falsely suggests that the registrant is related to another entity, or is confusingly similar to a name used in Québec by another entity, or is misleading in any other manner[837] and it adopted a two-step evaluation of the confusion likely to occur.[838] Each case of confusion or deception is decided using the specific applicable test and upon a close examination of the facts involved.

831. Sometimes, this issue of confusion is subject to a priori determination by the public officer in charge (before the issuance of the certificate of incorporation) – *see* the federal regime, Innovation, Science and Economic Development Canada- Corporations Canada, *Name Granting Compendium*, (2016) p 7 available at https://www.ic.gc.ca/eic/site/cd-dgc.nsf/eng/cs07270.html, and sometimes, this ground of ineligibility will only be examined by the public officer in charge after a change of name has been requested by an interested party – *see* Le Registraire Des Entreprises, *Les noms d'entreprises au Québec*, (2017) p 19, available at http://www.registreentreprises.gouv.qc.ca/fr/sepf/formulaires/in-531.aspx.

832. RSC 1985, c. T-13.

833. Subsection 16 (1) of the *Trade-marks Act,* RSC 1985, c. T-13.

834. Section 18 of the *Canada Business Corporations Regulations*, 2001, SOR/2001-512.

835. Subsection 9(1)(b) of the Ontario *Business Corporations Act* R.S.O. 1990, c. B.16.

836. *Business Corporations Regulation*, B.C. Reg. 65/2004, s. 7.

837. Section 17 of the *Act respecting the Legal Publicity of Sole Proprietorships, Partnerships and Legal Persons*, CQLR c P-44.1.

838. Sections 4–5 of the *Regulation respecting the application of the Act respecting the Legal Publicity of Sole Proprietorships, Partnerships and Legal Persons*, CQLR, c P-45, r 1.

Chapter 6. Industrial Designs

§1. Sources: Legislation

325. In 1867, the *British North America Act, 1867*,[839] (renamed in 1982 the *Constitution Act, 1867*),[840] granted legislative power over copyright to the Federal Parliament.[841] After Confederation, the legislation on designs was re-enacted by the Dominion Parliament, as an adjunct part to the trademark legislation, in the *TradeMark and Industrial Design Act* of 1868.[842] Separation from the trademark statute occurred in 1952, when the design registration sections were placed in the *Industrial Design and Union Label Act.*[843] The Union labels provisions were short lived[844] and in 1970, the title of the *Industrial Design Act* was adopted.[845]

326. In 1988, when the first phase of the copyright reform was introduced, the legislator brought two major modifications to the industrial designs regime.[846] First, a legislative definition of 'design' was introduced. Second, a new provision was enacted to deal with the overlapping between the *Copyright Act* and the *Industrial Design Act*. In recent years, the *Industrial Design Act* was again amended, mainly to enable Canada to meet its international obligations.[847] In 2014, the *Economic Action Plan 2014 Act, No. 2*[848] modified the *Act* to make it consistent with the *Geneva (1999) Act of the Hague Agreement Concerning the International Registration of Industrial Designs*.[849]

§2. Subject Matter of Protection

327. Since 1988, the *Act* states that design or industrial design 'means features of shape, configuration, pattern or ornament and any combination of those features

839. (1867) 30-31 Vict., c. 3 (U.K.).
840. *See* No. 1 of the Schedule to the *Constitution Act, 1982*, being Sch. B of the *Canada Act 1982*, 1982, c. 11 (U.K.).
841. Section 91(23).
842. 31 Vict. c. 55; RSC 1886, c. 63; RSC 1906, c. 71; RSC 1927, c. 201.
843. RSC 1952, c. 150.
844. They were repealed by s. 68 of the *Trademarks Act*, SC 1952-53, c. 49.
845. The *Industrial Design Act*, RSC 1970, c. I-8, is now c. I-9 of the RSC 1985. It is accompanied by *Industrial Design Regulations*, SOR/99-460, amended by SOR/2003-210, SOR/2007-92.
846. *An Act to amend the Copyright Act and to amend other Acts in consequence thereof*, RSC 1985, c. 10 [4th Suppl.], ss 11–18–19.
847. *See* among others *Intellectual Property Law Improvement Act*, SC 1993, c. 15, ss 12–24; *North American Free Trade Agreement Implementation Act*, SC 1993, c. 44, ss 161–173 and *World Trade Organization Agreement Implementation Act*, SC 1994, c. 47, s. 118.
848. SC 2014, c.39. Some modifications were also introduced by the *Economic Action Plan 2015 Act, No. 1*, SC 2015, c. 36, ss 44–49.
849. As of January 1, 2017, Canada had not yet joined the Hague System. The 2014 reform will come into force when the modifications to the regulations have been completed.

that, in a finished article, appeal to and are judged solely by the eye'.[850] It does not matter that the article is made by hand, tool or machine.[851]

328. The statutory definition is consistent with the concept of industrial design that was developed by the case law prior to the 1988 reform. The Supreme Court of Canada had given a definition: 'A "design" is, therefore, a pattern or representation which the eye can see and which can be applied to a manufactured article.'[852] The concept was analyzed by the Ex. C.R.:

> *The sort of design that can be registered is therefore a design to be 'applied' to 'the ornamenting' of an article. It must, therefore, be something that determines the appearance of an article, or some part of an article, because ornamenting relates to appearance. And it must have as its objective making the appearance of an article more attractive because that is the purpose of ornamenting. It cannot be something that determines the nature of an article as such (as opposed to mere appearance) and it cannot be something that determines how an article is to be created. In other words, it cannot create a monopoly in 'a product' or 'a process' such as can be acquired by a patent for an invention. There is, moreover, nothing in the legislation that limits the type of design that may be registered (as was suggested in argument) to those providing for something that is applied to an article after the article comes into existence. Section 11 contemplates a 'design' being 'applied' to the 'ornamenting' of any article. It is not restricted to a 'design' being 'applied' to an 'article'. [...]*
>
> The fact that a design relates to shape or configuration of an article is not, in itself, an objection to its registration. As long as it is a design to be applied 'to the ornamenting' of an article, it is eligible for registration even though it requires that its purpose of 'ornamenting' be accomplished in whole or in part by constructing the article, or parts of it, in a certain shape or shapes.[853]

329. The *Act* stipulates that no protection afforded by its provisions shall extend to features applied to a useful article,[854] which are dictated solely by a utilitarian function of the article, or extend to any method or principle of manufacture or construction.[855] However, features may be "simultaneously useful and visually appealing" and in such a case, the exclusion does apply.[856]

---

850. Section 2.
851. *See* the definition of 'article' provided by s. 2.
852. *Clatworthy & Son, Ltd. v. Dale Display Fixtures Ltd.*, [1929] S.C.R. 429, at 431.
853. *Cimon Ltd. v. Bench Made Furniture Corp.* (1964), [1965] 1 Ex. C.R. 811, at 831–833.
854. Section 2 defines a useful article as one that has a function other than merely serving as a substrate or carrier for artistic or literary matter. It includes a model of any such article.
855. Section 5.1. *See also* s. 11.1 as introduced by s 107 of the *Economic Action Plan 2014 Act, No. 2*, SC 2014, c.39.
856. *Zero Spill Systems (Int'l) Inc. v. Heide*, 2015 FCA 115.

§3. Conditions of Protection

330. Two conditions must be met in order to obtain a registration: the design must be original and the application for registration must be filed within one year from the date of the design's first publication.[857] Amendments voted in 2014 will require novelty instead of originality and will take into account the priority filing dates, if any, of the applicant.[858] The Act will provide that a design is registrable if (a) the application is filed in accordance with this Act; (b) the design is novel, within the meaning of section 8.2; (c) the design was created by the applicant or the applicant's predecessor in title; (d) the design does not consist only of features that are dictated solely by a utilitarian function of the finished article; and (e) the design is not contrary to public morality or order.[859]

331. The *Industrial Design Act* implies that, in order to be registered, a design must show a certain degree of originality. Section 4 requires that the applicant makes a declaration that the design was not in use to his or her knowledge by any person other than himself at the time of his or her adoption. Section 6 commands to the Minister to register a design if he or she finds that it is not identical with or does not so closely resemble any other design already registered as to be confounded therewith. Section 7(3) stipulates that the certificate of registration is a prima facie proof of originality. It means that the design must be substantially different from previous designs.[860] As the Supreme Court of Canada explained:

> It must be remembered, [...], that to constitute an original design there must be some substantial difference between the new design and what had theretofore existed. A slight change of outline or configuration, or an unsubstantial variation is not sufficient to enable the author to obtain registration. If it were, the benefits which the Act was intended to secure would be to a great extent lost and industry would be hampered, if not indeed paralyzed.[861]

857. This condition of protection will be examined in s. 4 of this chapter (Formalities (Procedure for Grant and Obtaining Protection)).
858. *See* s 105 of the *Economic Action Plan 2014 Act, No. 2*, SC 2014, c.39, introducing modifications to ss 5–8 of the *Act*.
859. S. 7 as modified by s 105 of the *Economic Action Plan 2014 Act, No. 2*, SC 2014, c.39.
860. H.G. Fox, *Canadian Law of Copyright and Industrial Designs* 665–666 (2d ed., Carswell 1967); Immanuel Goldsmith, *TradeMarks and Industrial Designs* ss 421–423 (Carswell 1982); John S. McKeown, *Fox Canadian Law of Copyright and Industrial Designs* 817 (3d ed., Carswell 2000).
861. *Clatworthy & Son Ltd. v. Dale Display Fixtures Ltd.*, [1929] S.C.R. 429, 433.

§4. Formalities (Procedure for Grant and Obtaining Protection)

332. To obtain protection of the design, an application must be filed within a year of the publication of the design anywhere in the world.[862] The 2014 reform will require that the application be filed within the priority period.[863]

Before 1993, the *Industrial Design Act* prescribed some marking requirements,[864] but it was not clear if the consequences of non-compliance were the loss of all statutory protection[865] or not.[866] Since 1993, the failure to mark will preclude the owner from obtaining any remedy other than an injunction, if the defendant can prove that he or she was not aware or had no reasonable grounds to suspect that the design was registered.[867]

§5. Ownership and Transfer (Assignment: Licences)

333. The proprietor of the design may apply to register the design.[868] The statute stipulates that the author of the design is the first proprietor of the design, unless the author has executed the design for another person for a good and valuable consideration, in which case the other person is the first proprietor.[869]

334. The statute allows for the assignment of designs, registered or not, for the whole or for any undivided part thereof.[870] It is now possible to transfer applications for registration, since section 4 allows the first proprietor or a subsequent proprietor to apply to register the design.[871] Before 1993, the registration of a design by an assignee was void because the application could be made only by the author or the person who had commissioned the design.[872] The assignment must be by an instrument in writing

862. Section 6. The *Industrial Design Regulations*, SOR/99-460, also regulates the content and form of the industrial design application.
863. *See* s 8.2 as introduced by s 105 of the *Economic Action Plan 2014 Act, No. 2*, SC 2014, c. 39.
864. Section 14, abrogated by the *Intellectual Property Law Improvement Act*, SC 1993, c. 15, s. 20.
865. *Allaire v. Hobbs Glass Ltd.*, [1948] Ex. C.R. 171, at 185–186; *Mainetti S.P.A. v. E.R.A. Display Co. Ltd.* (1984), 80 C.P.R. (2d) 206, at 222–224.
866. *Cimon Ltd. v. Bench Made Furniture Corp.* et al., [1965] Ex. C.R. 811, at 846; *L.M. Lipski Ltd. v. Dorel Industries Inc.* et al. (1988), 20 C.P.R. (3d) 226, at 236–244.
867. Section 17 as replaced by s. 21 of the *Intellectual Property Law Improvement Act*, SC 1993, c. 15.
868. Section 4.
869. Subsection 12(1).
870. Section 13 and s. 4.
871. Section 4 was amended by s. 13 of the *Intellectual Property Law Improvement Act*, SC 1993, c. 15.
872. *Melnor Manufacturing Ltd.* et al. *v. Lido Industrial Products Ltd.* (1969), 56 C.P.R. 212, [1969] 1 Ex. C.R. 76, aff'd (1970), 62 C.P.R. 216 (S.C.C.).

which must be registered.[873] The statute also allows for the grant of exclusive licenses, which must be registered.[874]

§6. Scope of Exclusive Rights

335. It is provided by section 11 of the *Act*, as amended by the *NAFTA Implementation Act*,[875] that during the existence of an exclusive right, no person shall make, import for the purpose of trade or business, or sell, rent, or offer or expose for sale or rent, any article to which the design or a design not differing substantially therefrom has been applied.[876]

§7. Limitations of the Scope of Protection

336. There is no limitation in the *Act* except to exclude features applied to a useful article that are dictated solely by a utilitarian function of the article, or any method or principle of manufacture or construction.[877]

§8. Duration of Protection

337. For designs registered after 1 January 1994, the protection runs for ten years from registration[878] and maintenance fees are due periodically.[879] Under the 2014 reform, the protection will start on the the date of registration or the prescribed publication date, whichever is later, and will end ten years after the date of registration of the design or fifteen years after the filing date of the application, whichever is longer.[880]

---

873. Section 13(1). After the coming into force of the 2014 reform, an unregistered transfer of a registered design will be void against a subsequent transferee if the transfer to the subsequent transferee has been registered : *see* subs. 13(4) as introduced by s. 108 of the *Economic Action Plan 2014 Act, No. 2,* SC 2014, c. 39.
874. Section 13(2), which does not seem to require that the exclusive licence be put in writing. Scholars tend to require a written document for an exclusive licence of an industrial design. *See* David Vaver, *Intellectual Property Law* 576 (2d ed., Irwin Law 2011). Some conclude that it is not clear whether a licence may be by parole. *See* John S. McKeown, *Fox Canadian Law of Copyright and Industrial Designs* 834 (3d ed., Carswell 2000).
875. SC 1993, c. 44, s. 164.
876. In determining whether differences are substantial, the extent to which the registered design differs from any previously published design may be taken into account: Section 11(2). For a recent application, *see* *Bodum USA, Inc. v. Trudeau Corporation (1889) Inc.*, 2012 FC 1128.
877. Section 5.1. *See also* our analysis in s. 2. Subject Matter of Protection.
878. Section 10.
879. Registration will expire if the maintenance fees are not paid within a six months period after the first five years term. *See* s. 10(3) of the *Industrial Design Act* and s. 18 of the *Industrial Designs Regulations.*
880. S. 106 of the *Economic Action Plan 2014 Act, No. 2,* SC 2014, c. 39.

§9. Infringement and Remedies

338. In an action for infringement of a registered design, the owner can ask for damages, punitive damages, an account of profits, delivery up and an order for the disposal of any infringing article or kit.[881] The plaintiff has the burden of proof of authorship and infringement, on balance of probabilities. The certificate of registration, in the absence of proof to the contrary, is sufficient evidence of the design, of the originality of the design, of the name of the proprietor, of the person named as proprietor being proprietor, of the commencement and term of registration and of compliance with the *Act*.[882] If the plaintiff cannot prove the actual loss due to the defendant's acts, he or she may be awarded nominal damages.[883]

339. Injunctions, both interlocutory and final, are available.[884] As mentioned previously,[885] since 1993, if the defendant can prove that he or she was not aware or had no reasonable grounds to suspect that the design was registered and if the articles bearing the design were not properly marked, the owner will not obtain any remedy other than an injunction.[886]

340. The action for infringement can be brought in the F.C. or in the courts of the provinces.[887] Section 18 provides for a limitation period of three years to actions for infringement.

§10. Overlapping and Relation to Other Intellectual Property Laws

I. Overlap with Copyright

341. Industrial designs may sometimes qualify as copyright works. The legal protection applicable to those designs has been substantially modified in 1988. The previous regime is still applicable to designs created before the legislative amendments were brought into force, which is created prior to 8 June 1988.[888]

342. Under the old regime, if the design was capable of being registered under the *Industrial Design Act* and was used or intended to be used as a pattern to be multiplied by an industrial process, then it was not subject to copyright protection by operation of subsection 64(1) of the *Copyright Act*.[889] Registration under the *Industrial*

881. Section 15.1.
882. Section 7(3).
883. John S. McKeown, *Fox Canadian Law of Copyright and Industrial Designs* 846 (3d ed., Carswell 2000).
884. Section 15.1.
885. *See* §4 Formalities (Procedure for Grant and Obtaining Protection) of this chapter.
886. Section 17 as replaced by s. 21 of the *Intellectual Property Law Improvement Act*, SC 1993, c. 15.
887. Section 15.
888. Section 64(4) of the *Copyright Act*, RSC 1985, c. C-42.
889. For an application of the rule, *see Milliken & Co. v. Interface Flooring Systems (Canada) Inc.* (2000), 251 N.R. 358 (F.C.A.).

Design Act had to occur within the prescribed period; otherwise the design would not be entitled to any protection. To determine if a drawing was intended to be used as a model, the courts considered the author's intention at the time of the creation.[890] Also section 11 of the *Industrial Designs Rules*[891] determined when a design was deemed to be used as a model or a pattern to be multiplied by any industrial process: (a) when the design was reproduced or was intended to be reproduced in more than fifty single articles;[892] and (b) when the design was to be applied to: (i) printed paper hangings; (ii) carpets, floor cloths, or oil cloths manufactured or sold in lengths or pieces; (iii) textile piece goods, or textile goods manufactured or sold in lengths or pieces; and (iv) lace, not made by hand. For a time, the rules were interpreted as requiring both conditions to exclude a design from the copyright protection.[893] Finally, the F.C.A. decided that the two conditions were not cumulative and so ruled in the case at hand that the designs of boats would not enjoy copyright protection.[894] By a strange twist of the law, if the design only had a utilitarian function, it was not capable of being registered as an industrial design and the logical conclusion was to grant it the full copyright protection.[895] The 1988 *Act* changed the rule for both designs created prior, on or after 8 June 1988: according to section 64.1 of the *Copyright Act*, no copyright infringement is done by taking the features dictated solely by a utilitarian function of an article[896] and using a method or principle of manufacture or construction. On the other hand, under the old regime, section 64 of the *Copyright Act*, denying copyright protection, applied even if the lack of registrability as an industrial design was due to a lack of novelty or an untimely application.[897]

343. In 1988, the legislator ended the copyright exclusion for industrial designs: instead it created a regime that avoids a double protection for the same act of copying. If, with the authorization of the copyright holder, a design or an artistic work is used for the manufacture of more than fifty copies of a useful article, then it is not a copyright infringement to manufacture the article, to make a drawing or a reproduction in any material form of the article.[898] Equally, anyone may do anything with the article that the copyright holder has the sole right to do, without committing a copyright violation.[899]

---

890. *King Features Syndicate Inc. v. O. & M. Kleeman*, [1941] A.C. 417 (H.L.), at 427–428.
891. Then CRC 1978, c. 964.
892. Unless all the articles bearing the design formed only a single set as defined in the regulation: Section 11(a).
893. *See* Myra J. Tawfik, *'The Law of Copyright and Industrial Designs in Canada'* C.I.P.Rev. 7 130, at 139 (1990).
894. *Doral Boats Ltd. v. Bayliner Marine Corp.* (1986), 10 C.P.R. (3d) 289 (F.C.A.), at 293–295.
895. Myra J. Tawfik, *'The Law of Copyright and Industrial Designs in Canada'* C.I.P.Rev. 7 130, at 141, 130 (1990).
896. Section 64.1 also covers a drawing, or a reproduction, of the utilitarian features of the article made by reference solely to the useful article.
897. *Doral Boats Ltd. v. Bayliner Marine Corp.* (1986), 10 C.P.R. (3d) 289 (F.C.A.), at 295–296.
898. According to s. 64(1), a "useful article" is an article that has a utilitarian function. It is not always easy to determine whether an object, such as a piece of jewellery, should be considered useful: *see Pyrrha Design Inc. v. 623735 Saskatchewan Ltd.*, 2004 FCA 423.
899. Section 64(2).

344. The *Act* restores the full copyright protection to certain categories of works, even if they were used for producing more than fifty useful articles; section 64(3) provides the list:

(a) *a graphic or photographic representation that is applied to the face of an article;*
(b) *a trademark or a representation thereof or a label;*
(c) *material that has a woven or knitted pattern or that is suitable for piece goods or surface coverings or for making wearing apparel;*
(d) *an architectural work that is a building or a model of a building;*
(e) *a representation of a real or fictitious being, event or place that is applied to an article as a feature of shape, configuration, pattern or ornament;*
(f) *articles that are sold as a set, unless more than fifty sets are made; or*
(g) *such other work or article as may be prescribed by regulation.*

II. Overlap with Patent

345. So long as the respective statutory requirements are met, an article can be protected both by the *Patent Act*[900] and the *Industrial Design Act.*[901] However, the protection of the design does not extend to the functional features of the article, or to any method or principle of manufacture.[902]

III. Overlap with Trademark

346. A design can also be registered under the *Trademarks Act*,[903] so long as it possesses the essential requirements set by the statute.[904] However, certain courts have ruled that if the design serves only the function of decoration, if is merely an ornamental design, it is not used as a trademark, thus not distinctive and not properly registrable as a trademark.[905]

900. RSC 1985, c. P-4.
901. John S. McKeown, *Fox Canadian Law of Copyright and Industrial Designs* 815 (3d ed., Carswell 2000).
902. Section 5.1. *see also* our analysis in s. 2. Subject Matter of Protection.
903. RSC 1985, c. T-13.
904. McKeown indicates that the registrations of a distinguishing guise as a design and as a trademark are not mutually exclusive: John S. McKeown, *Fox Canadian Law of Copyright and Industrial Designs* 815 (3d ed., Carswell 2000).
905. *W.J. Hughes & Sons 'Corn Flower' Ltd. v. Morawiec* (1970), 62 C.P.R. 21 (Ex. Ct.) (the registration as a trademark of the representation of a flower applied to cut glass tableware was held invalid); *Adidas (Canada) Ltd. v. Colins Inc.* (1978), 38 C.P.R. (2d) 145 (F.C.T.D.) (parallel stripes on sports clothing held not registrable as trademark); *Canada's Royal Gold Pinetree Mfg Co. Ltd. v. Samann* (1986), 9 C.P.R. (3d) 223 (F.C.A.) (representations of an evergreen tree for air deodorizing substances held properly registered as trademarks since the marks in issue were not merely or solely ornamental).

Chapter 7. Plant Variety Protection

§1. Sources: Legislation

347. In Canada, protection is available to plants breeders through the *Plant Breeders' Rights Act,*[906] which was substantially modified in 2015.[907] On the international level, Canada has adhered to the 1978 *International Union for the Protection of New Varieties of Plants (UPOV) Convention*[908] and has signed the *UPOV Convention*[909] on 19 March 1992.[910] The 2015 reform came into force on 27 February 2015 bringing the *Plant Breeders' Rights Act* in line with the 1991 *UPOV Convention.*[911]

§2. Subject Matter of Protection

348. The section 2 of the Canadian *Act* defines 'plant variety' as 'plant grouping within a single botanical taxon of the lowest known rank that, whether or not the conditions for the grant of plant breeder's rights are fully met, is capable of being (a) defined by the expression of the characteristics resulting from a given genotype or combination of genotypes, (b) distinguished from any other plant grouping by the expression of at least one of those characteristics, and (c) considered as a unit with regard to its suitability for being reproduced unchanged;'. The definition covers asexually and sexually reproduced plants.[912] To be eligible, a plant must belong to a

906. SC 1990, c. 20. It is accompanied by the *Plant Breeders' Rights Regulations*, SOR/91-594, amended by SOR/93-87, SOR/94-750, SOR/98-582.
907. *Agricultural Growth Act*, SC 2015, c. 2, ss 2–81.
908. *International Convention For The Protection Of New Varieties Of Plants* of 2 Dec. 1961, as revised at Geneva on 10 Nov. 1972, and on 23 Oct. 1978. The text of the Convention is available at www.upov.int/upovlex/en/acts.html. The treaty was ratified by Canada on 4 Feb. 1991, and the ratification was in force on 4 Mar. 1991: *Canada Treaty Series 1991*, 5, (1991).
909. *International Convention for The Protection of New Varieties of Plants*, of 2 Dec. 1961, as Revised at Geneva on 10 Nov. 1972, on 23 Oct. 1978, and on 19 Mar. 1991. The text of the Convention is available at www.upov.int/upovlex/en/acts.html.
910. *See* UPOV, *Records of the Diplomatic Conference for the Revision of the International Convention for the Protection of New Varieties of Plants*, Geneva 1991. http://www.upov.int/export/sites/upov/about/en/pdf/346_Repords_Dep_Conf_1991.pdf.
911. For a short summary of the legislative intent behing the 2015 reform, *see* Canadian Food Inspection Agency, *The Impact of the International Union for the Protection of New Varieties of Plants (UPOV) Conventions on Plant Breeders' Rights in Canada - Questions and Answers*, 24 May 2015, available online at http://www.inspection.gc.ca/plants/plant-breeders-rights/overview/impact-upov/eng/1409072983279/1409073464633. The ratification by Canada of the 1991 Act took effect on June 19, 2015: for the annoucement of the notification, *see* http://www.upov.int/upovlex/en/text_notification.jsp?id=117.
912. Section 4(2)(d) expressly refers to the sexual reproduction or vegetative propagation of plants.

category prescribed by regulation.[913] Initially the protection was available for only a limited number of species, considered to be of importance to Canada.[914] The categories were expanded on several occasions.[915] In 1998, the regulations were again amended to afford protection for all crops, excluding algae, bacteria and fungi.[916]

§3. Conditions of Protection

349. To be a protectable variety, a subject matter must meet several requirements. It must be distinct, stable and sufficiently homogeneous.[917] It must also be a new variety[918], meeting certain requirements concerning prior commercialization.[919] There is no requirement that the new variety has utility or industrial application.

350. To be distinct, the variety must be 'by reason of one or more identifiable characteristics, clearly distinguishable from all varieties, the existence of which is a matter of common knowledge at the effective date of application for the grant of the plant breeder's rights respecting that plant variety'.[920] To determine if the existence of a plant is a matter of common knowledge, one must consider whether the variety is already being cultivated or exploited for commercial purposes, or whether the variety is described in a publication accessible to the public.[921] A plant variety is considered stable if its essential characteristics remain true after repeated propagation.[922] A variety is sufficiently homogeneous if, in the event of its sexual reproduction or vegetative propagation in substantial quantity, any variations in characteristics of plants so reproduced or propagated are predictable, capable of being described and commercially acceptable.[923]

351. To be able to apply, the person must be a citizen, resident of Canada or a country of the Union or an agreement country or have an establishement in Canada or a country of the Union or an agreement country.[924] A country of the Union means a country that has ratified the *International Convention for the Protection of New Varieties of Plants of 2 December 1961*, and any revisions of that treaty, as published in the Canada Gazette, or any WTO member.[925]

352. A priority right is attached to the applications made in a country of the Union or an agreement country: such applicants may claim the benefit of the earlier date of filing if they file an application in Canada within twelve months.[926]

913. *See also* s. 4.
914. SOR/91-594.
915. Sch. I, SOR/93-87, s. 3; SOR/94-750, ss. 14–20; SOR/98-582, s. 3; SOR/2012-286, s. 45.
916. SOR/98-582, s. 3.
917. Subsection 4(2).
918. Par 4(2)a).
919. Subsection 4(3).
920. Subsection 4(2)b).
921. Section 5 of the *Plant Breeders' Rights Regulations*.
922. Par 4(2)(c).
923. Subsection 4(4).
924. Section 7.
925. Section 2 of the *Act* and section 4 of the *Plant Breeders' Rights Regulations.*
926. Section 11.

353. There are time limits for applying for a grant. Normally, the application must be filed in Canada within one year of the first sale in Canada by or with the concurrence of the breeder or its legal representative.[927] If priority can be claimed by reason of a preceding application in a country of the Union or an agreement country, the sale in Canada must not have occurred before the priority date.[928] If the sale by or with the concurrence of the breeder has occurred outside Canada, the time limits for application are, for woody plants, including their rootstocks, six years from the first sale, and for other plants, four years.[929]

§4. Formalities (Procedure for Grant and Obtaining Protection)

354. An application must be made to the Plant Breeders' Rights Office (PBRO), which is part of the Canadian Food Inspection Agency (CFIA).[930] It must contain specific information,[931] including the proposed denomination,[932] a description of the plant variety, the origin and the breeding history of the variety, a statement on the method for maintaining the variety.[933] The application can include a request for exemption from compulsory licensing.[934] A provisional protection is granted as of the filing date of the application.[935]

355. The proposed name must satisfy several conditions: it must not be likely to mislead or to cause confusion,[936] it must not be prejudicial to any prior right of another person to the use of any designation,[937] which presumably means that it must not be similar to a previously registered denomination, unless the two denominations are held by the same party. International uniformity is being sought: if a name has been proposed in a similar application in another Convention country, the same name must be used in the Canadian application.[938] The denomination will serve as a generic word for the plant variety: after the grant of the plant breeder's rights, use of that denomination is mandatory for designating the variety for the purposes of the sale of propagating material.[939] Use for designating another variety is actionable.[940] The *Trademarks Act* states specifically that a denomination cannot be adopted, registered or used as a trademark or a trade name.[941] If a trademark or a trade name is used in

927. Subsection 4(3).
928. Subsection 4(3).
929. Subsection 4(3).
930. Their official website is located at www.inspection.gc.ca/english/toce.shtml.
931. Section 9 of the *Act* and ss 19–21 of the *Plant Breeders' Rights Regulations*.
932. Subsection 14 (1) of the *Act*.
933. For a detailed description of those requirements, *see* the instructions given by the PBRO on the website.
934. Paragraph 19(1)(m) and s. 28 of the *Plant Breeders' Rights Regulations*.
935. Section 19 of the *Act*.
936. Subsection 14(3) of the *Act*.
937. Section 16 of the *Act*.
938. Subsection 14(4).
939. Section 15.
940. Subsection 53(2)(b).
941. *Trademarks Act*, RSC 1985, c. T-13, ss 10.1–11.1.

association with a denomination, the latter must be clearly recognizable.[942] The Commissioner may reject the proposed denomination if considered unsuitable for any reasonable cause.[943] The Commissioner has also the statutory authority to approve a change of denomination.[944]

356. The office will examine the application to verify if it is compatible with the *Act* and the *Regulations* and to determine whether the candidate variety meets the requirements for distinctness, uniformity and stability.[945] The protection is granted only after proper testing. Some countries have a 'state-run' testing system, but Canada has adopted a 'breeder-run' testing system. The tests and trials are conducted by the breeder or the applicant under the review of the PBRO, who will send an examiner to verify the tests. The Commissioner may accept foreign tests and trials.[946] After the examination of the application, a description of the variety is published in the Plant Varieties Journal[947]. A person who considers that an application as published ought to be refused may file an objection.[948] The applicant and the person making the objection will be given a reasonable opportunity to make representations.[949] When the Commissioner is satisfied that the rights ought to be granted to the applicant, an entry will be made in the Register[950] and a plant breeders' rights certificate will be issued.[951]

357. The *Act* imposes an obligation to maintain a stock of propagating material.[952] To ensure that the holder is causing the propagating material to be maintained, the Commissioner may ask to inspect the holder's facilities and may request samples of the material which shall exhibit the same characteristics as described in the application.[953] Failure to furnish a sample may result in the revocation of the rights.[954]

---

942. Subsection 14(6).
943. Subsection 14(2) of the *Act* and s. 22 of the *Plant Breeders' Rights Regulations*.
944. Subsection 14(5) of the *Act* and ss 23–24 of the *Plant Breeders' Rights Regulations*. When the Commissioner refuses to approve the change of denomination, adequate reasons must be provided: *see University of Saskatchewan v. Commissioner of the Plant Breeders' Rights Office* (2001), 11 C.P.R. (4th) 348 (F.C.T.D.).
945. Section 17.
946. Section 24.
947. Par 70 (1)b).
948. Section 22.
949. Subsection 22(4).
950. Sections 27(3) and 63.
951. Section 27.
952. Section 30.
953. Section 30. Section 13 of the *Plant Breeders' Rights Regulations* stipulates that the holder must comply with the request within sixty days after the date on which notice is given by the Commissioner.
954. Section 35.

§5. Ownership and Transfer (Assignment: Licences)

I. The Right to Grant

358. A breeder of a new variety or the legal representative of the breeder may make the application.[955] A breeder is someone who originates or discovers the plant variety or the employer of such a person.[956]

II. Assignment

359. The plant breeder's right is assignable as is the right to apply for a grant.[957] After the assignment, the Commissioner must be informed of the transfer within thirty days.[958] Section 26 of the *Regulations* requires the assignee to provide a letter of assignment signed by both the holder and the assignee, each in the presence of a witness and the effective date of the assignment.[959] However, the lack of registration will not bar an assignee to sue for infringement since section 41 of the *Act* gives a right to receive compensation for infringement to 'all persons claiming under the holder'.

360. Registration is also important for determining rights enforceable against subsequent assignees. Section 31(3) provides that:

> An assignment of plant breeder's rights is void against a subsequent assignee thereof for valuable consideration without notice who is registered as the holder of the rights unless, before the subsequent assignee is so registered, the person to whom that assignment is made is registered as holder of the rights.

III. Licences

361. The *Act* clearly admits the possibility of granting licences,[960] but does not require any particular form, nor does it provide for the registration of contractual licences. The *Act* only deals with the registration of compulsory licences.[961]

362. Section 41 gives a right to receive compensation for infringement to 'all persons claiming under the holder', which should include the licensee. Section 45

955. Section 7.
956. Section 2, definition of 'breeder'.
957. Section 31 and s. 7 which allows a representative to apply for the grant. Section 2 stipulates that a legal representative includes an assignee.
958. Section 31 of the *Act* and s. 12 of the *Plant Breeders' Rights Regulations*.
959. Subsections 26(d)(e).
960. Paragraph 5(1)(h) includes in the list of the plant breeder's rights, the right to authorize, conditionally or unconditionally, the doing of an act reserved to the holder. Subsection 33(1) confirms that the existence of a voluntary licence, even an exclusive one, will not affect the application for a compulsory licence. Section 45 seems to draw a distinction between a person authorized pursuant to para. 5(1)(h) or licensed to exercise plant breeder's rights.
961. *See* subs. 63(g).

specifies that unless their agreement otherwise prescribes, the licensee can call on the holder to take proceedings for infringement of the rights. If the holder refuses or neglects to take proceedings within fifteen days after being called on to do so, the licensee may institute the action in the name of the holder, making the holder a defendant.[962]

§6. Scope of Exclusive Rights

363. In the case of a variety for which plant breeders' rights have been granted before 27 February 2015, *the exclusive rights are :*

(a) *to sell, and produce in Canada for the purpose of selling, propagating material, as such, of the plant variety;*[963]
(b) *to make repeated use of propagating material of the plant variety in order to produce commercially another plant variety if the repetition is necessary for that purpose;*
(c) *where it is a plant variety to which ornamental plants or parts thereof normally marketed for purposes other than propagation belong, to use any such plants or parts commercially as propagating material in the production of ornamental plants or cut flowers; and*
(d) *to authorize, conditionally or unconditionally, the doing of an act described in paragraphs (a) to (c).*[964]

When the rights have been granted on, or after, 27 February 2015, the list is more extensive. The holder has the following exclusive rights :

(a) *to produce and reproduce propagating material of the variety;*
(b) *to condition propagating material of the variety for the purposes of propagating the variety;*
(c) *to sell propagating material of the variety;*
(d) *to export or import propagating material of the variety;*
(e) *to make repeated use of propagating material of the variety to produce commercially another plant variety if the repetition is necessary for that purpose;*
(f) *in the case of a variety to which ornamental plants belong, if those plants are normally marketed for purposes other than propagation, to use any such plants or parts of those plants as propagating material for the production of ornamental plants or cut flowers;*

962. Section 45 and s. 16 of the *Plant Breeders' Rights Regulations*. A holder who is made a defendant is not liable for any costs unless the holder takes part in the proceedings: Subsection 45(2).
963. It did not apply to sales of the propagating material outside of Canada, except if the material was brought to Canada and used for propagation: *See* the former subs. 5(2).
964. *See* the former subs. 5(1). The monopoly was only on the sale of the reproductive material and the production for the purpose of selling. The Act also specified at subs. 5(3) that the sale of propagating material granted to the purchaser the right to resell the material, but not to produce propagating material and then to sell it.

(g) *to stock propagating material of the variety for the purpose of doing any act described in any of paragraphs (a) to (f); and*
(h) *to authorize, conditionally or unconditionally, the doing of any act described in any of paragraphs (a) to (g).*[965]

364. In the case of a variety for which plant breeders' rights have been granted on, or after, 27 February 2015, the protection extends to (a) any other plant variety that is essentially derived from the plant variety if the plant variety is not itself essentially derived from another plant variety; (b) any other plant variety that is not clearly distinguishable from the plant variety; and (c) any other plant variety whose production requires the repeated use of the plant variety.[966] It also extends to any harvested material, including whole plants or parts of plants, that is obtained through the unauthorized use of propagating material of the plant variety, unless the holder had reasonable opportunity to exercise his or her rights to exercise their rights in relation to that propagating material.[967] However, farmers may save and use their own seed of protected varieties without committing infringement.[968]

365. In addition to the farmers' privilege, the *Act* provides for exceptions when the protected varieties are used for private and non-commercial purposes, for experimental purposes, for breeding and developing new plant varieties.[969] The Act also adopts the rule of exhaustion of rights after a sale in Canada, unless there is further propagation of the plant variety or unless the propagating material is exported, for purposes other than consumption, to a country that does not protect varieties of that plant genus or species.[970]

§7. Limitations of the Scope of Protection: Compulsory Licenses

366. If the Commissioner considers that it is appropriate to do so, he or she may issue a compulsory licence.[971] Although the statute does not require an abuse of the right holder, the PBRO indicates in their *Guidelines* that the licence will be granted to an applicant who can demonstrate to the Commissioner that the holder of the right has unreasonably refused to grant a licence.[972] The Commissioner will act to ensure that the variety is available to the public at reasonable prices, that the supply of the variety is widely distributed, that reproductive material is maintained in quality and that the royalty rates are kept reasonable.[973] The licence must be non-exclusive.[974]

965. Subsection 5(3).
966. Section 5.2.
967. Section 5.1.
968. Subsection 5.3(2)
969. Section 5.3.
970. Section 5.4.
971. Section 32.
972. Canadian Food Inspection Agency, *Guide To Plant Breeders' Rights In Canada*, 13 July 2015, available online at http://www.inspection.gc.ca/plants/plant-breeders-rights/overview/guide/eng/1409074255127/1409074255924#a9.
973. Subsection 32(2).
974. Subsection 32(6).

367. At the time of application, the applicant may request an exemption from compulsory licensing.[975] The *Plant Breeders' Rights Regulations* specify that the request may be granted if the applicant requires time to multiply and distribute propagating material of the variety.[976]

§8. Duration of Protection

368. In the case of a grant before 27 February 2015, the protection lasts for a period of up to eighteen years, starting at the date of issue of the rights certificate.[977] Rights granted on, or after, 27 February 2015 are protected for a period of up to twenty-five years for the variety of a tree and vine (including their rootstocks), and twenty years for all other varieties of plants (excluding algae, bacteria and fungi), effective from the date of issue of the rights certificate.[978] Annual maintenance fees must be paid.[979] The grant may be revoked in various instances: if there is failure to pay the annual maintenance fee,[980] failure to supply propagating material of the variety or to comply with the requests concerning the maintenance of propagating material,[981] or if the the variety is no longer uniform or stable.[982] At any time during the duration of the grant, the holder may surrender the rights on the variety.[983]

369. The Commissioner may also annul the grant if it is proven that the variety was not distinct when rights were granted, or if the variety was sold prior to time limits set in the *Act* or *Regulations*,[984] or if convention priority rights are established against the grant.[985]

§9. Infringement and Remedies

370. Actions for infringement may be brought by the right holder, or an assignee,[986] or a licence[987] or 'any person claiming under the holder'.[988] In proceedings for

975. *See* subs. 27 (2.1) and 75. (1)(k) of the *Plant Breeders' Rights Act*.
976. Section 28 of the *Plant Breeders' Rights Regulations*.
977. *See* former section 6.
978. Section 6.
979. Subsection 6.(2) of the *Act* and ss 29 and 30 of the *Plant Breeders' Rights Regulations*. The amount is indicated in Sch. II of the *Regulations*.
980. Paragraph 35(1)(d).
981. Sections 30 and 35(1)(a) and (b).
982. Paragraph 35 (1)(e). In the case of rights granted before February 27, 2015, the reasons for a revocation also include the failure to meet the conditions imposed by an order granting compulsory licence and breach of the undetaking not to market the plant for the duration of a prtoective direction *See* former s. 35 of the *Act*.
983. Section 38.
984. Section 34.
985. Section 13.
986. *See* § 5II *infra* .
987. *See* § 5III *infra* .
988. *See* s. 41.

infringement, the plaintiff, if successful, is entitled to damages, account of profits, injunction and delivery up.[989] The defendant may challenge the validity of the grant, but only on certain basis.[990] The Federal Court is also empowered to make a declaration of non-infringement at the request of anyone who has reasonable cause to believe that his or her actions might be alleged by the holder of plant breeder's rights to constitute an infringement.[991] In addition to actions defined as infringement under the *Act*, there are defined criminal offences concerning disclosure of information and improper use of a plant denomination.[992]

§10. Overlapping and Relation to Other Intellectual Property Laws

371. Both the *Plant Breeders' Rights Act*[993] and the *Patent Act*[994] may be used to gain protection for a new plant variety. Nothing in either *Acts* precludes a cumulative protection on a plant, by way of a patent and a breeder's rights certificates. In *Harvard College v. Canada (Commissioner of Patents)*,[995] the majority thought that the enactment of the *Plant Breeders' Rights Act* was an element showing that the *Patent Act* was not tailored to protect plants. It was a factor leading to the conclusion that Parliament had not intended higher life forms to be patentable. However in *Monsanto Canada Inc. v. Schmeiser*,[996] the Supreme Court upheld a patent on a gene which increased the plants' tolerance to herbicides. Arguably, patent protection is now available for plants as long as not the plant itself, but the genes and the plant cells are targeted in the claims.

989. Paragraph 41(2).
990. Subsection 43 (3).
991. Subsection 43.(4).
992. Section 53.
993. S.C.1990, c. 20.
994. RSC 1985, c. P-4.
995. [2002] 4 S.C.R. 45.
996. [2004] 1 S.C.R. 902.

Chapter 8. Chip Protection

§1. Sources: Legislation

372. In Canada, semiconductor chips are protected under the *Integrated Circuit Topography Act.*[997] The *Act* was adopted, among other reasons, to allow Canadian creators to gain protection in the United States.[998] The *Act* was put into force on 1 May 1993,[999] but has proved to be of little popularity: only thirty-eight registrations were made between 1993 and 1998,[1000] only a few in the following years.[1001] In 1999, the Government of Canada reported that the *Act* was fulfilling its objective of providing the appropriate legislative framework for the semiconductor industry and concluded that no amendments to the Act were needed.[1002]

373. Canada has not signed the *Treaty on Intellectual Property in respect of Integrated Circuits*, also called *Washington Treaty* or *IPIC Treaty* (signed at Washington on 26 May 1989), which is currently not in force. Some of the provisions of the *IPIC Treaty* were integrated into *NAFTA* and *Agreement on Trade-Related Aspects of Intellectual Property Rights* (*TRIPs Agreement)*[1003] to which Canada is bound.

997. SC 1990, c. 37. It is accompanied by the *Integrated Circuit Topography Regulations*, SOR/93-212, amended by SOR/2007-94.

998. A.A. Macchione, *'Parliamentary Review of the Provisions and Operation of the Integrated Circuit Topography Act and its Regulations'* C.I.P.Rev. 16 91, at 92(1999).

999. SI/93-68.

1000. Industry Canada, *Report to Parliament on Review of the Integrated Circuit Topography Act*, available http://strategis.ic.gc.ca/epic/internet/inippd-dppi.nsf/en/ip00128e.html.

1001. Canadian Intellectual Property Office, *Annual Report 2002–2003.* The low level of registrations seems to be the norm: there were only four in 2002–2003, three in 2001–2002, one in 2000–2001, six in 1999–2000, five in 1998–1999, three in 1997–1998, and nine in 1996–1997. In recent years (2010–2015), there were 5 applications. *See* the Canadian Intellectual Property Office, *Annual Report 2013–14 and Annual Report 2014–15, available online at https://www.ic.gc.ca/eic/site/cipointernet-internetopic.nsf/eng/h_wr00025.html#annualreports.*

1002. Industry Canada, *Report to Parliament on Review of the Integrated Circuit Topography Act*, (2001). It seems that the protection in United States of Canadian mask works have been more valued by rights holders. Between 1985 and 1996, there have been 138 registrations of Canadian mask works: *See* Carl A. Kukkonen, *'The Need to Abolish Registration for Integrated Circuit Topographies under TRIPS' IDEA* 38 105,111 (IDEA 1997).

1003. *See* Arts 35–38 of the *Agreement on Trade-Related Aspects of Intellectual Property Rights* (*TRIPs Agreement*), which was signed by Canada on 15 Apr. 1994 and ratified on 30 Dec. 1994. It was enacted into domestic law by the *World Trade Organization Agreement Implementation Act*, SC 1994, c. 47. The *North American Free Trade Agreement* (*NAFTA)* (32 I.L.M. 296) contains a c. 17 devoted to intellectual property matters and is reproduced at 32 I.L.M. 670. Art. 1710 deals with the layout designs of semiconductor integrated circuits. The agreement was signed on 17 Dec. 1992 by the governments of the United States, Mexico and Canada. It came into force on 1 Jan. 1994. *See* Index, *Canada Treaty Series 1994*, 1, (1998). It was enacted into Canadian domestic law by the *North American Free Trade Agreement Implementation Act*, SC 1993, c. 44.

§2. Subject Matter of Protection

374. The *Act* indicates that 'integrated circuit product' means a product, in a final or intermediate form, that is intended to perform an electronic function and in which the elements, at least one of which is an active element, and some or all of the interconnections, are integrally formed in or on, or both in and on, a piece of material.[1004] The 'topography' means the design, however expressed, of the disposition of (a) the interconnections, if any, and the elements for the making of an integrated circuit product; or (b) the elements, if any, and the interconnections for the making of a customization layer or layers to be added to an integrated circuit product in an intermediate form.[1005]

§3. Conditions of Protection

375. The conditions of protection are set forth in section 4. The topography must be original, the applicant must be a person entitled to register and the application must be filed within the specified time limit.[1006]

I. Originality

376. The legislation expresses in detail what is an original topography: a topography is not original if it has been produced by the mere reproduction of another topography or of any substantial part thereof.[1007] It must also be the result of an intellectual effort and must not be, at the time of its creation, commonplace among creators of topographies or manufacturers of integrated circuit products.[1008] Where a topography consists of a combination of elements or interconnections that are commonplace among creators of topographies or manufacturers of integrated circuit products, the topography will be considered to be original only if the combination, considered as a whole, is original.[1009]

377. This legislative notion of originality has been said to be a copyright-patent hybrid.[1010] The condition that a topography must not be commonplace seems to be a softer requirement than the novelty standard under the current *Patent Act* which states

1004. Section 2.
1005. *Ibid.*
1006. *See* §. 4. Formalities (Procedure for Grant and Obtaining Protection).
1007. Paragraph 4(2)(a).
1008. Paragraph 4(2)(b).
1009. Subsection 4(3).
1010. David A. Ruston, *'Bus Drivers and Other Conductors: A Review of Semi-Conductor Topography Protection'* C.I.P.Rev. 6 155, 158 (1990), discussing the originality and novel requirements under the *U.S. Semiconductor Chip Protection Act of 1984.*

that a patent will be invalid if it was disclosed in such a manner that the subject matter became available to the public anywhere in the world.[1011]

II. Person Entitled to Register

378. A topography is protected if the creator or the topography is connected to Canada.[1012] The protection also benefits the nationals of WTO members[1013] and the persons or entities connected to countries that are parties to a treaty affording protection to topographies of which Canada is also a party.[1014] The *Act* also contains a scheme of reciprocal protection for foreign chips: If the Minister of Industry certifies that a country or intergovernmental organization confers protection on Canadian nationals or connected legal entities, the Canadian *Act* will apply to protect the topographies of the persons or entities related to that country.[1015]

§4. Formalities (Procedure for Grant and Obtaining Protection)

379. The application for registration of the topography must be filed with the Registrar less than two years after the topography is first commercially exploited.[1016] It must contain specific information and documents as required by the legislation and regulations[1017] and be accompanied by the prescribed fee.[1018] The Registrar does not verify the accuracy of the information provided in the application.[1019] Once issued, the certificate is a prima facie evidence of the validity of the registration.[1020]

1011. Paragraph 28.2(1)(b), *Patent Act*, RSC 1985, c. P-4. On the difference between the novelty and the originality requirement of the *Integrated Circuit Topography Act*, *see* Stuart C. McCormack, *World Intellectual Property Guidebook: Canada* s. 2M [2] (Matthew Bender 1991).

1012. The creator of the topography must, at the time of its creation or on the filing date of the application, be a national of Canada, or an individual or legal entity that has in Canada a real and effective establishment for the creation of topographies or the manufacture of integrated circuit products. *See* subpara. 4(1)(c)(i). Even if the creator does not meet the nationality requirements, the topography will be registrable if the topography is first commercially exploited in Canada. *See* s. 4(4).

1013. Subparagraph 4(1)(c)(iv). In the *Guide to Integrated Circuit Topographies* (available at http://strategis.ic.gc.ca/sc_mrksv/cipo/ict/ict_gd_form-e.html, it is mentioned that if the creator of the topography has, at the time of creation or at the time of filing, a real and effective establishment for the creation of topographies or the manufacture of integrated circuit products in a country that is a member of the *World Trade Organization* (WTO), he can apply for registration.

1014. Subparagraph 4(1)(c)(ii).

1015. Subparagraph 4(1)(c)(iii). *See* for instance the *Order According Reciprocal Protection to Switzerland under the Act*, SOR/94-27.

1016. Paragraph 4(1)(b).

1017. Subsection 16(2) of the *Act* and ss 12–19 of the *Integrated Circuit Topography Regulations*.

1018. Subsection 16(3).

1019. Subsection 18(2).

1020. Subsection 19(3).

§5. Ownership and Transfer (Assignment: Licences)

I. Ownership

380. Section 16 grants to the creator of the topography or its successor in title the right to apply for registration. When the topography was created in the course of employment or pursuant to a contract, the employer or a party to the contract for whom the topography was created is deemed to be the creator of the topography unless the employer and the employee or the parties to the contract, as the case may be, otherwise agreed.[1021]

II. Assignment

381. The *Integrated Circuit Topography Act* states that a topography, whether registered or unregistered, is transferable, that is, assignable, either as to the whole interest or as to any part thereof.[1022] When the application is made by a successor in title, the application must describe the interest that the applicant holds in the topography.[1023] The *Act* does not prescribe any specific formalities to complete an assignment. Section 21 simply imposes on the Registrar the duty to register the particulars of any transfer when he or she is provided with satisfactory evidence.

III. Licences

382. Subsection 7(2) clearly recognizes the capacity of the owner to grant licences, in whole or for a partial interest. No formalities are required and under section 21, registration seems to be possible for all types of licences.

IV. The Right to Sue

383. The right to sue is granted to the owner of the registered topography (which would include an assignee) and to the licensee,[1024] unless otherwise agreed in the licensing agreement. The legislation does not indicate if the plaintiff must have registered its interest in order to be able to bring an action for infringement.

1021. Subsection 2(4).
1022. Subsection 7(1).
1023. Paragraph 16(2)(d).
1024. Subsection 8(1). Each owner of the registered topography must be or be made a party to any action for infringement. Subsection 8(2).

§6. Scope of Exclusive Rights

384. Section 3 enumerates the exclusive rights attached to a registered topography:

- a right to reproduce the topography or any substantial part;
- a right to manufacture an integrated circuit product incorporating the topography or any substantial part; and
- a right to import or commercially exploit the topography or any substantial part, or any integrated circuit product that incorporates the topography or any substantial part. A commercial exploitation occurs when one sells, leases, offers or exhibits for sale or lease, or otherwise distributes a product for a commercial purpose.[1025]

385. The legislation makes it clear that an independent creation of a topography is not an infringement.[1026] The protection enjoyed by a registered owner does not cover ideas, concepts, processes, systems, techniques or information that may be embodied in a topography or an integrated circuit product.[1027]

§7. Limitations of the Scope of Protection

386. Section 6 lists a number of limitations:

- a worldwide exhaustion defence when the registered topography has been put legally on the market;[1028]
- an exception for acts done privately and for non-commercial purpose;[1029]
- an exception for acts done for the sole purpose of analysis or evaluation or of research or teaching;[1030]
- an exception for reverse engineering;[1031]
- an exception for the temporary or accidental entrance in Canada of vehicles, vessels, aircrafts or spacecrafts which contain the registered topography.[1032]

§8. Duration of Protection

387. The protection starts on the filing date of the application and subsists for a period of ten years from the filing date or the date of the first commercial exploitation, whichever is the first.[1033]

1025. *See* the legislative definition of 'commercially exploit' in s. 2.
1026. Subsection 6(3).
1027. Subsection 3(3).
1028. Paragraph 6(2)(c).
1029. Paragraph 6(2)(d).
1030. Paragraph 6(2)(a).
1031. Paragraph 6(2)(b).
1032. Paragraph 6(2)(e).
1033. Section 5.

§9. Infringement and Remedies

388. An action for infringement may be brought in front of a provincial court or the F.C.[1034] A detention order may also be sought.[1035] In case of a successful action, the court may grant an injunction, order the payment of royalties, the recovery of damages or profits, punitive damages and the disposal of any article containing an infringing integrated circuit.[1036] There is a limited defence for an innocent infringer who did not know and had no reasonable grounds to believe that the integrated circuit product was manufactured and sold for the first time without the consent of the owner.[1037] Only injunctive relief is available if the action is brought more than three years after the acts of infringement, unless the infringement is of such a nature that, at the time of its commission, it would not have come to the attention of a reasonably diligent owner or a licensee.[1038] In that case, the action for infringement must be commenced within three years after the infringement came or should have come to the attention of the plaintiff.[1039]

§10. Overlapping and Relation to Other Intellectual Property Laws

389. Only the *Copyright Act* expressly excludes the copyright protection for topographies.[1040] Other intellectual property statutes are implicitly not applicable to topographies; thus the *Industrial Design Act*,[1041] which protects 'those features that, in a finished article, appeal to and are judged solely by the eye',[1042] could hardly cover a topography normally not visible without an electronic microscope.[1043] Also, the *Industrial Design Act* states clearly since 1988 that no protection will extend to features dictated solely by a utilitarian function of the article,[1044] eliminating any hope of using the *Act* to gain a monopoly on a topography.

1034. Section 23. The Federal Court has exclusive jurisdiction to order that a registration of a topography be expunged or amended because it is invalid or inaccurate. *See* subs. 23(2). The Registrar has only a limited power to amend an entry in the register, notably to correct any typographical or clerical error. *See* subs. 21(2).

1035. Section 14.

1036. Section 9.

1037. Sections 10–11. The defence will not benefit an infringer dealing with marked integrated circuit products: *see* subs. 11(2).

1038. Subsection 12(1).

1039. Subsection 12(2).

1040. Section 64.2, *Copyright Act*, RSC 1985, c. C-42.

1041. RSC 1985, c. I-9.

1042. Section 2 of the *Industrial Design Act*.

1043. Johanne Daniel, 'Les origines de l'adoption d'un régime de protection 'sui generis' des topographies de circuits intégrés' in *Nouvelles technologies et propriété*, ed. Ejan Mackaay (Montréal: Ed. Thémis, 1991), 71.

1044. Section 5.1. *See also* s. 11.1 as introduced by s 107 of the *Economic Action Plan 2014 Act, No. 2*, SC 2014, c.39.

390. In theory, the *Patent Act*[1045] and trade secrets protection may be used to shield some aspects of a topography from copying but in practice, very few layouts of integrated circuits will meet the novelty condition and present the necessary inventive step of the patent regime.[1046] The time-consuming nature of the formalities for obtaining patent protection may also be considered a serious disincentive, since a topography may have a commercial life of less than one year.[1047] As far as trade secrets are concerned, the fact that integrated circuits layouts may be reverse engineered means that, after a few months of free sales on the market, the protection will become ineffective.[1048]

1045. RSC 1985, c. P-4.

1046. Johanne Daniel, *'Les origines de l'adoption d'un régime de protection 'sui generis' des topographies de circuits intégrés'* in *Nouvelles technologies et propriété* 71 (Ejan Mackaay ed., Éditions Thémis, 1991).

1047. Leon Radomsky, *'Sixteen Years After The Passage Of The U.S. Semiconductor Chip Protection Act: Is International Protection Working?'* in *Berkeley Tech. L.J.* 15 1049, 1054 (2000).

1048. J. Daniel, 'Les origines de l'adoption d'un régime de protection 'sui generis' des topographies de circuits intégrés' in *Nouvelles technologies et propriété*, 60 (Ejan Mackaay ed., Éditions Thémis, 1991).

Chapter 9. Trade Secrets/Confidential Information

§1. Sources: Legislation

391. At the provincial level, few provisions deal with the protection of trade secrets. Protection is for instance provided in statutes which impose an obligation to disclose information[1049] or statutes which establish the right to access information or personal data.[1050] Otherwise, the general rules of the common law (in the common law provinces) and of the civil law (in Québec) will apply to the wrongful appropriation of a trade secret or confidential information. In Quebec, two provisions of the *Civil Code of Québec* clarify the civil law rules applicable to the illegal exploitation of a secret.[1051]

392. At the federal level, statutes also grant access to information[1052] and outline some exemptions for trade secrets, confidential information and some other sensitive information.[1053] The general criminal law will also apply when the facts surrounding the wrongful appropriation of information present the necessary elements of an offence.[1054] Specific offences have also been enacted.[1055]

393. Also at the federal level, section C.08.004.1 of the *Food and Drug Regulations*[1056] provides for the protection of undisclosed tests or other data necessary to determine the safety and effectiveness of a drug containing a new medicinal ingredient. These data and tests, which must be submitted to obtain a notice of compliance (NOC)

1049. *See* for instance s. 39 of the *Telecommunications Act*, SC 1993, c. 38; Section 67 of the Québec *Act respecting Occupational Health and Safety*, CQLR c S-2.1.

1050. *See* for instance ss 5(2B) and 21 of the Nova Scotia *Freedom of Information and Protection of Privacy Act*, S.N.S. 1993, c. 5; Section 14 of the Prince Edward Island *Freedom of Information and Protection of Privacy Act*, R.S.P.E.I. 1988, c. F-15.01; Section 17 of the Saskatchewan *Local Authority Freedom of Information and Protection of Privacy Act*, SS 1990–91, c L-27.1; Sections 18–19 of the Saskatchewan *Freedom of Information and Protection of Privacy Act*, SS 1990–91, c. F-22.01; Sections 17–18 of the Ontario *Freedom of Information and Protection of Privacy Act*, R.S.O. 1990, c. F.31; Sections 10–11 of the Ontario *Municipal Freedom of Information and Protection of Privacy Act*, RSO 1990, c M.56; Section 18 of the Manitoba *Freedom of Information and Protection of Privacy Act*, CCSM c F175; Section 16 of the Alberta *Freedom of Information and Protection of Privacy Act*, RSA 2000, c F-25; Section 21 of the British Columbia *Freedom of Information and Protection of Privacy Act*, RSBC 1996, c 165.

1051. Sections 1472 and 1612 of the *Civil Code of Québec*.

1052. *Personal Information Protection and Electronic Documents Act*, SC 2000, c 5; *Access to Information Act*, RSC, 1985, c A-1.

1053. *Personal Information Protection and Electronic Documents Act*, SC 2000, c 5, s 9; *Access to Information Act*, RSC, 1985, c A-1, s. 20; for a recent application of the federal exemption, *see Merck Frosst Canada Ltd. v. Canada (Health)*, 2012 SCC 3, [2012] 1 S.C.R. 23.

1054. *See* Section I Criminal Action of §2 Protection of Trade Secrets/Confidential Information of this chapter.

1055. *See* s. 19 of the *Security of Information Act*, RSC 1985, c O-5, concerning economic espionage.

1056. *Food and Drug Regulations* (CRC, c 870). For further analysis, *see* footnote 531 of this monograph.

authorizing the marketing of the drug in Canada, are in principle entitled to an eight-year term of data protection from the issuance of the first NOC.[1057]

394. Furthermore, Canada is a party to some multinational conventions which impose on the adhering countries an obligation to provide an effective protection against unfair competition. Such obligation exists in Article 10*bis* of the *Paris Convention for the Protection of Industrial Property* (*Paris Convention*).[1058] Canada has also entered into the *Agreement Establishing the WTO*, which includes the *Agreement on Trade-Related Aspects of Intellectual Property Rights* (*TRIPs Agreement*)[1059] and is party to the *NAFTA* which regroups in a specific chapter on intellectual property, provisions similar to those adopted in the *TRIPs Agreement.*[1060] Both international texts require the countries to protect undisclosed information and data or information submitted to governments or governmental agencies to obtain the approval of the marketing of pharmaceutical or agricultural chemical products.[1061]

§2. Protection of Trade Secrets/Confidential Information

395. Trade secrets can be protected by criminal actions and civil actions.

I. Criminal Action

396. The general provisions of the *Criminal Code*[1062] apply to the wrongful appropriation of information. However, all the elements of the offence must be established to convict a defendant. In *R. v. Stewart*,[1063] the Supreme Court of Canada decided that a confidential list of the names, addresses and telephone numbers of a hotel's employees may not be object of a theft for the purposes of section 283(1) of *Criminal Code*, because the necessary elements of a theft were not present: confidential

1057. An additional six-month extension is available for some results of clinical trials concerning the use of the drug in pediatric populations.

1058. Canada acceded to the Stockholm version on 7 Apr. 1970, and the accession came in force on 7 Jul. 1970; as regards the substantive provisions, Canada acceded to Arts 1–12 at the Stockholm level on 23 Feb. 1996 and the accession became effective on 26 May 1996: *see* WIPO *WIPO-Administered Treaties*, www.wipo.int/treaties/en/.

1059. The agreement was signed by Canada on 15 Apr. 1994 and ratified on 30 Dec. 1994. It was enacted into the domestic law by the *World Trade Organization Agreement Implementation Act*, SC 1994, c. 47.

1060. Canada, United States and Mexico, 17 Dec. 1992, Index, *Canada Treaty Series 1994*, 1, 32 I.L.M. 296. The c. 17 is the one devoted to intellectual property matters and is reproduced at 32 I.L.M. 670. The agreement was signed on 17 Dec. 1992 by the governments of the United States, Mexico and Canada. It came into force on 1 Jan. 1994. *See* Index, *Canada Treaty Series 1994*, 1, (1998). Its goal is to create a free trade zone between the three countries. It was enacted into Canadian domestic law by the *North American Free Trade Agreement Implementation Act*, SC 1993, c. 44.

1061. *See* Art. 39 of the *TRIPs Agreement* and Art. 1711 of *NAFTA*.

1062. RSC 1985, c. C-46.

1063. [1988] 1 S.C.R. 963.

information is not a form of property and the 'taking' of this intangible would not deprive the alleged owner of the use or possession of the information. Similarly, the court ruled that the appropriation of the information did not amount to a fraud contrary to section 338(1) of the *Criminal Code*, since it had not resulted in a risk of economic loss amounting to deprivation. Thus only usurpation of trade secrets resulting in economic losses could in the proper circumstances constitute a fraud.

II. Civil Action

397. Various forms of civil action may be used to protect confidential information and trade secrets, in both the common law and the civil law systems. But in both systems, the ambit of the protection depends on whether confidential information can be characterized as moveable property or not. Up to now, higher courts have either refused to treat trade secrets and confidential information as property,[1064] or preferred to leave the legal issues to be decided on a case-by-case approach.[1065] But even if information is not considered property, protection can be provided by civil actions. In the common law system, one would look possibly at breach of confidence,[1066] breach of contract, breach of fiduciary duty, unjust enrichment and unlawful interference with contractual relations. In civil law, one may have to resort to extra-contractual liability, breach of contract, breach of an obligation of good faith, and parasitism.[1067]

1064. *See* in the Québec civil law system, *Tri-tex Co. Inc. v. Ghaly*, [1999] R.J.Q. 2324, (1999), 1 C.P.R. (4th) 160 (Qué. C.A.).

1065. In *Cadbury Schweppes Inc. v. FBI Foods Ltd.*, [1999] 1 S.C.R. 142, the court said: 'It would be contrary to the authorities [...] to allow the choice of remedy to be driven by a label ('property') rather than a case-by-case balancing of the equities.[...] Application of the label 'property' in this context would add nothing except confusion to the task of weighing the policy objectives furthered by a particular remedy and the particular facts of each case.' (at para. 48)

1066. *Lac Minerals Ltd. v. International Corona Resources Ltd.*, [1989] 2 S.C.R. 574; *Cadbury Schweppes Inc. v. FBI Foods Ltd.*, [1999] 1 SCR 142.

1067. You can find additional information about the civil law protection of trade secrets in Québec in Mistrale Goudreau, « Marques de commerce et concurrence déloyale » in JurisClasseur Québec - Propriété intellectuelle, Montréal, LexisNexis Canada, looseleaf.

Chapter 10. Geographical Indications and Appellations of Origin

§1. Sources: Legislation

398. The *TRIPs Agreement*[1068] established binding international obligations regarding the protection of geographical indications[1069] and following the ratification of the international text, Canada introduced in the *Trademarks Act*[1070] a protective scheme for geographical indications in relation with wines and spirits.[1071] Furthermore, on 30 October 2015, the *EU-Canada Comprehensive Economic and Trade Agreement* (CETA) was signed.[1072] This agreement requires some majeur modifications to the protective scheme. As of 1 January 2017, an implementation bill has passed second reading in the House of Commons.[1073]

399. In addition to the special geographical indications scheme, the regime for certification marks in the *Trademarks Act* can provide an effective means of protection. However, in the absence of registration and lack of evidence that ordinary consumers in the market for that type of product would likely be deceived as to the source of the product, an indication may be appropriated by a Canadian enterprise, despite the protests of the foreign authority responsible for the sign.[1074]

400. The misappropriation of a geographical indication can also be barred by an action for passing off, since Canadian law has accepted the validity of the concept of shared goodwill as dealt with by the House of Lords in *Erven Warnink B.V.* et al. *v. J. Townend & Sons (Hull) Ltd.* et al.[1075] Canadian courts have endorsed the requirements

1068. Canada, United States and Mexico, 17 Dec. 1992, Index, *Canada Treaty Series 1994*,. 1, 32 I.L.M. 296. The Ch. 17 is the one devoted to intellectual property matters and is reproduced at 32 I.L.M. 670.

1069. *See* ss 22–24 of the *TRIPs Agreement*.

1070. RSC 1985, c. T-13.

1071. *World Trade Organization Agreement Implementation Act*, SC 1994, c. 47, s. 192.

1072. But as of January 1, 2017, it had not been ratified : *see* Global Affairs Canada, International Trade Minister introduces legislation to Parliament to implement CETA, http://www.international.gc.ca/media/comm/news-communiques/2016/10/31a.aspx?lang=eng .

1073. S 61 and ff of Bill C-30 (First Session, Forty-second Parliament, 64-65 Elizabeth II, 2015–2016–2017). *See* the status of the bill in Legisinfo online at http://www.parl.ca/LegisInfo/BillDetails.aspx?Language=en&Mode=1&billId=8549249. Section 131 and ff incorporates some provisions of the *Canada–Korea Economic Growth and Prosperity Act* (SC 2014, c 28) relative to geographical indications.

1074. *Consorzio del Prosciutto di Parma v. Maple Leaf Meats Inc.* (2002), 18 C.P.R. (4th) 414 (F.C.A.). This case, among others, prompted the European Union to steps up bid for better protection of geographical indications. *See* the press release of 28 Aug. 2003, 'WTO talks: EU steps up bid for better protection of regional quality products' http://europa.eu/rapid/pressReleasesAction.do?reference=IP/03/1178.

1075. [1980] R.P.C. 31 (H.L.)

set out for this extended form of passing off.[1076] However, if Canadian companies have made extensive use of the indication and have built up a reputation and clientele of their own, the marks used in Canada are unlikely to be confused with the original and the action will be dismissed.[1077]

401. There are also provincial statutes which afford legal protection. In Quebec, the *Act Respecting Reserved Designations and Added-value Claims*[1078] creates a system to recognize designations which are attributed to agricultural and food products as an attestation of their method of production, region of origin or specificity.[1079] In particular, section 63 of the *Act* forbids the use of a reserved designation in the advertising, labelling or display of any product, or in commercial documents of any nature relating thereto, unless the product has been certified by an accredited certification body.

§2. Subject Matter of Protection

402. For the purpose of the *Trademarks Act*, 'geographical indication' means an indication that 'identifies the wine or spirit as originating in the territory of a WTO Member (or a region or locality of that territory) where a quality, reputation or other characteristic of the wine or spirit is essentially attributable to its geographical origin'.[1080] In the CETA implementation bill, an indication in respect of an agricultural product or food can also be protected.[1081]

403. To be protected as a geographical indication under the *Act*, an indication originating outside Canada must be protected by the laws applicable to the WTO Member of origin[1082] and must have been put on the list kept under the supervision of the Registrar of Trademarks.[1083]

§3. Conditions of Protection

404. The request to add an indication to the Canadian list must be submitted by a responsible authority for the wine or spirit in question. The *Trademarks Act* designates the responsible authority as the person, firm, or other entity that, in the opinion of the Minister of Industry Canada, is, by reason of state or commercial interest, sufficiently connected with and knowledgeable of that wine or spirit to be party to any proceedings

1076. *Consumers Distributing Co. v. Seiko Time Canada Ltd.*, [1984] 1 S.C.R. 583 at para. 34; *Ciba-Geigy Canada Ltd. v. Apotex Inc.*, [1992] 3 S.C.R. 120 at para. 31.

1077. *Institut nat. des appellations d'origine des vins & eaux de vie v. Andrés Wines Ltd.* (1987), 60 O.R. (2d) 316, 16 C.P.R. (3d) 385 (Ont. H.C.), aff'd (1990) 30 C.P.R. (3d) 279 (Ont. C.A.).

1078. S.R.Q. ch. A-20.03 (S.Q. 2006, c.4).

1079. *See* s. 1 of the *Act.*

1080. Section 2.

1081. Section 61 of Bill C-30 (First Session, Forty-second Parliament, 64-65 Elizabeth II, 2015–2016–2017).

1082. Section 2.

1083. Section 11.12. For an example of the protection it provides, *see Scotch Whisky Assn. v. Glenora Distillers International Ltd.*, 2009 FCA 16, at para. 4.

in respect of an objection to the addition of the indication to the list.[1084] The only ground of opposition is that the indication is not a geographical indication.[1085] Lack of distinctiveness or confusion is not relevant. The CETA implementation bill will widen the grounds of opposition, particularly in the case of an indication identifying an agricultural product or food.[1086]

§4. Scope of Exclusive Rights

405. Once entered on the list, the indication becomes a 'protected geographical indication'.[1087] In the present regime, no person can adopt or use it, as a trademark or otherwise, in relation with a wine or a spirit not originating in the relevant territory[1088] even if the public is not confused. The *Act* also prevents the registration of any trademark consisting, in whole or in part, of a protected geographical indication, if the trademark is to be registered in association with a wine or a spirit not originating in a territory indicated by the geographical indication.[1089] In the CETA implementation bill, the prohition extends to protected geographical indication identifying an agricultural product or food of a category set out in the schedule (and to translations put on the list) kept under the Act.[1090]

406. However, exceptions exist. For wine and spirit, if a Canadian has used a protected geographical indication in a continuous manner in relation to any business or commercial activity in respect of goods or services in good faith before 15 April 1994, or for at least ten years before that date, it may continue to use the sign.[1091]

407. Also, because some geographical terms had been used in Canada as generic terms rather than indications of the place of origin of products, the *Act* provided for some limitations. Subsection 11.18(2) allows for the adoption, use or registration, as a trademark or otherwise, of terms customary in common language in Canada as the common name for the wine or spirit, or customary names of some grape varieties.[1092] Furthermore, subsections 18(3) and 18(4) of the *Act* enumerate lists of generic names for wines and spirits for which the adoption, use or registration as a trademark or

1084. Section 11.11.
1085. Subsection 11.13(2).
1086. Section 62 of Bill C-30 (First Session, Forty-second Parliament, 64-65 Elizabeth II, 2015–2016–2017).
1087. Section 2.
1088. Sections 11.14, 11.15. The prohibition extends to any translation of the geographical indication. It does not cover use of a person's name, or use in a comparative advertising not placed on labels or packaging of the product (*See* s. 11.16).
1089. Paragraphs 12(1) g) h).
1090. Section 64 of Bill C-30 (First Session, Forty-second Parliament, 64-65 Elizabeth II, 2015–2016–2017).
1091. Section 11.17.
1092. The grape varieties must have been existing in Canada on or before the day on which the *TRIPs Agreement* comes into force.

otherwise, is permitted.[1093] In 2004, an agreement between the European Community and Canada brought a significant reduction of these lists.[1094]

408. The CETA implementation bill will also create exceptions to allow the use of some indications and some terms considered to be generic and to preserve some Canadian trademark rights.[1095]

1093. Section 11.18.

1094. *See* the Council Decision of 30 Jul. 2003 on the conclusion of the agreement between the European Community and Canada on trade in wines and spirit drinks, 2004/91/EC, OJ L 35, 6.2.2004, 1.

1095. Sections 54–64 of Bill C-30 (First Session, Forty-second Parliament, 64-65 Elizabeth II, 2015–2016–2017).

Selected Bibliography

Amani, Bita & Carys Craig. *Trade-Marks and Unfair Competition Law in Canada: Cases and Commentary*.

2nd ed. Toronto: Carswell, 2014.

Baribeau, Marc. *Principes généraux de la Loi sur le droit d'auteur*. Québec: Publications du Québec, 2013.

Barrigar, Robert H. *Canadian Patent Act Annotated*. Aurora, Ont.: Canada Law Books, 1994.

Burshtein, Sheldon. *The Law of Domain Names & Trade-marks on the Internet*. Toronto: Carswell, 2005.

Cameron, Donald M. (ed.). *Canadian Trade-Mark Law Benchbook*. 2nd ed. Toronto: Carswell, 2014.

Cameron, Donald M. (ed.). *Canadian Copyright/Industrial Designs Benchbook*. Toronto: Carswell, 2015.

Chromecek, Milan & McCormack Stuart C. *World Intellectual Property Guidebook: Canada*. New York: Matthew Bender, 1991.

Cornish, Diane E. *Licensing Intellectual Property*. Scarborough, Ont.: Carswell, 1995.

Fox, Harold G. *Canadian Law of Copyright and Industrial Designs*. 2nd ed. Scarborough, Ont.: Carswell, 1967.

Fox, Harold G. *Canadian Patent Law and Practice*. 4th ed. Scarborough, Ont.: Carswell, 1969.

Fox, Harold G. *Canadian Law of Trade Marks and Unfair Competition*. 3rd ed. Scarborough, Ont.: Carswell, 1972.

Gervais, Daniel J. *Collective Management of Copyright and Related Rights*. Alphen aan den Rijn, The Netherlands: Kluwer Law International, 2006.

Gold, Richard & Bartha-Maria Knoppers (dir.). *IP and Bioethics*. Markham, Ont.: LexisNexis, 2008.

Goldsmith, Immanuel. *Patents of Invention*. Scarborough, Ont.: Carswell, 1981.

Goldsmith, Immanuel. *Trademarks and Industrial Designs*. Scarborough, Ont.: Carswell, 1982.

Hagen, Gregory R. et al. *Canadian Intellectual Property Law: Cases and Materials*. Toronto: Emond Montgomery Publications, 2013.

Handa, Sunny. *Copyright Law in Canada*. Markham, Ont.: Butterworths, 2002.

Harris, Lesley Ellen. *Canadian Copyright Law.* 4th ed. Hoboken, New Jersey: John Wiley & Sons, Inc. 2014.

Henderson, Gordon. *Trade-marks Law of Canada*. Scarborough, Ont.: Carswell, 1993.

Henderson, Gordon. *Patent Law of Canada*. Scarborough, Ont.: Carswell, 1994.

Henderson, Gordon. *Copyright and Confidential Information Law in Canada*. Scarborough, Ont.: Carswell, 1994.

Herman, Lawrence L. *Canadian Trade Law: Practice and Procedure*. Toronto: Carswell, 2008.

Howell, Robert G. *Database protection and Canadian Laws: (State of Law as of 15 June 1998)*. Ottawa: Industry Canada 1998.

Hughes, Roger T. *Hughes on Copyright and Industrial Design*. Scarborough, Ont.: Butterworths, 1993.

Hughes, Roger T. *Hughes on Trade Marks*. 2nd ed. Scarborough, Ont.: Butterworths, 1984.

Hughes, Roger T. & John H Woodley. *Hughes and Woodley on Patents*. 2nd ed. Scarborough, Ont.: Butterworths, 1985.

Hughes, Roger T. et al. *Canadian Forms and Precedents – Commercial Transactions – Intellectual Property*. Markham, Ont.: LexisNexis Canada, 2007.

Hutchison, Cameron. *Digital Copyright Law.* Toronto: Irwin Law, 2016.

Jolliffe, Scott & Kelly Gil. *Fox Canadian Law of Trade Marks and Unfair Competition*. 4th ed. Toronto: Carswell, 2002.

Gervais, Daniel & Elizabeth F. Judge *Intellectual Property: The Law in Canada*. 2nd ed. Toronto: Carswell, 2011.

Gervais, Daniel J & Elizabeth F. Judge. *Le droit de la propriété intellectuelle*. Cowansville, Qué.: Yvon Blais, 2006.

Kratz, Martin P.J. *Canada's Intellectual Property Law in a Nutshell*. 2nd ed. Toronto: Carswell, 2010.

Kratz, Martin P.J. *Protecting Copyright and Industrial Design*. 2nd ed. Toronto: Carswell, 1999.

Kratz, Martin P.J. *Obtaining Patents*. 2nd ed. Toronto: Carswell, 1999.

Lehaire, Benjamin. *L'action en concurrence déloyale en droit civil québécois*. Montréal: Ed Yvon Blais, 2015.

MacOdrum, Donald. *Fox on the Canadian Law of Patents*. 5th ed. Scarborough Ont.: Carswell, 2013.

McKeown, John S. *Fox Canadian Law of Copyright and Industrial Designs*. 4th ed. Scarborough Ont.: Carswell, 2000.

McKeown, John S. *Brand Management in Canadian Law.* Toronto: Thomson Reuters Canada Limited, 2016.

Selected Bibliography

Perry, Stephen J. & Currier, T. Andrew. *Canadian Patent Law.* 2nd ed. Markham, Ont.: LexisNexis Canada, 2014.

Richard, Hughes G. & Laurent Carrière. *Canadian Copyright Act Annotated.* Toronto: Carswell, 1992.

Richard, Hughes G. *Canadian Trade Marks Act Annotated.* Toronto: Carswell, 1990.

Sanderson, Paul & Ronald N.Hier. *Musicians and The Law in Canada: A Guide to the Law, Contracts, and Practice in the Canadian Music Business.* 4th ed. Toronto: Carswell, 2014.

Sarna, Lazar & Hillel Neuer. *Annotated Copyright Act.* Montréal, Qué.: Jewel Publications, 1989.

Scassa, Teresa. *Canadian Trademark Law.* 2nd ed Markham, Ont.: LexisNexis Canada, 2015.

Stratton, Bruce. *Annotated Patent Act.* Toronto: Carswell, 2009.

Tamaro, Normand. *Loi sur le droit d'auteur, texte annoté.* 10th ed. Cowansville, Qué.: Yvon Blais, 2015.

Tamaro, Normand. *The 2017 Annotated Copyright Act.* Toronto: Carswell, 2016.

Vaver, David. *Intellectual Property Law: Copyright, Patents, Trade-Marks.* 2nd ed. Toronto: Irwin Law, 2011.

Vaver, David. *Copyright Law.* Toronto: Irwin Law, 2000.

Vincke, Christian. *Problèmes de droit d'auteur en éducation.* Québec: Éditeur officiel du Québec, 1977.

Selected Bibliography

Index

The numbers here refer to paragraph numbers.

Index

Index

Index

Index

www.ingramcontent.com/pod-product-compliance
Lightning Source LLC
Chambersburg PA
CBHW071340230926
51846CB00002B/399
9789041194749